THE WORK ETHIC
Working Values and Values That Work

THE
Work Ethic

WORKING VALUES
AND VALUES THAT WORK

David J. Cherrington

A DIVISION OF AMERICAN MANAGEMENT ASSOCIATIONS

Library of Congress Cataloging in Publication Data
Cherrington, David J
The work ethic.

Includes index.
1. Work. 2. Labor and laboring classes—United
States. 3. Job satisfaction—United States.
4. Social values. I. Title.
HD4905.C44 658.3'14 80-65871
ISBN 0-8144-5549-2

First Printing

ACKNOWLEDGMENTS

I am grateful for the generous contribution of many people. I am greatly indebted to Jan Erteszek for his personal encouragement and the financial contribution he provided to establish the Erteszek Research Fund at Brigham Young University for the study of organizations and values. Many of my colleagues, both at Brigham Young University and elsewhere, have made valuable contributions by assisting with the research or reading some of the research articles. Special recognition goes to the original members of the research team who worked with me in designing the questionnaire and analyzing the data: Spencer J. Condie and J. Lynn England in sociology, Robert J. Crawford in economics, and N. Dale Wright in public administration. Several people read earlier drafts of this book and provided helpful comments. Special thanks go to three reviewers: J. Owen Cherrington, Mary Kay Stout, and William R. Newton.

Typing a lengthy manuscript is always a difficult chore. I appreciate the cheerful service provided by all the secretaries in the South Word Processing Center who not only accomplished the task but said they enjoyed doing it. And since all significant accomplishments require a team effort, I am grateful to the other members of my team—Marilyn, David, Nathan, Jennifer, and Jill. Finally, thanks go to the thousands of people described herein who were willing to share their feelings and attitudes about work. Without their questionnaire responses and interview comments, the research described in these chapters would not have been possible.

PREFACE

This book was motivated by the comments of numerous supervisors who expressed concern about the work ethic. The following statements illustrate the frustration they feel in supervising a workforce with different values from their own:

"Last year our management team put together a set of goals that we wanted to accomplish over the next year. Generally, we did quite well. We were able to meet all our plant expansion and financial goals without much difficulty. In fact, the only goals we didn't meet were those dealing with our employees: and there we got worse. Our absenteeism has gone up, turnover is still just as bad, and our average skill level has actually decreased because of all the changes we've had to make in manpower. But our most serious problem is how we've mortgaged our future to avoid grievance hassles with our union. We made concessions to some employees on disciplinary matters when the employees should have been fired. We keep saying our people are our greatest asset, but they are also our greatest liability."

"In recent years there has been an enormous increase in our disciplinary problems: drugs, alcohol, damaged equipment, insubordination. You name it. One of our worst disciplinary problems is sleeping on the job. And I mean really sleeping, not just dozing off for a couple of minutes. One employee had a roll of foam rubber in his locker and we learned that he frequently rolled it out and slept through the last half of his shift. Our company policy has not changed, and we still dismiss people for disciplinary reasons. But our supervisors are apparently not aware of the number of people who get dismissed, because they seem to think there is nothing they can do about disciplinary problems. There is a saying going around, 'The only things that are fireproof around here are the employees.' "

A humorous illustration of the change in work values is found in the absenteeism record of a young assembly-line worker. During the first few months on the job, this new employee was absent an average of one day each week. Finally, his supervisor decided to find out the cause and asked the employee why he was averaging four days of work a week. The answer came without hesitation, "Because I can't make enough money by working only three days a week."

Other illustrations are not so humorous. At an assembly plant, a supervisor was hospitalized for three weeks with a skull fracture and concussion. The incident resulted from a dispute with an employee. The supervisor claimed that the employee was intentionally working slowly to reduce the speed of the entire section. Co-workers agreed that the employee did a lot of fooling around, took extended breaks to go to the restroom or drinking fountain, and occasionally sat around doing nothing during work periods. The supervisor tried to get the employee to work faster by verbal pressure. The employee felt hassled, lost his temper, and finally struck the supervisor with a two-foot length of lead pipe. The employee was fired, the supervisor returned to work three months later, and it looked for a time as if the incident was over. Six months later, however, the company learned that it was being sued. To everyone's surprise, the company lost a lengthy legal dispute and was forced to reinstate the employee and pay back wages. As soon as he received his 22 months of back pay, he quit.

At the other end of the scale are people who work at a

self-imposed frantic pace day after day. This comment was made by an employee of a management consulting firm:

"Before I came to work here I heard about people who were married to their job. I didn't understand what it meant until I started here. Now I know; it's unbelievable. Most of the men I work with are working their fool heads off. Everyone works at least 60 hours a week and some put in 80 hours or more week after week. I really respect most of them; they are a great group of men. They don't have any vices: they don't drink; they don't smoke; and they don't fool around. In my opinion their only weakness is work—that's all they can do. I've heard some of them don't have a very good family life and I can see why. If you're working as long as some of these men do I don't see how you could have any family life at all."

This book looks at the values of people who work and examines some fundamental questions. What is the meaning of work in the lives of workers? Why do some employees see work only as a means to an end and an unpleasant means at that, while other employees view work as a desirable activity providing meaningful self-fulfillment? How are positive work values developed and what can supervisors do to strengthen employees' work habits? When does work become excessive and create a workaholic?

These questions are discussed in the following chapters. Except for the definitions of the work ethic in Chapter 2, each chapter is largely self-contained. Therefore, the chapters do not necessarily have to be read in order. Someone who is interested in the problems of excessive work can turn directly to the final chapter, "The Workaholic and Leisure." Or someone who is interested in how work values influence career development and education can turn to Chapter 10.

One further comment should be added. This book was not designed to provide a balanced analysis of the role of work in the lives of American workers. Little is said about the masses of average or good performers who dominate the workforce.

ix

Workaholics are discussed only in part of the final chapter. Most of the book focuses on outstanding performers who have strong work values and inadequate performers who have largely rejected the traditional work ethic. Generally, the intent is not to describe the role of work as it is, but as it might be.

David J. Cherrington

CONTENTS

THE WORK ETHIC
Working Values and Values That Work

1

NEW JOBS,
NEW WORKERS,
NEW VALUES

During the 1530s, Martin Luther taught that work was a calling from God—that one served God best, not by fleeing to a monastery, but by diligently laboring in one's daily occupation. This was a reasonable philosophy at the time, since the medieval caste system had most people locked into a fixed occupation. Knowing that they were doing what God wanted must have made people's lives more meaningful. In the 1750s, Benjamin Franklin wrote that the road to success was through industry and thrift. His advice to work hard made a lot of sense to the early Americans, who came to settle a vast wilderness. Early Puritan ministers taught that Christians had two callings: a general calling to serve God and a personal calling to perform their daily labors. This belief helped a group of deeply religious people integrate the survival demands of the physical world with their spiritual desires to serve God.[1]

Hard work, diligence, and industry have always been consistent with the social and economic demands of the past. But what about work today? The medieval caste system no longer exists. The vast wilderness has vanished. And the survival demands of work have diminished along with the pivotal importance of religion in most Americans' lives. What, then, are the work values of today's workers, and are they relevant to today's socioeconomic system? Is work one of the most important parts of a person's life? Do workers feel a sense of pride and craftsmanship in their work? Do people who do careless work feel guilty? What is the proper balance between work and leisure for improving the quality of a person's life?

The American work ethic is undergoing a significant change. This change is having a dramatic impe t on the meaning of work and the quality of peoples' lives. It is also having an enormous impact on organizations and their ability to survive and function effectively. The change is not a recent development—the work ethic has been evolving for over three centuries. What is new is the rate of change. More change has occurred in the past 30 to 40 years than in the previous 300 to 400 years. Old values have been freely challenged and re-confirmed, changed, or discarded.

While work values have been changing, so have jobs and workers. Working conditions and the job itself have changed so much in the past 100 years that the world of work is not really the same. Industrialization and technology have made it possi-ble for most workers to produce more in two hours, usually with less effort, than their grandparents produced in the normal 12-hour day. The loss of a job used to pose a serious threat to the financial security of workers and their families. Today, however, many workers can collect as much as 90 percent of their regular take-home pay through unemployment compen-sation and union layoff benefits.

New entrants into the workforce are also different today than they were 100 or even 20 years ago. There is a greater diversity in their educational training—some are still unable to read or write while others have completed 6 to 10 years of education beyond high school. Today's workers tend to come from larger cities and smaller families, more often with both parents working. Their life expectancy is 20 to 25 years longer and their reasons for work fall in different categories than earlier generations.

NEW JOBS

That the past two centuries have seen dramatic changes in the nature of work comes as no surprise. The surprising thing is how much change has taken place. Many jobs performed today did not exist 10 years ago. Furthermore, many of these changes have undoubtedly influenced the meaning of work.

The average workweek has become shorter for each succeeding generation. The average worker today works about 38 hours.[2] Very few employees work more than five days a week, and many work a four-day week. But it hasn't always been that way. In 1822, Philadelphia carpenters demanded that their workday be reduced to 12 hours. They were expected to work from sunup to sundown.[3]

In the nineteenth century the workweek for most occupations was at least 60 hours, and often longer. In the steel industry, for example two men typically staffed one job around the clock. Each worked a 12-hour shift, seven days a week. The shifts rotated every two weeks, with one man having 24 hours free while the other worked 24 consecutive hours.[4] In retail stores, such as Carson, Pirie, Scott in Chicago, sales personnel worked 84 hours each week—six 14-hour days. Company rules stated that the store was not to be open on Sunday except for emergencies. Salesmen were allowed one evening for courting, and two if they had attended Sunday school. Leisure hours, after a 14-hour workday, were to be spent primarily in reading worthwhile books.[5]

The average workweek in most companies was over 50 hours until the 1930s. Henry Ford was one of the earliest industrial leaders to reduce the workweek in his factories to 40 hours. He reasoned that more leisure time and relatively high wages would increase the demand for cars. During the Depression, legislation (the National Industrial Recovery Act of 1933, Public Contracts Act of 1936, and Fair Labor Standards Act of 1938) helped to standardize the five-day, 40-hour week.[6]

Legislation has not only influenced the hours of work; it has also influenced the meaning of holding a job. The "privilege" of having a job and the personal responsibility of jobholders to develop the necessary skill and prove their worth have shifted toward the "right" to have a job and society's responsibility to provide training and guarantee full employment. This shift has been encouraged by social legislation, such as the Employment Act of 1946, which established the goal of full employment, and the Manpower Development and Training Act of 1972, which established training programs for people who did not have adequate skills.

The meaning of work has also been influenced by a shift in the power positions of the employer and the employees. If workers today feel that management is unresponsive to their interests, they can petition the National Labor Relations Board for a representation election. They can force management to bargain in good faith with a labor organization representing them. The position of unions today differs dramatically from what it was in the early 1800s, when a strike was considered a criminal conspiracy in restraint of trade. Only in relatively recent times has picketing been considered lawful. For many years "peaceful picketing" was looked upon as a contradiction in terms.

Federal laws have significantly changed other aspects of work. Until recent times, most employees worked from day to day with little job security. Their financial welfare was continually threatened by death, disability, or termination. Hazardous working conditions were often considered a normal part of the job, and the employee's only alternative was to quit. Job safety and security have been strengthened in recent years through legislation. The Occupational Safety and Health Act makes unsafe working conditions unlawful; unemployment compensation is provided for workers who lose their jobs; Social Security benefits provide income to retirees and death benefits to surviving family members, and workers' compensation benefits cover accidents and long-term disability.

Technology has dramatically changed the nature of work. When Americans established their political and economic independence two centuries ago, about 90 percent of them obtained their income from agriculture. Early American farming was a labor-intensive industry. Food was grown and processed without the aid of tractors to turn the soil, specialized equipment to harvest the crops, and trucks to haul the produce to market. Today, rather than toiling at the end of a sickle, the farmer rides atop a massive machine that cuts wide swaths through a field of wheat and threshes it at the same time. Where plowing was once a strenuous task of guiding a horse and plow along a furrow, many farmers now sit in enclosed cabs with power controls and stereophonic music.

Similar technological changes have occurred in mining and manufacturing. The number of workers employed in mining has not changed much over the century, but the methods have changed considerably because of technological innovations. A century ago, for example, coal miners often worked with family members in small groups, picking at a vein of coal, shoveling it into buckets, and carrying them to the top of the mine. The work was strenuous, the conditions were uncomfortable, and the environment was dangerous. Mining is still a hazardous occupation, but mechanical equipment has taken the picks, shovels, and buckets out of the miners' hands. Operating mechanical equipment is very different work from swinging a pick. Factory work has also changed. Automation and mechanical equipment have reduced the level of toil and effort. Even the manufacturing of mechanical equipment has become automated. Skilled machinists have been replaced by computers that guide automated machines as they produce other machines.

Many of the most difficult and unpleasant jobs have been eliminated through automation, but some still remain. Today "dirty" jobs are performed by about 10 to 15 percent of the American workforce, and there is growing concern whether organizations will be able to staff these jobs in the future. Examples of dirty jobs are carrying food trays, pushing brooms, shoveling dirt, and performing countless other physical and menial tasks that haven't changed substantially for centuries. It has been suggested that mechanization has gone about as far as it can to eliminate menial jobs and that new incentives, such as more money and opportunities for advancement, will be needed to attract people to these jobs. This implies that employees doing dirty jobs will work strictly for money or other incentives, not because they believe their work is important, satisfying, or fulfilling. The current social dilemma seems to be who should do these jobs. A growing number of college graduates with degrees in liberal arts are finding that dirty jobs are the only ones available to them.[7]

NEW WORKERS

Long days and hard labor make the lives of early Americans seem rather harsh and unpleasant. The pain, however, was often cut short by death. The average life expectancy in 1979 was 72.3 years of age, but in 1910 it was only 47.3, largely because of the high infant mortality.[8]

Longer life expectancy is having a significant influence on the composition of the workforce and the aspirations of workers. Until recently, very few workers planned ahead for their retirement. Retirement, as a separate phase of life as we know it today, was not the norm for older Americans. Age 65 was not established as the age of retirement, and people continued to work in whatever capacity their health permitted. In 1900, only 4 percent of the population was over 65 years of age, and 67 percent of the men over 65 were still working. In 1977, 11 percent of the population was over 65 years of age, and even though they tended to have better health, only 20 percent of the men were still working.[9]

A growing trend today is for workers to choose early retirement. Many people retire at age 62, and a growing percentage are retiring in their 50s. These changes are placing a serious drain on Social Security funds. As recently as 1955 there were 7 workers for each person collecting Social Security. By 1960 the ratio was 4 to 1, by 1978 it was 3 to 1, and the ratio is estimated to be no more than 2 to 1 between 2000 and 2005. Mandatory retirement laws have been changed to encourage older workers to remain on the job. But the trend toward early retirement continues.[10]

Early retirement possibilities have encouraged workers to begin planning for their retirement earlier in their careers, an activity that used to be restricted to career personnel in the military. Thus, rather than serving as a major source of life's satisfaction, work is becoming a preparatory phase for retirement. Employees are increasingly concerned about company benefit plans, pensions, profit sharing, stock options, and vesting rights.

Another significant change in the composition of the workforce is the growing percentage of female employees. Since 1947 the male workforce has increased by 26 percent, but the female workforce has increased by more than 200 percent. Nearly 45 percent of today's workforce is female.[11]

The growth in female employment is being accompanied by other population changes. Marriages and childbearing are being postponed. The birth rate and family size are declining. From 1970 to 1977, the population of unmarried women in their early twenties rose from 36 to 45 percent; and among those who had married, the proportion without children rose from 36 to 43 percent. The number of births per 1,000 population was 14.8 in 1978—well below 25.1 in 1945, typical of the "baby boom" years, and 30.1 in 1910, typical of earlier growth years.[12] These changes have important implications for the career development of women and their activities in the workforce. The effects of female employment on the work ethic, however, are not clear. Will day-care centers be able to teach values as effectively as mothers in the home? Will two working parents have a greater impact than one working parent as role models for future workers?

Many observers claim that new entrants into the workforce today are brighter and better educated than any previous group. The data, however, do not do much to support this claim. The change, at least, is small when the median years of school completed is compared for the 25- to 29-year-olds. In 1950 the median was 12.0; in 1977 it had risen to only 12.9.[13]

The average educational level of the workforce is rising, a change that results primarily from the retirement of older workers, who tend to have less education than the new younger workers who are replacing them.

The percentage of new entrants who have never held permanent jobs seems to be increasing. Most students who enter the workforce have had previous experience from only summer jobs and part-time employment. High youth unemployment, limited work opportunities, the willingness of parents to give children spending money, and child labor laws that discourage teenage employment all reduce the opportunities for youth to obtain early work experiences.

NEW VALUES

Many managers have complained that today's workforce does not have the same values as previous generations. Some insist that the deterioration of the work ethic is a serious indictment of a society that grew and flourished from the ideals of rugged individualism and hard work. The evidence indicates that the claims of these managers are generally correct. Members of today's workforce, especially young workers, do not have the same attitudes as previous generations toward the importance of work, pride, and craftsmanship. Their reasons for holding a job are different, and work itself serves a different purpose for many of today's employees.

Changes in the nature of work have seriously challenged the relevance of the traditional work ethic. Why should work be an important part of your life when the workweek is becoming continually shorter and the four-day workweek is being considered to allow greater leisure pursuits? Why should you believe in the dignity of labor when minimum wage laws eliminate "dirty" jobs, automation eliminates repetitive jobs, welfare and unemployment compensation reward people for not working, older workers are encouraged to take early retirement, and mandatory retirement ages are set? Why should children be taught to work when child labor laws prevent them from getting a job? How can you take pride in your work when products are mass-produced, no one notices your performance, and you are paid for your time, not your efforts? Why should you be dependable and punctual when executives set their own work hours and companies are reluctant to fire an employee for absenteeism or sloppy work?

Still, managers insist that they want employees who are dependable, reliable, and punctual. They are looking for workers who are outstanding producers and who take pride in their work. They want employees who think work is an important part of their life and who will go out of their way when necessary to make changes and meet emergencies. In short, they want employees who espouse the work ethic.

There is tremendous uncertainty about the working values of today's workers. The disagreement over what workers think about work is well illustrated in the recent literature. During the 1960s, very little was written about the work ethic in the popular literature. In fact, the *Reader's Guide to Periodical Literature* indicated there were only three articles about the work ethic in the latter half of the 1960s and nothing from January 1963 to March 1967.

During the 1970s, the situation changed. Hundreds of articles, books, and television specials discussed the work ethic. In 1971 and 1972, the meaning of work was the topic of a presidential address; the subject of a special report issued by the Department of Health, Education, and Welfare; the focus of a bestselling book; and a central issue in an unauthorized but highly publicized strike at an auto assembly plant. Most management journals published a series of articles discussing the work ethic. It was also discussed in various newspaper articles and editorials. But there was not much agreement in all the publicity.

A review of the articles indicated that there were dramatic differences of opinion on the status of the work ethic in the 1970s. At least three distinct themes were described. One theme suggested that the traditional work ethic was alive and well—that people were as strongly committed to the values of pride, craftsmanship, and initiative as ever. A second theme implied that the work ethic was dead or dying and was an archaic belief that today's workers no longer accepted. A third theme stated that the value of work was based on the value of the job—that personal values might still be centered in work, but only if the job was enriched with a lot of variety, responsibility, and autonomy. Each theme was defended with both logic and personal observation.

Alive and Well.   One of the most widely broadcast affirmations of the vitality of the work ethic was a radio address by President Richard M. Nixon on September 6, 1971. Nixon extolled the work ethic, which is so "ingrained in the American character that most of us consider it immoral to be lazy or slothful. America's competitive spirit, the work ethic of this people, is alive and well on Labor Day, 1971. The dignity of work, the value of achievement, the morality of self-reliance—none of these is going out of style."[14]

This address was criticized by the press and others. In an article entitled "Nixon in the Pulpit: Economic Evangelism," *Time* magazine claimed that "the speech contained much muddled logic" and suggested that the greatest threat to the work ethic was not indolence but technological revolution. The address was also criticized as naive by an educational journal: "The calls from the White House to solve our problems by simply having everyone return to the good old American work ethic show no recognition of what the trouble is all about."[15]

Also in support of the traditional work ethic was an article called "The Work Ethic Is Alive and Well," describing the positive responses of railroad employees to a merger.[16] A merger in 1970 of four major lines required extensive job changes, relocation, and consolidation of seniority lists. Many employees accepted the changes and began to learn new skills. Others were bitter and attempted to sue the company. One episode resulting from the merger reinforced the importance of work. All employees had been assured that the merger would not lead to the loss of a job or a reduction in pay. However, the consolidation of the clerical functions left a group of 61 former clerks without anything to do, although they were guaranteed jobs and pay for life. At first these employees were told to simply stay home and draw their paychecks twice a month until a job became vacant. The senior employees, however, complained loudly about this policy. So the employees were instructed to report to a vacant office, Room 101, for eight hours a day and do whatever they wanted: read, knit, play cards, listen to the radio. After only a few days, one employee complained to a local newspaper. Her letter began "From Cell Block 101: 'Help'." The employees were interviewed by reporters and a lot of publicity followed. Employees commented: "I get out at night feeling more exhausted that I ever did before. I come home and drop exhausted. I found myself fighting with friends I worked with for two years." "We were like freaks." "Who wants to sit down all day?" These workers wanted to work and complained bitterly about having nothing to do.

Numerous authors claimed that the work ethic was alive and well. A personnel director suggested that people need to work and want to work; therefore, the work ethic can be an employee motivator. "It is clear that people have not lost interest in work, despite popular opinion. The work ethic is alive and well and ought to be relied on as a basic motivator of people." A businessman stated: "It's my conviction and that of many alert, progressive, and effective managers that the 'work ethic' is very much alive in American industry." A medical doctor argued that harmful stress is created not by hard work but by the frustration of failure. The title of his article was "But Hard Work Isn't Bad for You."[17]

Some authors even claimed that work was still generally accepted as a religious commandment. One minister indicated that work would never be abolished by technology, and with the proper Christian attitude work would become enriching to the soul. "Let us have no delusions about dispensing with work. . . . It is a necessity that matches our situation, and no law or political delusion can abolish it." The religious im-

11

portance of work was emphasized in a *Senior Scholastic* editorial entitled "Why Do We Work So Hard?" Quoting Thomas Carlyle, the editorial stressed: "Older than all the preached gospels was this unpreached, inarticulate but ineradicable, forever-enduring gospel: work, and therein have well-being."[18]

Dead or Dying.   Not everyone agreed that the traditional work ethic was alive and well in the 1970s. Many authors claimed that it was dead or dying. Some mourned its loss as a cherished public virtue. Others seemed delighted to see it go. For example, a senior pastor in a campus ministry condemned work and the achievement motive for creating such intense pressures that people felt compelled to fill even leisure hours with active pursuits. "Work is not to be worshipped and glorified. It is not the measure of a man or the sign of his election. Work saves no one from sin, death, or the power of the devil, John Wesley and Benjamin Franklin notwithstanding. . . . What I am saying is that it is high time we pointed out that the so-called 'Protestant ethic' was bad religion in the first place, and that in its modern secular form as the 'work ethic' it is a superstition that sanctifies violence and exploitation."[19]

A sociologist called for a moratorium on further research into the Protestant work ethic. After reviewing numerous studies comparing the work values and behaviors of Catholics and Protestants, Andrew Greeley claimed it was no longer a fruitful topic of research. He said there were no systematic or significant differences in the work values or work behaviors of Catholics or Protestants. Instead, there was greater variation within each group than between the two groups.[20]

One observer noted that even though work was still important, its importance had diminished drastically: "Since returning to the United States after a year abroad, I have sensed a remarkable deterioration taking place in the world of work right here at home. There is [a] growing belief that the American will to work . . . is increasingly becoming a thing of the past." To support his accusation, this observer noted that in 1972 more people were drawing money from the government for not working than during the Great Depression of the 1930s. In the 1960s absenteeism doubled and turnover more than tripled among auto workers, the highest-paid factory workers in the country. In 1968, and again in 1971, college seniors were asked if they thought hard work paid off. In just three years, the percentage agreeing dropped from 68 percent to 38 percent.[21]

An unauthorized strike in 1972 became a catalyst for many business executives and behavioral scientists to question the values of the workforce. Workers at the General Motors assembly plant in Lordstown, Ohio, went on strike for 22 days. The issue was *not* pay, benefits, or any of the traditional grievances. The workers went on strike over what has been called dehumanizing work. Chevrolet Vegas were coming off the line at the rate of 101.6 an hour—a pace that required each worker to perform the same specialized task every 36 seconds. The line had been recently redesigned to represent the best in engineering knowledge. The workers were mostly young employees who had the health and stamina to make Lordstown the most productive assembly plant in the world. But for 22 days they produced nothing. The initial complaint was that the line was moving faster than it should. Later analyses concluded that the problem was the very existence of a line at all—any assembly line. All assembly-line work was condemned as monotonous, boring, and dehumanizing. A new emotion-laden concept was added to the vocabulary of ethics in the 1970s. In political circles it was Watergate; in military circles it was My Lai; and in labor circles it was Lordstown.[22]

The dehumanization associated with assembly-line work was extended to other jobs. Clerical positions were soon seen as nothing more than disguised stations in a paper- and punchcard-dominated assembly line. The following comment of an insurance company executive indicates that the boredom and dehumanization of assembly-line work is not governed by the color of your collar:

"I worked on an assembly-line job before I started college, and if there was anything that kept me going in

13

college it was knowing that if I flunked out I'd probably be back there on that line. . . . About two years after I finished college I started to realize that my job here was just another assembly-line job. Information comes down the line to me, I add my two bits' worth to it, and send it on. That's all this company is—just one long assembly line.''

During the 1970s, all forms of work were questioned, and many observers concluded that the work ethic had been destroyed by highly specialized, routine work. This idea was promoted effectively by the bestselling book *Working*.[23] Studs Terkel interviewed hundreds of workers who performed dozens of different jobs. The taped interviews were casual and informal to encourage workers to talk about the frustrations of their work. Terkel concluded that work ''as we know it today'' is an instrument of violence to humanity. While some workers found meaning and satisfaction in their work, the majority expressed anger, resentment, and frustration. Work was a series of daily humiliations for workers on all kinds of jobs: steel workers, receptionists, farm workers, spot welders, executives, prostitutes, washroom attendants, on and on. Terkel said that in giving his Labor Day homily it was unfortunate that President Nixon did not encounter some of the people he interviewed. It is also unfortunate that Terkel did not encounter more of the outstanding workers I interviewed and describe in Chapters 6 and 7.

Job Enrichment.   The most prevalent theme advocated by a majority of the articles on work was that the value of work depended on the nature of the job. These authors treated the work ethic not as a general philosophy about work but as a specific job attitude like satisfaction with pay or satisfaction with the supervisor. Work was important to an employee with a high-status, easy job. Work was meaningless to an employee with a menial, repetitive job. If there was a decline in the work ethic (and most agreed there had been), the responsibility rested at the feet of managers who had created meaningless jobs, worthless products, and impersonal organizations.

14

The rationale for equating the value of work with a satisfactory job was that everyone has the same basic needs. All workers, it was assumed, have the same objectives: "equal pay for equal work and equal opportunities for advancement; jobs that are worthy of respect and lead to careers; better-paying jobs that provide more interesting work, greater autonomy, and more schooling; jobs that are minimally involving in terms of work and hours; jobs which allow for more leisure time; and many other combinations."[24]

But what are the implications of equating the value of work with the value of a job? Most jobs are better today than they were in the past. Does this mean the work ethic is stronger? Some say yes: "What is happening is that the work ethic is undergoing a radical transformation. Workers, particularly younger ones, are taking work *more* seriously, not less. Many may have abandoned the success ethic of their elders, but they still believe in work. Young and old are willing to invest more effort in their work, but are demanding a bigger payoff in satisfaction." Others claim the changes made work less important: "There has been less emphasis on the meaning of work, and people have begun to turn to other forms of expression to realize achievement, mastery, self-worth, and pleasure."[25]

In summary, there was a lot of disagreement about the values of workers in the 1970s. Some claimed that the traditional work ethic was still alive and well; others said it was dead or dying. Still others pointed to the goals of various job enrichment programs and said these were the new work values. Most agreed that the work ethic was not the same as it had been in earlier generations. But there was very little agreement about what the new values were.

THE FUTURE OF THE WORK ETHIC

The work ethic today is not the same as it was in early America. The jobs are different, the workers are different, and the values have changed. The consensus of most supervisors I have worked with in management training is that about a third of the employees entering the workforce are achievement-oriented, hardworking young people. The most highly praised workers seem to be college graduates with degrees in the physical sciences and engineering. Another third are just the opposite—they have poor attendance records, their performance is not acceptable, they have a negative view of management, and they think their attitudes and behavior are acceptable. ("If you don't like what I do, that's tough. It's your problem.") Between these extremes is another third who can be motivated to perform well if they receive the proper supervision and associate with a good work group. Supervisors have been particularly concerned about the middle and bottom groups. Within the past decade, they think the size of the bottom group has grown and is exerting a larger influence on the middle group.

The development of strong work values and highly productive work behavior depends very heavily on the development of self-discipline, self-control, and personal initiative. These characteristics are generally determined by socialization processes during youth. However, the values of adults can also be developed and changed. The initial experiences a new employee receives when entering the workforce as a permanent full-time member tend to be the most pronounced forces in the acquisition of new values.

Such values are not acquired overnight through some quick and easy training program or slick presentation. Positive work values are acquired over an extended period of patient and persistent effort. The principles involved in the development of positive work values are principles of good supervision.

Thus the future of the work ethic depends heavily on the quality of supervision today. Work values are learned values. Employees will learn the values they are taught in their environment. Federal legislation, government regulations, company policies, and social expectations all contribute significantly to the environmental forces that influence the meaning of work. But the immediate supervisor usually represents the biggest force in the development of a worker's values.

16

The key to developing good work values lies in the quality of supervision. Most employees think they "work" for their company, but it is their immediate supervisor who translates the influence of the company into the employee's life. It is the immediate supervisor who makes job assignments, gives instructions, and evaluates performance. And it is the immediate supervisor who helps the employee understand the purpose of the job and offers compliments for good performance. The immediate supervisor can either amplify or blunt top management's efforts to create a healthy climate, improve performance, and eliminate waste. Workers frequently justify their behavior by saying, "Why should I worry about the number of rejects when my supervisor doesn't give a damn?"

REFERENCES

1. See Max Weber, "Die Protestantische Ethik und der Geist des Kapitalismus," *Archiv fur Sozialwissenschaft,* Vols. 20, 21 (1904, 1905). Translated by Talcott Parsons, *The Protestant Ethic and the Spirit of Capitalism* (New York: Charles Scribner's Sons, 1958), Chapter 3. See also Benjamin Franklin "The Way to Wealth," *Writings II* (1758), in *Benjamin Franklin: The Autobiography and Other Writings* (New York: Signet, 1961). pp. 182–196; and Cotton Mather, *A Christian at His Calling* (Boston: Green and Allen, 1701).
2. Janice N. Hedges and Stephen J. Gallogly, "Full and Part Time: A Review of Definitions," *Monthly Labor Review,* Vol. 100, No. 3 (March 1977), pp. 21–28.
3. Cited in William F. Glueck, *Personnel: A Diagnostic Approach,* rev. ed. (Dallas: Business Publications, 1978), p. 125.
4. Margaret F. Byington, *Homestead: The Households of a Mill Town* (New York: Arno Press, 1910).
5. Company rules published by Carson, Pirie, Scott. Reproduced in Edgar F. Huse and James L. Bowditch, *Behavior in Organizations: A Systems Approach to Managing* (Reading, Mass.: Addison-Wesley, 1973), p. 3.
6. See Archibald A. Evans, "Work and Leisure, 1919–1969," *International Labor Review,* Vol. 99 (January 1969), pp. 35–59.
7. See Edmund Faltermayer, "Who Will Do the Dirty Work Tomorrow?" *Fortune,* Vol. 89 (January 1974), pp. 132–138; and David Konisberg, "Laboring over the Work Crisis," *American Way* (December 1978), pp. 47–48.
8. National Center for Health Statistics, U.S. Department of Health,

17

Education, and Welfare. Reported in *The World Almanac and Book of Facts, 1979* (New York: Newspaper Enterprise Association, 1979), p. 956.

9. "Guide to Growing Older," in *Information Please Almanac: Atlas and Yearbook, 1979* (New York: Viking Press, 1979), p. 659.

10. *Ibid.*, pp. 661–662.

11. See Allyson Grossman, "Women in the Labor Force," *Monthly Labor Review*, Vol. 98 (November 1975), pp. 3–16.

12. Manuel D. Plotkin, "Changing Population Patterns," in *The World Almanac and Book of Facts, 1979, op. cit.*, p. 205.

13. *Statistical Abstracts of the United States* (1978), p. 143.

14. Excerpted in *U.S. News and World Report* (September 20, 1971), p. 34.

15. *Time* (September 20, 1971), pp. 11–12; Erwin R. Smarr and Philip J. Escoll, "Humanism and the American Work Ethic," *Today's Education*, Vol. 63 (January–February 1974), pp. 83–85.

16. Thomas C. DeButts, "The Work Ethic Is Alive and Well," *Personnel*, Vol. 52 (September–October 1975), pp. 22–31.

17. Stanley J. Schwartz, "The Work Ethic Can Be an Employee Motivator," *Industry Week*, Vol. 181 (April 8, 1974), pp. 35–38; DuPree Jordan, Jr., "Let's Hear It for the Work Ethic," *Administrative Management Society Report*, Vol. 34 (November 1973), pp. 67–70; Hans Selye, "But Hard Work Isn't Bad for You," *Reader's Digest*, Vol. 102 (June 1973), pp. 124–125.

18. Byron C. Lambert, "On Avoiding Work," *Christianity Today*, Vol. 15 (August 27, 1971), pp. 7–8; "Why Do We Work So Hard?" *Senior Scholastic*, Vol. 101 (November 6, 1971), p. 9.

19. Gordon J. Dahl, "Time, Work, and Leisure Today," *Christian Century*, Vol. 88 (February 10, 1971), pp. 185–189.

20. Andrew Greeley, "The Protestant Ethic: Time for a Moratorium," *Sociological Analysis*, Vol. 25, No. 1 (Spring 1964), pp. 20–33.

21. Carl F. H. Henry, "The Ailing World of Work," *Christianity Today*, Vol. 14 (January 2, 1970), pp. 22–23; Floyd G. Lawrence, "Our Forgotten Strength: The Will to Work," *Industry Week*, Vol. 174 (September 4, 1972), pp. 1–16.

22. See Paul Dickson, *The Future of the Workplace* (New York: Weybright and Talley, 1975), p. 14.

23. Studs Terkel, *Working* (New York: Avon Books, 1972).

24. Alan Gartner and Frank Riessman, "Is There a New Work Ethic?" *American Journal of Orthopsychiatry*, Vol. 44, No. 4 (July 1974), pp. 563–567.

25. Donald M. Morrison, "Is the Work Ethic Going Out of Style?" *Time* (October 30, 1972), pp. 96–97; James F. Murphy, "The Future of Time, Work, and Leisure," *Parks and Recreation*, Vol. 8 (November 1973), pp. 25–26.

2

DEFINING
THE WORK ETHIC

One of the major reasons for the diversity of opinion about the work ethic is that it has been defined in so many different ways. There is no single "work ethic" that workers either accept or reject; there are numerous different values of work. A worker might accept some values as important justifications for work and reject others. The belief that labor in your "daily calling" is the only acceptable way to live before God implies a very different meaning of work than the belief that labor is important because it produces wealth. A person might espouse either of these values or reject both. In this chapter, the work ethic is defined and the meaning of work is examined by placing it along a continuum of importance.

THE PROTESTANT WORK ETHIC

The work ethic has been defined very narrowly to refer to a positive attitude about work—a belief that work itself is important and that doing a good job is essential. On the other hand, the work ethic has been defined very broadly to refer to the Protestant work ethic as described by Max Weber, the great German scholar. His famous treatise in 1904–1905, *The Protestant Ethic and the Spirit of Capitalism,* is the focal point of a debate that has raged for seven decades.[1] The Protestant work ethic encompassed an entire philosophy of life which Weber related to religious and economic activity. Therefore, when people talk about the Protestant ethic, they are referring to a broad philosophy that might include numerous beliefs about work and related topics.

The broader meaning of the work ethic typically refers to one or more of the following beliefs:

1. People have a moral and religious obligation to fill their lives with heavy physical toil. For some, this means that hard work, effort, and drudgery are to be valued for their own sake; physical pleasures and enjoyments are to be shunned; and an ascetic existence of methodical rigor is the only acceptable way to live.

2. Men and women are expected to spend long hours at work, with little or no time for personal recreation and leisure.

3. A worker should have a dependable attendance record, with low absenteeism and tardiness.

4. Workers should be highly productive and produce a large quantity of goods or service.

5. Workers should take pride in their work and do their jobs well.

6. Employees should have feelings of commitment and loyalty to their profession, their company, and their work group.

7. Workers should be achievement-oriented and constantly strive for promotions and advancement. High-status jobs with prestige and the respect of others are important indicators of a "good" person.

8. People should acquire wealth through honest labor and retain it through thrift and wise investments. Frugality is desirable; extravagance and waste should be avoided.

One of the most popular instruments for measuring these attitudes is the Protestant Ethic Scale. This questionnaire, shown in Figure 2.1, consists of items related to most of the preceding beliefs.[2]

When talking about the work ethic, people could be referring to any of these attitudes. The concept is difficult to understand because so many different ideas are thrown together. Although they might be related in the value systems of most people, these ideas need to be studied separately. The following discussion focuses specifically on the meaning of work. Other considerations, such as wealth and commitment, are examined only as they relate to this basic issue.

CONTINUUM OF IMPORTANCE

To understand the meaning of work, it is necessary to recognize the different values that attach to it. The meaning of work can be placed along a continuum of importance, as shown in Figure 2.2. This continuum ranges from a low end (G), where work is undesirable and has no meaning or importance, to a high end (A), where the importance of work is exaggerated (to the extent that it impairs a person's physical and emotional health). The traditional work ethic is defined by Points B and C along the continuum. At these points work is highly regarded either as a terminal value (where work itself is valued as a desirable activity) or as an instrumental value (where work is valued because it produces desirable consequences).

Movement along the continuum is characterized primarily by two factors: the rewards of work and a time perspective. The rewards (or outcomes) from work can be positive, such as self-esteem, promotion, service to the community, and the accomplishment of a personal goal. Or the rewards can be negative, such as boredom, fatigue, and a loss of personal freedom. The time perspective refers to the specificity or generality of the value and the immediacy of reward. The value can be specifically associated with a particular job (such as taking food to a customer), or it can be generalized to a broad group of related activities (such as providing service to customers).

The time perspective is specific if the meaning of work is associated with the outcomes of a particular task and the rewards are received within a short time. (*Example:* "If I serve

21

Figure 2.1. The Protestant Ethic Scale.

	I Strongly Disagree			I Strongly Agree		
1. Most people spend too much time in unprofitable amusements.	−3	−2	−1	+1	+2	+3
2. Our society would have fewer problems if people had less leisure time.	−3	−2	−1	+1	+2	+3
3. Money acquired easily (for example, through gambling or speculation) is usually spent unwisely.	−3	−2	−1	+1	+2	+3
4. There are few satisfactions equal to the realization that you have done your best at a job.	−3	−2	−1	+1	+2	+3
5. The most difficult college courses usually turn out to be the most rewarding.	−3	−2	−1	+1	+2	+3
6. Most people who don't succeed at life are just plain lazy.	−3	−2	−1	+1	+2	+3
7. The self-made man is likely to be more ethical than the man born to wealth.	−3	−2	−1	+1	+2	+3
8. I often feel I would be more successful if I sacrificed certain pleasures.	−3	−2	−1	+1	+2	+3
9. People should have more leisure time to spend in relaxation.[a]	−3	−2	−1	+1	+2	+3

[a]Scoring reversed.

Scoring: After items 9, 13, and 15 are multiplied by −1, a constant of 4 is added to each response and the responses are summed. The lowest possible score is 19; the highest possible score is 133. Mirels and Garrett reported that for a sample of 54 male students the mean and standard deviations were X = 85.7 and *sd* = 15.5; and, for 55 female students, X = 85.5 and *sd* = 16.2.

	I Strongly Disagree				I Strongly Agree		
10. Anyone who is able and willing to work hard has a good chance at succeeding.	-3	-2	-1		$+1$	$+2$	$+3$
11. People who fail at a job have not tried hard enough	-3	-2	-1		$+1$	$+2$	$+3$
12. Life would have very little meaning if we never had to suffer.	-3	-2	-1		$+1$	$+2$	$+3$
13. Hard work offers little guarantee of success.[a]	-3	-2	-1		$+1$	$+2$	$+3$
14. The credit card is a ticket to careless spending.	-3	-2	-1		$+1$	$+2$	$+3$
15. Life would be more meaningful if we had more leisure time.[a]	-3	-2	-1		$+1$	$+2$	$+3$
16. The man who can approach an unpleasant task with enthusiasm is the man who gets ahead.	-3	-2	-1		$+1$	$+2$	$+3$
17. If a man works hard enough, he is likely to make a good life for himself.	-3	-2	-1		$+1$	$+2$	$+3$
18. I feel uneasy when there is little work for me to do.	-3	-2	-1		$+1$	$+2$	$+3$
19. A distaste for hard work usually reflects a weakness of character.	-3	-2	-1		$+1$	$+2$	$+3$

Source:
Developed by Herbert L. Mirels and James B. Garrett. "The Protestant Ethic as a Personality Variable." *Journal of Consulting and Clinical Psychology,* Vol. 36, No. 1 (1971), pp. 40–44. Used with permission of the authors and the American Psychological Association.

Figure 2.2. The meaning of work: continuum of importance.

	Point	
Work Is Extremely Desirable		*Workaholic*
	A	Displaced Terminal Value Reward = removal of guilt, fear, or uncertainty Time perspective = general
		Work Ethic
	B	Terminal Value—Part of the Character Ethic Reward = work itself is a positive virtue of good character Time perspective = general
	C	Generalized Instrumental Value Reward = service to others: society, community, or company Time perspective = general
		Worth Ethic
	D	Self-Evaluation Reward = self-esteem Time perspective = general or specific
	E	Specific Instrumental Value Reward = money, status, recognition, promotion Time perspective = specific
		Leisure Ethic
	F	Unfortunate Obligation Reward = leaving work and using money from work to pursue nonwork activities Time perspective = specific
	G	Mind-Numbing Violence Reward = none; all work is punishing Time perspective = general
Work Is Extremely Undesirable		

Continuum of Importance

the food fast, I get a tip.'') The time perspective is general if the meaning of work is derived from a broad system of values. (*Example:* "When I do my job well I feel proud of myself, the customers are pleased, or I will get ahead in life.") In the general time perspective, the extrinsic rewards are not received immediately, but are obtained several years later and possibly in the next life. However, there are also intrinsic rewards associated with the general time perspective, such as joy in serving others and pride in doing a job well. Since these rewards are self-administered, they are received immediately, both during the activity and after it is done.

There are seven points along the value continuum. These points are not entirely distinct—there is a lot of overlap, both in the way they are defined and in the degree to which they are accepted by individual workers. These seven points represent the major ways work values have been discussed in the recent literature.

Workaholic.   At Point A, on one end of the continuum, work is so important to the person that he or she is addicted to it. Here work is a displaced terminal value. The meaning and purpose of work are distorted, and life is out of balance. The person works because of an uncontrollable compulsion. If there is no productive work to do, work will be created to fill the available time. This is the person who works long hours at the job, brings work home in the evenings, and dislikes taking a vacation, not because of a desire to create a meaningful product but because of an inner need to work. Deriving extreme pleasure from work does not make a person a workaholic.

It is the compulsion to work that identifies workaholics. If they are not working, they feel nervous and guilty. If their work schedule is interrupted, they get irritable and cross. The rewards of work are the removal of guilt, fear, and personal uncertainty. Work is a way to avoid confronting other concerns in life. In an unstructured social situation, workaholics feel unsure of themselves and uncertain of their abilities. Back on the job, they know what to do and can bury themselves in their work. (The symptoms of workaholics and their inability to retain meaning in their work are discussed in Chapter 12.)

Terminal Value.   At Point B on the continuum, work is a terminal value. Here the person believes that dedicated work is a desirable activity in and of itself. Dedicated work is considered a mark of good character and has been described by such positive labels as industry, perseverance, diligence, initiative, and devotion to one's calling. For people who accept this belief, dedicated work is a positive virtue, much like honesty or loyalty. Implicit in this belief is an ethical demand that a person *ought* to be diligent and industrious. This set of values has been called the character ethic and is described in Chapter 3.

The most widely accepted justification for a belief in the terminal value of work is that it is a religious principle. "Six days shalt thou labor and perform all thy work" (Exodus 20:9). According to Max Weber's classic discussion of the Protestant work ethic, work in your daily occupation was a "calling" from God. Thus the only way to live acceptably before God was through devotion to your calling. God demanded more than single good works; He demanded a methodical life of good works combined into a unified pattern of work and worship.

There are also nonreligious justifications for work as a terminal value. Some people believe, independent of religion, that work is a moral obligation. For example, they might believe that work is necessary for the survival of the individual and society—that unless productive work is done, humankind cannot survive. For such people, work is a natural law that governs life. It produces a feeling of dignity, self-respect, and independence. Therefore, they believe that everyone should feel a moral obligation to work.

Generalized Instrumental Value.   At Point C on the continuum, work is a generalized instrumental value—it is considered a positive activity because it contributes, at least indirectly, to other worthwhile goals. Here the rewards of work come from its contribution to society, the community, or the company. Work itself is not considered a personal virtue, nor is it a form of worship. But it is instrumental in achieving other virtues. Some of the positive values thought to be furthered by dedicated work include greater national productivity, organizational effectiveness, personal happiness, self-discipline and the development of character, improved health, and service to society as a result of one's accomplishments.

Self-Evaluation. At Point D on the continuum, work is valued because of its role in building a person's self-esteem. A worker develops feelings of competence and mastery by successfully accomplishing a task. Therefore, work is important to some people because it helps them feel competent and worthwhile. Other people prefer to evaluate themselves by non-work activities. For these people, work is not as important.

This point has been identified separately and placed in the middle of the continuum because so many articles have discussed the relationship between work and self-esteem. It should be noted, however, that work activity influences self-esteem at every point along the continuum. Even people whose primary life interests are hobbies and leisure activities experience changes in their self-esteem as a result of their competence or incompetence at work. As work becomes increasingly important to the individual, the relationship between effective performance and high self-esteem becomes stronger. But even at the bottom of the continuum, where work is undesirable, people's self-esteem will be influenced by their work performance.

The time perspective at this point might be either specific or general. With a specific time perspective, people evaluate themselves by their performance on a specific task. (*Example:* "I am a good welder," or "I am a competent insurance salesman.") With a general time perspective, people evaluate themselves in terms of general characteristics. (*Example:* "I am a dependable worker," "I am a valuable member of this company," or "I am a competent person who can get things done.") With a general time perspective, the importance of work to a person is quite similar to that described at Point C—generalized instrumental value. With a specific time

27

perspective, the importance of work to a person is quite similar to that described at Point E—specific instrumental value.

Specific Instrumental Value. At Point E on the continuum, work is a specific instrumental value. Work is positive because it contributes to the worker's level of rewards and job satisfaction. The time perspective is limited to the specific task. Thus the value of work does not go beyond the contribution it makes to the worker on a particular job. For example, work might acquire temporary value because it contributes to a person's financial position, social status, level in the company, social power, or job satisfaction.

Here work is valued because it contributes to the personal worth of the worker. For this reason, this value has occasionally been called the worth ethic—the job is worth doing because of its immediate rewards and satisfactions. If work does not result in some obvious signs of output or personal benefit, it loses its value. In essence, the worker thinks: "I will work hard at this job if it is worth doing—if the activity itself is enjoyable or if it will benefit me monetarily, increase my social status, or provide some other tangible reward." When work has meaning only as a specific instrumental value, it has no enduring value or nobility of purpose. The rewards tend to be immediate, specific, and usually self-serving.

Unfortunate Obligation. At Point F on the continuum, work is undesirable and disliked, although it could be neutral. The person's primary interests in life are away from the workplace. But the person realizes that money from work is required for other pursuits. Therefore, work represents an unfortunate obligation. Here, the major rewards for work are monetary; and the primary satisfactions come from leaving work and pursuing other interests. Since leisure activities represent the person's primary interests, this value has been called the leisure ethic.

The time perspective at this point is limited to a specific activity. A task is disliked because it prevents the worker from pursuing some other interest. Most of the job enrichment literature assumes that highly specialized, alienating jobs have caused workers to view work as an unfortunate obligation. Years of work on meaningless jobs have destroyed the value of work and forced the worker to look elsewhere for fulfillment in life. The literature suggests, however, that job enrichment can restore meaning to work and that workers can be moved from Point F on the continuum up to Points D and E. The relationship between job enrichment and work values is discussed in Chapter 11.

Mind-Numbing Violence.   At Point G on the continuum, work is described as a form of mind-numbing violence to humanity. This description comes from Studs Terkel's book *Working*. Here there are no rewards associated with work; all work is punishing and undesirable. An intense dislike of work is illustrated by the comments of a steelworker:

> The first thing happens at work: When the arms start moving, the brain stops. I punch in about ten minutes to seven in the morning . . . at seven it starts. My arms get tired about the first half-hour. After that they don't get tired any more until maybe the last half-hour at the end of the day. I work from seven to three-thirty. My arms are tired at seven-thirty and they're tired at three o'clock. I hope to God that I never get broke in, because I always want my arms to be tired at seven-thirty and three o'clock [laughs]. 'Cause that's when I know there's a beginning and there's an end. That I'm not brainwashed. In between, I don't even try to think. . . . Unless a guy's a nut, he never thinks about work or talks about it. Maybe about baseball or about getting drunk the other night or he got laid or he didn't get laid. I'd say one out of a hundred will actually get excited about work.[3]

DESIRABILITY OF THE
MEANINGS OF WORK

Placing the meaning of work along a continuum may convey the mistaken impression that one end is good and the other end is bad. Consequently, one final point should be noted. As defined in this chapter, the work ethic does not refer to a compulsion to work—the meaning of work to a workaholic. This definition is important in later chapters. The benefits of work to the individual, the company, and society are not so positive when the work ethic includes workaholism. The distinction between the work ethic and the worth ethic is also critical in understanding the development of work values and evaluating the usefulness of job enrichment programs.

REFERENCES

1. Max Weber, "Die Protestantische Ethik und der Geist des Kapitalismus," *Archiv fur Sozialwissenschaft,* Vols. 20, 21 (1904, 1905). Translated by Talcott Parsons, *The Protestant Ethic and the Spirit of Capitalism* (New York: Charles Scribner's Sons, 1958), Chapter 3.

2. Herbert L. Mirels and James B. Garrett, "The Protestant Ethic as a Personality Variable," *Journal of Consulting and Clinical Psychology,* Vol. 36, No. 1 (1971), pp. 40–44. Other instruments measuring work values and attitudes have been developed by Stephen Wollack, James G. Goodale, Jan P. Wijting, and Patricia C. Smith, "Development of the Survey of Work Values," *Journal of Applied Psychology,* Vol. 55, No. 4 (1971), pp. 331–338; Robert Dubin, "Industrial Workers' Worlds: A Study of the 'Central Life Interests' of Industrial Workers," *Social Problems,* Vol. 3 (1956), pp. 131–142; Milton R. Blood, "Work Values and Job Satisfaction," *Journal of Applied Psychology,* Vol. 53, No. 6 (1969), pp. 456–459; Thomas M. Lodahl and Mathilde Kejner, "The Definition and Measurement of Job Involvement," *Journal of Applied Psychology,* Vol. 49, No. 1 (1965), pp. 24–33.

3. Studs Terkel, *Working* (New York: Avon Books, 1972), p. 5.

3

THE WORK ETHIC
IN EARLY AMERICA

There was no uncertainty in early America about the work ethic and its importance; it was the only sure pathway to eternal salvation and worldly success. The signposts marking the way were clear and unmistakable. Like a brightly lighted beacon, the moral preeminence of work beamed unwaveringly from all the early moralists. Influential statesmen, clergymen, and authors all taught that success came through hard work, diligence, perseverance, honesty, and thrift. Young people were confronted on all sides with advice about dedicated work, the wise use of time, and the importance of good character. Work was accepted as both a terminal value and a generalized instrumental value.

For early Americans, work was a necessary and important part of life. It was more than accepted as the common lot of mankind; it was highly esteemed as a noble activity. The moral importance of work stood virtually unchallenged as an accepted social value. Dignity and honor accompanied any honest job, whether it entailed working with your head or your hands. Jobs that required greater skill and training were justly paid a higher wage. But regardless of the wage paid, all honest jobs were imbued with dignity and value.

Living on public welfare was a totally foreign concept.

31

Social welfare programs for the poor were designed to provide only temporary help until secure employment could be obtained. Most welfare programs were created to help new immigrants. People were expected to work and to provide for their own support regardless of wealth or social status. Living in idleness and luxury on inherited wealth was not socially acceptable, especially in the North, although it was not much of an issue in America until the end of the nineteenth century.

Absenteeism was tolerated reluctantly when there were valid excuses. But there was no good excuse for tardiness. Punctuality was a highly esteemed virtue and a mark of good character. Skilled tradesmen were applauded for their craftsmanship, and they took pride in the high quality of their work. Young tradesmen served long apprenticeships, a sacrifice which only strengthened their feelings of loyalty and commitment to their trade. Poor-quality work was called slothfulness and condemned as loudly as idleness.

The hours of work were from sunup until sundown. Idleness and drunkenness were equally sinful, and people of all ages were admonished to fill their hours with worthwhile pursuits. While there was an implicit value attached to being busy and constantly at work, there was a greater value attached to being efficient and productive. The purpose of efficiency was to allow for leisure activities. But leisure was to be spent in education and other worthwhile pursuits rather than in idleness or fanciful play.

Occupational advancements were looked upon favorably, such as acquiring greater skills, learning a new trade, obtaining an education, and being promoted to a position of greater responsibility. Advancing within your occupation not only meant greater wealth and personal success; it was also a mark of good character. It meant that you could now make a greater contribution to society. Such opportunities were highly coveted. Educational opportunities especially were limited and, consequently, highly valued.

The ethical standards of society were set by the middle classes, who controlled the major institutions of social influence, including the factories, schools, colleges, churches, political offices, and publishing companies. The interlocking set of individuals who controlled these institutions were called "moralists, keepers of their countrymen's moral conscience."[1] This group of people felt greatly concerned about the social ethics and personal morals of Americans. They used the institutions at their command to inculcate their ethical standards in society. They proselyted with a missionary zeal. Although they were primarily Northerners, their opinions and influence carried uncommon weight throughout the United States.

Knowing what the early settlers of America thought about work is interesting today not only because of *what* they believed, but *why*. They believed in hard work, diligence, thrift, and industry for several reasons, but principally for one major reason. Above all, work was commanded by God; it was the common lot of humanity and accepted as a divine command. Dedicated labor was the sure pathway to eternal salvation.

There were other justifications for work in addition to the religious calling. Dedicated work was considered an economic necessity and a form of public usefulness. It was also identified as the only acceptable road to social and financial success as well as the primary antidote for moral laxity. But during the early days of colonization, all these justifications fit together in a unified, consistent philosophy of life. Hard, dedicated work was consistent with the needs of society, the goals of the individual in this life, and eternal salvation in the life to come.

THE CHARACTER ETHIC

Max Weber credited the origin of the work ethic to Martin Luther's interpretation of "calling" in Luther's translation of the Bible from the Latin Vulgate into German in 1521 to 1522. According to Luther, man was summoned by God to a secular calling which today we would call a job. Luther believed that by laboring in your calling you expressed brotherly love through the services and products you produced for society. Later, however, the fulfillment of worldly duties under all circumstances was strongly emphasized as the only way to live acceptably before God. All legitimate callings were presumed to have equal worth in the sight of God. Thus the Protestant Reformation, supported by Luther's own translation of the Bible, was credited with originating the concept of worldly work as a calling from God. This concept provided a religious justification not only for work but also for the rigid social class system that dominated medieval history.[2]

The early immigrants to America were primarily Protestant separatists. Consequently, the work values of these early settlers were labeled the "Protestant work ethic" by Max Weber. Some writers have preferred to use the term "Puritan ethic," because intense discussions about the importance of work can be traced to the philosophical writings of the early Puritan founders.[3] More recently, "character ethic" has been used, perhaps more appropriately, since these work values are not unique to either Protestantism or Puritanism.[4] The character ethic taught that the way to success and wealth, and the only way to live a righteous life, was through working hard and cultivating the virtues of frugality, industry, diligence, prudence, and honesty. The "character ethic" is an especially appropriate label, since it emphasizes the integration and justification for this set of virtues. The work ethic and other virtues of moral living comprised a unified and consistent set of values for every decent person.

The character ethic was a well-established cultural tradition, especially in England, for many years before the early immigrants left Europe for religious freedom and economic opportunity. In the 80 years after Elizabeth ascended the throne in 1558, more than 20 works were printed which taught the same philosophy—that God was best served by laboring unceasingly in an earthly calling, and that success came through hard work, frugality, and perseverance. The work ethic in Europe was taught by clergy and laity alike, but its most ardent proponents were influential members of the clergy, and eternal salvation was a powerful incentive for believing in the doctrines they taught.

In early America the work ethic was a central part of religion. The gospel of work was taught week after week from the pulpits. William Penn (1644–1718) reminded the Quakers of Philadelphia that "Diligence is a Virtue useful and laudable among Men: It is a discreet and understanding Application of one's Self to Business; and avoids the Extreams of Idleness. . . . Frugality is a Virtue too, and not of little Use in Life. . . . It is proverbial, *A Penny sav'd is a Penny got*."[5]

One of the greatest apostles of the work ethic in early America was Cotton Mather (1663–1728), an influential Puritan leader in New England. In 1701 Mather published a popular treatise titled *A Christian at His Calling,* in which he stressed that "every Christian hath a general calling, which is to serve the Lord Jesus Christ, and save his own soul, in the services of religion. . . . But then, every Christian hath also a personal calling, or a certain particular employment, by which his usefulness in his neighborhood is distinguished." According to Mather, a Christian laboring at his two callings was like a man in a boat rowing for heaven: "If he mind but one of his callings, be it which it will, he pulls the oar but on one side of the boat and will make but a poor dispatch to the shore of eternal blessedness."[6]

Popular writings also abounded with advice about the virtues of hard work. According to Max Weber, the most influential popular proponent of the American work ethic was Benjamin Franklin (1706–1790). Many of Franklin's ideas appeared in *Poor Richard's Almanac,* a publication he started in 1732 and continued until 1758. Franklin taught that wealth was the result of virtue and the proper display of character. In *Advice to a Young Tradesman,* he argued that the way to get ahead was as plain as the way to market: "It depends chiefly on two words, *industry* and *frugality;* that is, waste neither time nor money, but make the best use of both." In Franklin's *Autobiography,* eleven more virtues were added to the list: temperance, silence, order, resolution, sincerity, justice, moderation, cleanliness, tranquility, chastity, and humility.[7] With Franklin, the work ethic shifted from a direct form of worshiping God to an indirect way of rendering service to God by developing one's character and doing good to one's fellowmen.

After Franklin, the religious justification for the work ethic was gradually replaced with other practical justifications. Many eighteenth- and nineteenth-century moralists continued to emphasize the importance of diligent work in a religious life. But the most powerful justification for work was its role in the development of good character. The road to success was still paved with the character ethic. And though hard work was less an indication of serving God, it remained an indication of social usefulness and the appropriate design for success.

During this period, children's schoolbooks were an especially strong influence on the development of moral values. The most well-known and widely read children's books were *McGuffey's Eclectic Readers,* by William Holmes McGuffey (1800–1873). Over 122 million copies of these six readers were sold, with peak years falling in the 1870s and 1880s. It has been suggested that from 1850 to 1925 four-fifths of the schoolchildren in America studied from *McGuffey's Eclectic Readers*.[8] In story after story, diligence and the development of good character were repeatedly rewarded, while carelessness, disobedience, and dishonesty brought unhappiness and shame. Numerous stories illustrated the rewards of industry. In short, *McGuffey's Eclectic Readers* taught children to do the right things and develop the proper attributes of character, regardless of peer pressure.

CHALLENGES TO THE WORK ETHIC

Until 1850, the moral preeminence of work stood essentially unchallenged as an accepted social value. Between 1850 and 1920, however, the work ethic collided with the industrial revolution in America. Factories grew larger, became more numerous, and employed large numbers of workers. Industrialization and new working conditions created problems for the nineteenth-century moralists who wanted to continue proclaiming the moral vitality of work. By 1920, the work ethic stood firm in spite of its critics. But it had become idealized as a general social value and was tied less to the day-to-day context of actual work. During this period the work ethic was challenged by the realities of factory work.[9]

The factory wage system posed an especially serious challenge to the moral importance of work. Factory wages became a major issue largely because of the debates about slavery. A worker who was chained to a factory wage system was no more free than the slave chained to a master. Such a system destroyed the economic freedom of the worker and the meaning of work. "To put a man upon wages is to put him in the position of a dependent," wrote Samuel Eliot in 1871; the longer a man holds the position, the more his capacities for independent judgment atrophy and "the less of a man, in fine, he becomes."[10]

If work was to be worthwhile, it required the self-direction and autonomy of the worker. Several schemes were tried during this period to restore individual freedom to the worker: workers' cooperatives, profit sharing, stock purchase plans, industrial democracy, and piece-rate incentive plans. None of these schemes restored the conditions of freedom and autonomy that had existed earlier in the shops and cottage system. In the shops, workers were paid for what they produced; in the factories, they were paid for their time. One system rewarded diligent work; the other approximated conditions of bondage. Piece-rate incentives were the most enduring and widely accepted change to the factory wage system. But they failed to restore a sense of freedom to the worker. Piece rates were established on specialized jobs that placed increasingly tight restrictions on the movements of workers.

A second challenge to the work ethic resulted from the efficiency of the factory system and the materialism it produced. Between 1860 and 1920 the population of the United States tripled, while the volume of manufactured goods increased between twelve- and fourteenfold. The economy changed from one of excess demand to one of excess supply in various major industries. The efficiency of industrialization changed ideas about the permanence of scarcity and economic necessity. The importance of diligence and industry was not quite so obvious. Society became more concerned with how equitably products were allocated and consumed than with the ever-pressing need to produce more. Excess capacity made it harder and harder to insist that compulsive activity, work, and usefulness were the highest goals of life. The ultimate effect of excess capacity was to create a materialistic society with more leisure time and more goods and services. The importance of working hard diminished and the importance of enjoying the fruits of your labor increased.

Another challenge to the work ethic came from the growing uncertainty that hard work would bring economic and social success. While Horatio Alger stories continued to dominate the success literature, some moralists began to notice that heroic rises were the exception, not the rule. Most people who made it to the top did not start at the bottom; they started much higher, with the advantages of wealth, family influence, and better education.[11]

The most dramatic success philosophy to challenge the work ethic was the personality ethic. The personality ethic began to blossom during the 1920s and emerged full-blown in 1936, when Dale Carnegie's book *How To Win Friends and Influence People* was published. The book was an enormous success. During the next 35 years, over 8 million copies were sold. The personality ethic taught that the way to success was through other people. A pleasing personality could help you get along with others and sell products that were in competition with other products.[12]

The principles of the personality ethic were designed to improve social interaction. Carnegie offered six ways to make people like you, twelve ways to win people to your way of thinking, and nine ways to change people without giving offense or arousing resentment. Success came not by working hard but by knowing how to smile, nod approvingly, and get other people to talk about themselves. Honesty, which was of central importance to the work ethic, was more than ignored in the personality ethic. It was inconsistent with the goals of avoiding arguments, agreeing with others, and getting others to think that the ideas were theirs.

In the work ethic of early Americans, "true success" not only meant wealth and happiness on earth; more important, it meant an other-worldly reward of eternal salvation. In the personality ethic, "true success" meant something very different. The literature of the personality ethic emphasized accumulating wealth for its own sake—a goal that lacked the nobility of benefiting society, worshipping God, or helping others through charitable contributions or personal service. By avoiding arguments, speaking the other fellow's name, and emphatically admitting your mistakes, you increased your chances of making a sale, impressing the boss, or making friends. But the ultimate goal of the personality ethic was a self-seeking accumulation of status, wealth, or power.[13]

With the advent of the personality ethic, the moral preeminence of work no longer stood unchallenged as a noble social virtue. Working long and hard was no longer seen as the only road to success. Rather, success depended on a pleasing personality, the ability to get along with others, and knowing the right person.

An abundant society and the advent of the personality ethic raise several serious questions about the status of the work ethic today. What are workers today being taught about work and the development of character? What are the values of today's workers? These issues are the focus of the next chapter.

REFERENCES

1. Two of the best reviews of the work ethic in early America are Richard M. Huber, *The American Idea of Success* (New York: McGraw-Hill, 1971) and Daniel T. Rodgers, *The Work Ethic in Industrial America, 1850–1920* (Chicago: University of Chicago Press, 1978).

2. Max Weber, "Die Protestantische Ethik und der Geist des Kapitalismus," *Archiv fur Sozialwissenschaft,* Vols. 20, 21 (1904 and 1905). Translated by Talcott Parsons, *The Protestant Ethic and the Spirit of Capitalism* (New York: Charles Scribner's Sons, 1958).

3. John D. Long, "The Protestant Ethic Reexamined," *Business Horizons,* Vol. 15, No. 2 (1972), pp. 75–81.

4. A lengthy and well-documented description of the character ethic is presented in Huber, *op. cit.*

5. William Penn, "The Advice of William Penn to His Children," in Frederick B. Tolles, *Meeting House and Counting House: The Merchants of Colonial Philadelphia, 1682–1763* (Chapel Hill: University of North Carolina Press, 1948), pp. 45–48.

6. Cotton Mather, *A Christian at His Calling* (Boston: Green and Allen, 1701), pp. 38–39.

7. Benjamin Franklin, *Advice to a Young Tradesman* (1748). See *Benjamin Franklin: The Autobiography and Other Writings* (New York: Signet, 1961), pp. 185–187.

8. William H. McGuffey, *McGuffey's Eclectic Reader,* Vols. 1–6 (New York: American Book Co., 1879, 1896, 1907, 1920). Statistics are quoted from Huber, *op. cit.,* pp. 23–24; and John H. Westerhoff III, *McGuffey and His Readers* (Nashville: Abingdon Press, 1978). Quotation comes from Hugh Fullerton, "That Guy McGuffey," *Saturday Evening Post* (November 26, 1927).

9. The effects of the industrial revolution on the work ethic are analyzed by Rodgers, *op. cit.*

10. Samuel Eliot, "Relief of Labor," *Journal of Social Science,* Vol. 4 (1871), p. 139.

11. See Huber, *op. cit.;* and Rodgers, *op. cit.*

12. Dale Carnegie, *How to Win Friends and Influence People* (New York: Simon & Schuster, 1936).

13. The concept of "true success" is discussed by Huber, *op. cit.*

THE WORK ETHIC
TODAY

There is a lot of disagreement about the work ethic today. As described in Chapter 1, some observers believe the work ethic in America is alive and well, and joyfully exclaim, "Long live dignity in labor!" Others think the work ethic is dying or dead and say without regret, "May it forever rest in peace." Between these extremes are many other attitudes. This chapter summarizes several studies of the values and attitudes of American workers.

SURVEY OF WORKER ATTITUDES

In 1975, my colleagues and I surveyed the attitudes and values of a large sample of American workers. We wanted to measure an assortment of attitudes toward one's specific job, toward the company, toward the community, and toward work in general. Our goal was to study the meaning of work in the lives of workers. What do today's workers think about hard work? Do they take pride in their work? Is pride in craftsmanship as important as money and fringe benefits? How do today's workers feel about welfare?

To answer these questions, we surveyed 3,053 workers in 53 companies throughout the United States. The companies were predominantly manufacturing plants, although they included three mines, three insurance companies, several banks, one construction company, one hotel, two airlines, two printers, one hospital, and one school district. The participants were selected from a list of 200 companies compiled by an advisory group of businesspeople. We attempted to select organizations of various sizes from both rural and urban areas as well as from numerous regions of the United States.[1]

To ensure a broad sampling of responses, we limited the number of workers surveyed in any particular company to 80 employees, except when different divisions of the same company located in different communities were sampled. Within each company, the goal was to obtain 50 percent operative employees in production or assembly-line jobs, 20 percent supervisors or foremen, and 30 percent employees in middle management or in clerical or staff positions.

To minimize potential selection biases, a random method of selecting participants was used whenever possible. In some instances, however, it was necessary to deviate from a strictly random selection to accommodate the production demands of the company. On assembly-line jobs, for example, either an entire line or section of a line was stopped while the employees completed the questionnaire, or workers were taken off the line one by one as supervisors or maintenance personnel could replace them. In most instances, small groups of employees assembled in a lunchroom or conference room, where they were given the questionnaires and brief instructions by the researchers. The employees were assured that the questionnaire was for research purposes only and that it would be anonymous. When the questionnaires were completed, usually in about 45 minutes, they were handed directly to the researcher.

The survey consisted of 191 questions about workers' attitudes toward their jobs, their company, their community, and work in general. Also included were several demographic questions. The questionnaire was pilot-tested with employees in two organizations and then modified slightly to clarify or eliminate some ambiguities.

TODAY'S WORK ETHIC

When the 3,053 responses to each question were averaged, the character ethic appeared to be flourishing among this sample of workers. For example, the workers were presented with a list of work-related outcomes and asked to indicate the desirability or importance of each outcome on a scale that ranged from 0 (extremely undesirable) to 100 (extremely desirable). They were free to choose any number they wanted from 0 to 100 with the only restriction that they not use the same number more than once. Their responses indicated how desirable and important the rewards were they received from working. These data help to answer the question: "Why do people work?"

The Rewards of Work.   Surprisingly, money was not the most desirable work outcome. The most desirable work-related outcome was "feeling pride and craftsmanship in your work" (86.6). As shown in Table 4.1 all four intrinsic rewards were highly valued: it was very important for people to feel pride and craftsmanship in their work, to feel more worthwhile, to be recognized and respected by others, and to be of service to others. These intrinsic rewards are apparently very important reasons for working. People work, in part, because of the positive feeling they get from doing a good job.

The second most desirable work outcome was "getting more money or a larger pay increase" (81.2). No doubt, money is an important work outcome. It is much more important than fringe benefits and promotions and essentially as important as the intrinsic rewards. People need money to live, and getting more money is a very desirable reward for working. If a job did not pay well, no matter how intrinsically rewarding it was, a worker would probably be forced to leave it for some other form of profitable employment. The other two extrinsic rewards, fringe benefits and promotions, were rated slightly desirable but closer to neutral.

The survey data indicated that supervisors still have the capacity to reward or punish their subordinates. Supervisors'

Table 4.1. Desirability of 13 work outcomes: average responses of 3,053 American workers.

Extremely Undesirable					Neutral				Extremely Desirable	
0	10	20	30	40	50	60	70	80	90	100

Intrinsic Rewards

Feeling pride and craftsmanship in your work	86.6
Feeling more worthwhile	80.4
Being recognized and gaining the respect of others	78.7
Being of service to others	78.3

Extrinsic Rewards

Getting more money or a larger pay increase	81.2
Receiving more fringe benefits	68.9
Being promoted more quickly	68.0

Other Work Outcomes

Having your supervisor compliment you	71.4
Being chewed out by your supervisor	18.6
Being given more responsibility	70.6
Having leisure and free time	58.7
Feeling tired from a day's work	43.3
Being fired	7.9

compliments were quite desirable work outcomes (71.4), and being chewed out was a very undesirable outcome (18.6). Workers generally desired more responsibility in their work (70.6), but they did not want work to interfere with their leisure and free time (58.7) or make them feel tired at the end of the day (43.3).

Pride in Craftsmanship. Another indication of strong positive support for the importance of work was shown by the responses to several statements about pride in craftsmanship. The workers were asked to indicate how much they agreed with each statement by using a scale which ranged from 1 (strongly disagree) to 7 (strongly agree), with 4 as neutral. As shown in Table 4.2, the statement that garnered the greatest agreement was "A worker should feel a sense of pride in his work" (6.61). Most workers also strongly agreed with a similar statement: "A worker should do a decent job whether or not his supervisor is around" (6.60). When the statement was reversed—"There is nothing wrong with doing a poor job at work if a man can get away with it"—most workers strongly disagreed (1.51). The data clearly indicated that most of these American workers were strongly committed to pride in craftsmanship. They thought they should enjoy their work and receive recognition for doing a good job. But doing a good job was important, they said, even if they disliked their work.

Moral Importance of Work. A commitment to high-quality work is a major part of the traditional work ethic. The other major part is the moral importance of work. This refers to the moral obligation people feel to have an occupation and contribute some product or service to society. As shown in Table 4.3, the survey data indicated that while most workers felt a strong commitment to pride in craftsmanship, they were much less enthusiastic about the moral importance of work. For many employees, work embodied certain positive social

Table 4.2. Pride in craftsmanship:
average responses of 3,053 American workers.

Strongly Disagree			Neutral			Strongly Agree
1	2	3	4	5	6	7
A worker should feel a sense of pride in his work						6.61
A worker should do a decent job whether or not his supervisor is around						6.60
There is nothing wrong with doing a poor job at work if a man can get away with it						1.51
An individual should enjoy his work						6.36
Even if you dislike your work you should do your best						6.00
Getting recognition for my own work is important to me						6.00

Table 4.3. Moral importance of work:
average responses of 3,053 American workers.

Strongly Disagree			Neutral			Strongly Agree
1	2	3	4	5	6	7
A good indication of a man's worth is how well he does his job						5.82
Working hard makes a man a better person						5.46
Work should be one of the most important parts of a person's life						4.92
Rich people should feel an obligation to work even if they do not need to						4.08
An unproductive worker is not loyal to his country						3.96

rewards but was not the ultimate in their existence. Work contributed to making an individual a better person, and doing a good job was an indication of an individual's worth. But work for the sake of working was not an important value.

In early America, the road to success followed the path of hard work, diligence, thrift, and perseverance. In America today, the same path is still largely seen as the way to success, as shown in Table 4.4. When asked what determines success, workers indicated that success generally was not a matter of luck. Knowledge and education, usually considered the solution to discrimination and dead-end jobs, were seen as only slightly associated with success. The major determinant of occupational success was the amount of effort put into one's work.

The rewards for doing a good job were not especially promising in the eyes of most workers. The relationship between doing an especially good job and receiving various outcomes is shown in Table 4.4. In general, there was a strong relationship between doing a good job and feeling intrinsically rewarded. But the extrinsic rewards were not as likely. Even the reactions of supervisors were not especially predictable.

To summarize these reward contingencies broadly, the major reasons for working hard are not pay, promotions, and supervisor compliments, since workers believe these rewards

Table 4.4. Road to success: average responses of 3,053 American workers.

Strongly Disagree			Neutral			Strongly Agree
1	2	3	4	5	6	7

Success in an occupation is mainly a matter of luck	2.51
Success in an occupation is mainly a matter of how much you know	4.30
Success in an occupation is mainly a matter of how much effort you put into it	5.70

Never			Uncertain		100% Certain	
1	2	3	4	5	6	7

If you do an especially good job, what are the chances that:

You will get a larger pay increase	4.16
You will receive more fringe benefits	3.00
You will be promoted more quickly	3.83
You will feel greater pride in craftsmanship	6.01
You will feel more worthwhile and be a better person	5.91
You will be recognized and gain the respect of others	5.05
Your work will benefit others	5.78
Your supervisor will compliment you	4.90
You will be given more responsibility	5.13
You will feel tired at the end of the day	4.72

If you do a rather poor job, what are the chances that:

You will be fired	4.18
You will be chewed out by your supervisor	5.03
You will feel guilty	5.71
Your fellow workers will get on you	3.77

are not very likely. The major reasons are the intrinsic feelings of pride in craftsmanship, being of service, and feeling worthwhile—outcomes much more closely associated with doing a good job. Likewise, if workers do a poor job they are likely to feel guilty and may get chewed out by their supervisors. But it is not too likely that they will get fired for doing a poor job and even less likely that their fellow workers will care.

Most of the attitudes toward the specific job and the

company were positive, but closer to neutral. For example, "Considering everything about the company, I'm very well satisfied with it" was slightly positive (4.97), and "My company is just a place to work and is separate from my personal interests' was slightly negative (3.60). (Company and community attitudes will be discussed later.) In spite of relatively neutral attitudes toward the company, most workers reported quite favorable attitudes about the value and importance of doing a good job.

These findings indicate that the work ethic continues to be a significant force in the lives of many American workers. Work per se does not possess the strong moral imperative that was characteristic of the pronouncements of early American moralists. But pride in craftsmanship is still highly valued and generally associated with doing a good job; the road to success is still largely paved with dedicated efforts; and work is still a fairly important part of workers' lives.

Finding favorable attitudes within a mixed group at one particular time, however, says very little about what is happening to the work ethic today. Are attitudes more or less favorable now than they were in past decades? Are the social, economic, and family forces that created the current favorable work attitudes capable of passing on these values to future generations? In short, is there a "generation gap" in the work values of today's workers? The evidence presented in the following sections suggests that in some areas there is not much difference between the values of younger and older workers. But in other areas there are significant differences that might have profound implications for the quality of an individual's work life and the effectiveness of organizations.

THE VALUES OF YOUNG WORKERS

The attitudes of different age groups were compared to examine the relationship between age and work values. The sample was divided into thirds. The younger group ranged from 17 to 26 years of age, the middle group from 27 to 40, and the older group from 41 to 65. When it was found that the younger group included 51 percent females while the middle group had only 30 percent females and the older group 36 percent females, the differences in both age and sex were analyzed to avoid the problem of unequal distribution of females in the three groups.

Do workers of different ages and sexes have different work attitudes and values? We were interested in several factors, such as attitudes toward pay and other work-related outcomes; work values; attitudes toward the company and the role of business in society; attitudes about welfare; and attitudes about fellow workers and social pressures. The results are summarized in Tables 4.5 to 4.18 at the end of this chapter.

The Meaning of Money.   Younger workers are frequently criticized for being interested only in money—"What's in it for me?" Do younger workers attach greater value and importance to money than older workers, and if so, why? The survey results indicated that getting more money was more important to younger workers, male and female, than to older workers (Table 4.5). A reasonable explanation is that younger workers make less money, yet need more money than older workers to buy a house, furniture, and other major first-time purchases. The average monthly take-home pay for young males ($590) was only 64 percent that of older males ($923) and 67 percent that of middle-aged males ($877). Because their income is lower, younger workers are less satisfied with their pay, even though they tend to think it is equitable and fair. Considering all the responses, we concluded that the accumulation of wealth appears to hold the same meaning for both older and younger workers. Money is important to workers of all ages and only slightly more important to younger workers. It is important not only for what it can obtain but also for what it signifies in terms of status, prestige, and approval of work performance.

Pride in Craftsmanship.   The questionnaire contained several items designed to measure pride in craftsmanship. On all the questions, significant differences were reported between

49

the three age groups (Table 4.6). The direction of the differences was extremely consistent as well—younger workers were less work-oriented than middle-aged workers and middle-aged workers were less work-oriented than older workers. Compared with older workers, younger workers felt that pride in craftsmanship and joy in being of service were less desirable, having leisure and free time were more desirable, and doing a poor job was more acceptable. Younger workers also reported that if they did an especially good job they would not be as likely as older workers to feel more worthwhile or to think their work benefited others.

These results have serious implications for the motivation of younger workers. They suggest that intrinsic work rewards are not as desirable and that the relationship between good performance and receiving intrinsic rewards is more uncertain for younger workers. Unless they can obtain other valued rewards for their efforts, younger workers are likely to be less motivated than older workers.

Two interesting differences were found between the work attitudes of males and females. Males tended to agree more strongly that work should be one of the most important parts of life. This difference is understandable, since women tend to play a much larger role in raising children and running a home. However, on most of the questions regarding pride, doing a good job, and serving others, females were more work-oriented than males, as illustrated by Figure 4.1. Women agreed more strongly that you should do your best even if you dislike your work and even if your supervisor is not around. When asked to evaluate their own performance, women reported higher performance levels than men. Also, leisure and free time were less important to women. We concluded that older workers are more work-oriented than younger workers, and that females endorse pride and diligence slightly more than males.

Moral Importance of Work. In the American culture the importance of doing a good job appears to be widely accepted, especially by older workers. But the moral importance of work

Figure 4.1. Pride in craftsmanship.

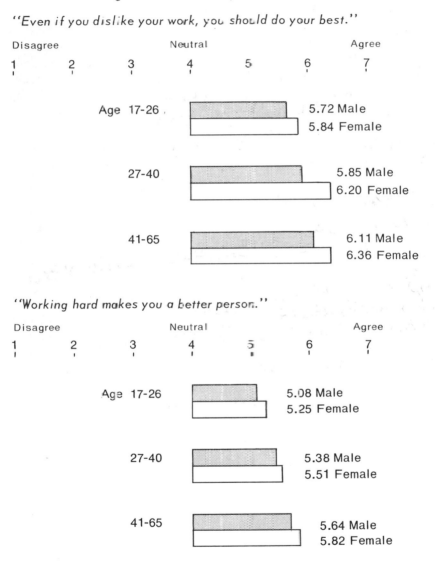

"Even if you dislike your work, you should do your best."

Disagree			Neutral			Agree
1	2	3	4	5	6	7

Age 17-26
5.72 Male
5.84 Female

27-40
5.85 Male
6.20 Female

41-65
6.11 Male
6.36 Female

"Working hard makes you a better person."

Disagree			Neutral			Agree
1	2	3	4	5	6	7

Age 17-26
5.08 Male
5.25 Female

27-40
5.38 Male
5.51 Female

41-65
5.64 Male
5.82 Female

is not as widely believed. Young workers particularly seem to question the value of work. On six statements related to the value of work, younger workers were significantly less work-oriented than older workers (Table 4.7).

One question asked whether work was related to the measure of a person's "worth." The responses to this question indicated that older workers and younger workers used different criteria in measuring worth. In America there has been a noticeable move toward an egaliterian philosophy: all people are not only created equal, but when carried to the extreme they remain equal—equal in employment, equal in housing, equal in pay, equal in education, and equal in value. According to this philosophy, everyone has the same worth regardless of his or her performance. While younger workers were inclined to accept egalitarianism, older workers did not particularly espouse this philosophy. They felt that a good indication of a person's worth was how well he or she performed a job. This attitude is rather close to the early Puritan philosophy that people's social usefulness is determined in part by the service they perform.

The belief that work should be one of the most important parts of a person's life was not as well accepted by younger workers as by older workers. And when asked if rich people should feel an obligation to work, young workers tended to say no while older workers tended to say yes. Older and younger workers also disagreed about the loyalty of unproductive workers to their country. (This item was included in the questionnaire because subsequent research was scheduled to cover several countries in the Far East. In some of these countries, especially Taiwan and Japan, slothfulness used to be, and to some extent still is, considered a sign of disloyalty.) Among American workers, older workers tended to feel that unproductive workers were not loyal, while younger workers felt that poor performance had very little to do with loyalty. One older worker, after looking at these results, said he thought younger workers should go back to the newspapers written during World War II and read some of the editorials condemn-

Figure 4.2. Moral importance of work.

"Work should be one of the most important parts of a person's life."

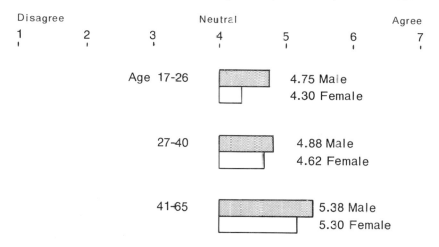

Disagree   Neutral   Agree

1   2   3   4   5   6   7

Age 17-26   4.75 Male / 4.30 Female

27-40   4.88 Male / 4.62 Female

41-65   5.38 Male / 5.30 Female

"An unproductive worker is not loyal to his country."

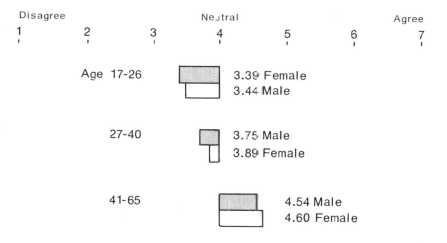

Disagree   Neutral   Agree

1   2   3   4   5   6   7

Age 17-26   3.39 Female / 3.44 Male

27-40   3.75 Male / 3.89 Female

41-65   4.54 Male / 4.60 Female

ing workers who restricted productivity because of group-enforced quotas. The results are illustrated in Figure 4.2.

Leisure and Free Time.   Many observers of today's work values say that the most significant change is the desire for more leisure. Employees increasingly want more free time away from work and the opportunity to pursue leisure activities. The survey confirmed this observation (Table 4.8). Workers of all ages indicated that leisure and free time were desirable, but they were much more desirable to younger workers than older workers. Furthermore, when they were asked about being expected to do additional work, younger workers tended to feel it was slightly undesirable while older workers tended to say it was slightly desirable.

These results confirm the impression of numerous supervisors, who find it increasingly difficult to alter job assignments and fill overtime schedules. One supervisor said, "When I have to find people to work overtime I can just about predict which ones will do it by knowing whether they have their boats, campers, trail bikes, or snowmobiles paid off. If they do, it's almost impossible to get them to come in to work. They want to stay home and enjoy their toys." The increased opportunity for leisure activities, accompanied by the range of leisure products available, is a significant change in the American culture. Mass advertising, especially television commercials, subtly suggests that the pursuit of leisure is life's ultimate goal.

Promotions and Social Status.   An important issue that separates the personality ethic and the character ethic is whether a person should work hard even at the risk of losing friends. The character ethic encourages young men and women to avoid peer influences and petty jealousies that might keep them from developing such virtues as perseverance, industry, and determination. The personality ethic glorifies the importance of making friends and maintaining social relationships. The survey confronted this issue directly by asking workers whether it was more important to them to get along with friends or to work hard at a job. Younger workers were close to neutral on this issue, while older workers indicated that it was more important to work hard (Table 4 9).

These findings are consistent with the attitudes discussed earlier about the importance of hard work and pride in craftsmanship. Younger workers still support the character ethic, but not as strongly as older workers. Their attitudes are more consistent with the personality ethic than are those of older workers.

Accepting the personality ethic means trying to get along well with friends. It also means striving for a promotion or higher social status. The survey indicated that young workers wanted to be promoted more quickly, but they did not want a promotion if it interfered with other things in life. Many supervisors think these "other things" are leisure activities. But more than just leisure and free time are involved. Many workers, both old and young, place a lower value on promotion than they do on family, religion, and the quality of work life.

In short, social status is less important to younger workers than it is to older workers. Furthermore, younger workers have less loyalty and commitment to the company and are less willing to assume added responsibilities. Consequently, many young workers respond to a promotional opportunity with much less enthusiasm than do older workers. One steel company executive reflected on this phenomenon:

"We're running into a problem we've never had before and we don't know what to do about it. What it amounts to is that some of our new people won't accept a promotion. A few years ago we had trouble promoting some guys from the union into management. That was a real shocker and it made us sit back and ask what has happened to the old American dream of getting ahead. No one used to turn down a promotion. But now it's even worse. We're starting to find a sizable number of individuals who refuse a promotion within the union ranks, even when it means more money. We've interviewed a lot of those who have turned it down. They say they don't need the money that bad and they don't want the responsibility of a higher-level job. A few years ago everyone wanted a promotion. We can't understand what has changed. Our company will be in serious trouble if this keeps up.''

Personal Responsibility Versus Welfare.   If workers had the option of quitting their jobs and living on welfare, would they do it? Are younger workers more inclined to accept welfare than older workers? If a person needs more money, what is the most acceptable way to get it? The survey indicated that for all workers the most acceptable way to get more money was to work more hours, take a second job, or get more training or education (Table 4.10). All these alternatives are consistent with the character ethic's advice to work harder and become more skillful. However, accepting welfare from both the government and the church, as well as help from family and friends, was more acceptable to younger workers than to older ones. From interviews with workers after they completed the questionnaire, we learned that all workers were willing to accept Social Security payments, since they felt they had earned them. But older workers had more reservations than younger workers about accepting unemployment compensation and other welfare payments. Older workers had mixed attitudes about Medicare. Some thought it was a degrading government dole; others thought it was society's attempt to rectify the inequity of exorbitant medical costs.

Family Orientation.   The American family has changed in recent years, although the change has not been as dramatic in America as it has in European countries such as Sweden, where a growing number of husbands remain at home while the wives go out to work. In America the percentage of working wives has increased significantly, but husbands and wives have not traded places as the family breadwinner. If the wife works, the husband usually works also. If one spouse must stay home to care for the children, it is almost always the wife who does so in America.

56

The time may come, however, when increasing percentages of men remain at home to care for children while their wives work. The women's movement in America has called for more shared responsibilities in marriage, with husbands taking part in caring for the children, preparing meals, and cleaning house. But it is unlikely that many husbands will stay at home and more likely that both wife and husband will work and utilize day-care centers, limit the size of their family, or work different shifts.

The American divorce rate has increased dramatically in recent years. This alarming increase in separations has led some to conclude that the family unit will not survive in the future. "Living arrangements," where couples live together without a formal marriage contract, and group marriages, where two or more members of each sex jointly live together, are being tried as alternatives to the traditional family unit.

Although the number of divorces has increased significantly, the number of marriages has also increased. Being married continues to be the preferred way of living for most Americans. Many observers predict that the family unit will survive and will continue to be the dominant life pattern of most Americans. The biggest change will be the dissolution of the extended family. Couples will live together with decreased association with parents, brothers, sisters, and other relatives.[2]

Changes in the family are having at least two profound effects in the workplace. First, all workers increasingly feel that work should not interfere with their family life. When the wife's primary role was the responsibility of the home, the husband could invest more time and energy in his work. But as husband and wife increasingly share family responsibilities, the job commitments of both are reduced. According to the survey, all workers, and especially young workers, felt that family life was more important than work (Table 4.11).

The second major change comes from the increasing number of women who choose to work during their childbearing years or who work while they have small children at home. Personnel policies have changed to allow for maternity leaves—which range from only a couple of weeks in some companies to a couple of years in others. The conflicts between job demands and family responsibilities will probably increase as a larger percentage of women enter the workforce. This tension will be particularly intense for women who are not willing to sacrifice career advancement during their childbearing years.

Most workers, and especially older workers, still believe that mothers of small children should remain at home rather than go out to work. Older male workers felt it was not desirable for a wife to have to work to supplement the family's income. These attitudes were not shared as strongly by younger workers and females. Clearly, older males seemed to espouse the traditional model of the family more than young workers and female workers.

Community Involvement.   The quality of a person's life is greatly influenced by the quality of the community in which he or she lives. A friendly community that is free of crime and that efficiently provides public services contributes greatly to individual happiness. Creating a good neighborhood requires the involvement and commitment of community members. The survey indicated that the commitment of young workers was much lower than that of older workers. These attitudes may improve somewhat over time, since commitment usually increases with exposure to a cause. But for the present, the differences between older and younger workers were dramatic (Table 4.12).

Younger workers are more mobile and do not feel tied to their community. Unlike older workers, they do not plan to live in the community the rest of their lives and would readily move if offered a better job. Young workers reported that they were less willing to become involved in activities to improve the community. They were also less willing to get politically involved by either running for public office or voting in local elections; and they were not as likely to donate to charitable organizations that benefit the community.

Business and Free Enterprise.　During the Vietnam War era, the student protests and mass demonstrations revealed a negative sentiment not just toward the war but also toward business and the American system of free enterprise. Recruiters for numerous large corporations were as unwelcome on college campuses as recruiters for the military. This antibusiness sentiment was so alarming to many executives that they launched campaigns against "economic illiteracy."

The survey indicated that the value of America's free enterprise system is being challenged not only by high school and college students but also by younger workers who are employed in the companies that are part of the system (Table 4.13). The most dramatic differences in the attitudes of workers centered on the role of the company in the community and economy. When asked if the community was a better place to live because of the company, younger workers slightly disagreed, middle-aged workers slightly agreed, and older workers strongly agreed. The results were about the same when workers were asked if the company was essential to the local economy. These results clearly suggest that younger workers have significantly different attitudes from older workers about the role of businesses in society. Younger workers are more likely to question the usefulness of their company and to challenge its contribution to the community.

Company Loyalty and Commitment.　Numerous characteristics of an organization influence a worker's loyalty and commitment, such as company size, friendliness of coworkers, and nature of the work. In addition to these company variables, numerous individual variables influence company commitment, one of which is age. The survey indicated that younger workers were less loyal and committed to the company than older workers (Table 4.14). Older workers felt that the company was more than just a place to work. They had a psychological investment in the company and were more willing than younger workers to subordinate their personal interests to the needs of the company when necessary.

Job Satisfaction.   It is generally assumed that job-related attitudes are determined by the kind of job a worker has. "Rotten" jobs are expected to create negative attitudes and good jobs are expected to create positive attitudes. On the whole, these assumptions are correct. The job itself and the worker's suitability to it are probably the most important determinants of job-related attitudes. Nevertheless, it also seems reasonable to assume that people who are highly work-oriented and who believe that they should always do their best will feel more positive about their jobs than less work-oriented people.

The survey results indicated that older workers were more satisfied with their jobs than younger workers (Table 4.15). Older workers said that their jobs were more attractive, more interesting, and more exciting. There was a definite trend in the attitudes of the three age groups. Older workers had more favorable attitudes toward their jobs than did middle-aged workers, and middle-aged workers had more favorable attitudes than younger workers. The differences among the three groups were very consistent, and the results were the same even when the socioeconomic status levels of the jobs were controlled. (The analysis is described at the end of the chapter).

Company Satisfaction.   It also seems reasonable to assume that an employee's attitude toward the company is largely determined by the company. But again, age is a significant factor. The questionnaire contained numerous statements about attitudes toward the company. On every item the responses of older workers tended to be much more favorable than the responses of younger workers (Table 4.16). Older workers thought the company showed more respect for their personal rights and treated them more fairly than did younger workers. Older workers also expressed more confidence in the judgment of top management. When asked how their company compared with others in the area, younger workers rated the company lower than older workers.

Job Enrichment.   Many have argued that today's young workers want more enriched jobs: more autonomy, more responsibility, and more opportunities to participate in decision making. The survey results indicated that all workers sought more enriched jobs. However, younger workers felt that their jobs were more strongly in need of enrichment than did older workers. In particular, younger workers wanted more participation in decision making (Table 4.17). Methods for enriching jobs and the role of job enrichment in changing work values are discussed in Chapter 11.

CONCLUSIONS

The results of the survey suggest the following conclusions. Workers of all ages and both sexes feel that pride in craftsmanship and doing one's best are important and desirable. Hence, at least part of the character ethic is not dead; it continues to be accepted by most workers. However, sizable and consistent differences exist between younger and older workers. Some of these differences can be explained by social and economic circumstances. Money, for example, is more important to young workers than to older workers, because young workers make less money and need money for major first-time purchases. Likewise, younger workers are more interested in having their jobs enriched, because their jobs are the ones most in need of enrichment.

On the other hand, some basic differences exist in the attitudes of older and younger workers that cannot be attributed to economic circumstances. These differences, which appear to be related to age, include the following:

- Younger workers do not believe hard work and pride in craftsmanship are as important as older workers believe them to be.
- Younger workers have less favorable attitudes toward their jobs, the company, and top management than do older workers; these differences cannot be entirely attributed to the kinds of jobs they are assigned.
- Younger workers are much less committed to the company than older workers, and they report less favorable

61

attitudes about its role in the community and the economy.

- Younger workers regard government or church welfare and help from family and friends as more acceptable than older workers do.
- Younger workers are more concerned than older workers about having their fellow workers like them; they feel it is more important to get along with friends than to work hard on the job.

ELIMINATING OTHER EXPLANATIONS

The differences in work values between older and younger workers are caused by something related to age, but what? Is it just the maturation process or something else?

There are several explanations for the differences which are not specifically a function of age. Four variables closely related to age are income, education, seniority, and occupational level. Compared with younger workers, older workers generally have higher incomes, more seniority, higher-level jobs in the organization, and less education.

To examine the relationship between age and work values, my colleagues and I analyzed the survey data using a multiple regression analysis. A multiple regression analysis computes an equation which shows the relationship between a dependent variable (such as pride in craftsmanship) and a set of independent variables (such as age, income, sex, seniority, education, and occupational level). The regression equation determines an index called a beta coefficient. This index is a standardized weight which ranges from $+1.00$ to -1.00 and shows the relative contribution of each independent variable to the dependent variable.

The regression analysis indicated that age was significantly related to work values even when other variables—income, seniority, sex, education, and occupational status—were controlled. The beta coefficients for these variables, as they pre-

Figure 4.3. Beta coefficients predicting moral importance of work.

Age
.305

Education
− .031

Occupation
− .020

Seniority
− .018

Sex
.014

Income
.006

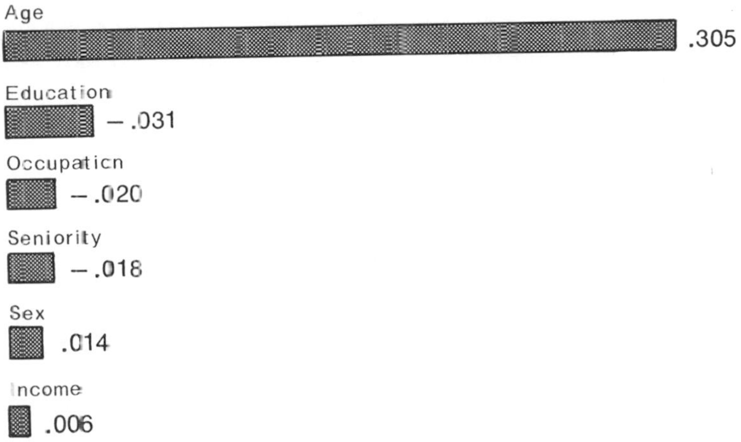

dict the moral importance of work. are shown in Figure 4.3. Furthermore. age was significantly related to attitudes about the job, the company, and the community. Older workers had stronger work values and more favorable attitudes toward the job, the company, and the community than did younger workers (Table 4.18).

Income was related to attitudes about pay, which would be expected. Occupational status was significantly related to job satisfaction and company attitudes, which was also not surprising. The important finding, however, was that age was significantly related to both work values and job attitudes even when other variables were controlled. This means that older workers are more work-oriented even when their higher income level, higher job level, and lower education level are held constant. People with higher-level jobs might be expected to feel more satisfied with their job and the company. But at any given organizational level, older workers reported more satisfaction than younger workers.

The conclusion to be drawn here is that older workers generally have stronger work values and more favorable job attitudes than younger workers because of something to do with their age. These differences cannot be explained entirely, or even primarily, by different levels of income, education, seniority, or occupational status. The differences are largely a function of something related to age. The next chapter examines three age-related hypotheses to explain these differences.

REFERENCES

1. Data were also collected from outside the United States but were not included in the analysis reported in this chapter. For a more complete description of the data collection process and the questionnaire, see David J. Cherrington and associates, "Work Values," Erteszek Working Paper Series, Graduate School of Management, Brigham Young University, Provo, Utah, 1976.
2. See Donald Moffitt, *The Wall Street Journal Views America Tomorrow* (New York: AMACOM, 1977).
3. The regression analysis is reported more completely in David J. Cherrington, Spencer J. Condie, and J. Lynn England, "Age and Work Values," *Academy of Management Journal,* Vol. 22, No. 3 (1979), pp. 617–623.

Table 4.5. The meaning of money.

	Age			
	17–26	*27–40*	*41–65*	
Getting more money or a larger	86.2	82.4	75.8	Male
pay increase[a]	85.5	81.8	78.6	Female
Receiving more fringe benefits[a]	74.1	69.1	64.9	
	69.9	68.4	69.4	
My pay: Satisfying/dissatisfying[b]	4.05	4.24	4.56	
	4.32	4.48	4.58	
My pay: Reasonable/unreason-able[b]	4.31	4.52	4.64	
	4.51	4.64	4.85	
My income is much lower than	4.10	3.86	3.81	
most of my neighbors'[c]	3.86	3.42	3.55	
How would you describe your	4.90	4.94	4.56	
need for additional income?[d]	4.66	4.80	4.63	
When you are making enough	2.99	3.21	3.41	
money to get along, making more	3.08	3.08	3.29	
money isn't very important anymore[c]				
When a man is looking for a job,	3.55	3.31	3.32	
money should be the most	3.38	3.38	3.41	
important consideration[c]				
Average monthly take-home pay	$590	$877	$923	
	$423	$523	$509	

[a]100-point scale (0 = undesirable, 100 = desirable.)
[b]7-point scale (1 = unfavorable, 7 = favorable).
[c]7-point scale (1 = disagree, 7 = agree).
[d]7-point scale (1 = low, 7 = high).

Table 4.6. Pride in craftsmanship.

	Age			
	17–26	*27–40*	*41–65*	
If you do an especially good job what are the chances that you will feel greater pride in craftsmanship?[a]	5.69 5.84	6.02 6.22	6.09 6.12	Male Female
If you do an especially good job what are the chances you will feel more worthwhile and be a better person?[a]	5.51 5.75	5.93 6.17	5.98 6.04	
If you do a rather poor job what are the chances you will feel guilty?[a]	5.23 5.74	5.73 5.91	5.79 5.79	
Feeling pride in craftsmanship in your work[b]	83.7 84.2	86.8 87.7	87.3 88.8	
Being of service to others[b]	75.3 78.2	77.3 80.7	78.6 80.4	
A worker should do a decent job whether or not his supervisor is around[c]	6.36 6.66	6.56 6.72	6.61 6.73	
A worker should feel a sense of pride in his work[c]	6.36 6.57	6.60 6.70	6.66 6.75	
Even if you dislike your work you should do your best[c]	5.72 5.84	5.85 6.20	6.11 6.36	
There is nothing wrong with doing a poor job at work if a man can get away with it.[c]	1.88 1.57	1.51 1.44	1.38 1.34	

[a]7-point scale (1 = never, 7 = 100% certain).
[b]100-point scale (0 = undesirable, 100 = desirable).
[c]7-point scale (1 = disagree, 7 = agree).

Table 4.7. Moral importance of work.

	Age			
	17–26	*27–40*	*41–65*	
Working hard makes a man a	5.08	5.38	5.64	Male
better person	5.25	5.51	5.82	Female
A good indication of a man's worth	5.39	5.67	6.04	
is how well he does his job	5.67	5.94	6.20	
Rich people should feel an	3.91	4.09	4.44	
obligation to work even if they	3.80	3.73	4.16	
do not need to				
Work should be one of the most	4.75	4.88	5.38	
important parts of a person's life	4.30	4.62	5.30	
An unproductive worker is not	3.39	3.75	4.54	
loyal to his country	3.44	3.89	4.60	
I would quit my job if I inherited	4.05	3.62	3.81	
a lot of money	4.22	3.80	3.90	

Note: 7-point scales where 1 = disagree and 7 = agree.

Table 4.8. Leisure and free time.

	Age			
	17–26	*27–40*	*41–65*	
Having leisure and free time	66.4	63.0	57.9	Male
	56.8	53.7	48.9	Female
Being expected to do more work	45.7	52.6	54.7	
	51.2	54.9	53.5	

Note: 100-point scale where 0 = undesirable and 100 = desirable.

Table 4.9. Promotions and social status.

	17–26	27–40	41–65	
		Age		
It is more important to get along with your friends than to work hard at a job[a]	3.59	2.97	2.79	Male
	3.30	2.68	2.76	Female
A person should try to get promoted at work even if it interferes with other things in life[a]	3.13	3.21	3.29	
	2.83	2.81	3.16	
My friends would not think much of me if I did not have a good job[a]	3.10	3.39	3.52	
	2.85	2.70	2.77	
Being promoted more quickly[b]	77.0	72.6	60.1	
	68.3	69.6	60.8	

[a]7-point scale (1 = disagree, 7 = agree).
[b]100-point scale (0 = undesirable, 100 = desirable).

Table 4.10. Personal responsibility versus welfare.

Suppose you were not making enough money working in your present job to support yourself and your family. How desirable are the following alternatives?[a]

	17–26	27–40	41–65	
		Age		
Accept government welfare	2.51	2.11	2.12	Male
	2.30	1.98	2.01	Female
Accept church welfare	2.21	1.99	1.92	
	2.32	1.88	1.92	
Accept help from family or friends	3.00	2.68	2.42	
	3.32	2.77	2.39	
Get more training or education	6.00	5.94	5.77	
	6.00	6.02	6.02	
Work more hours or get a second job	5.15	5.27	5.31	
	5.18	5.33	5.49	
Have my spouse work part or full time	4.61	4.38	4.20	
	5.45	5.48	5.32	
Change jobs	5.49	5.63	4.92	
	5.47	5.33	4.82	

[a]7-point scale (1 = undesirable, 7 = desirable).

Table 4.11. Family orientation.

	Age			
	17–26	*27–40*	*41–65*	
Work should not interfere with a	5.67	5.35	5.25	Male
person's family life	5.71	5.73	5.48	Female
It is more desirable for a mother	5.59	5.91	6.08	
with small children to stay at home than to go out to work	5.32	4.47	5.55	

Note: 7-point scales where 1 = disagree and 7 = agree.

Table 4.12. Community involvement.

	Age			
	17–26	*27–40*	*41–65*	
If I were offered a better job I	3.40	3.77	4.32	Male
wouldn't take it if I had to move	3.70	4.12	4.49	Female
I plan to live in this community the	3.40	4.14	4.82	
rest of my life	3.38	4.27	5.16	
I feel very much that I belong in	4.02	4.67	5.21	
this community	4.43	4.79	5.51	
I would be willing to run for polit-	3.65	4.10	3.83	
ical office if I could help this community	3.02	3.26	3.32	
I gladly donate to charitable or-	4.33	4.86	5.40	
ganizations	4.56	5.22	5.65	
I always vote in the local elections	4.30	5.12	5.94	
	4.21	5.13	5.77	

Note: 7-point scales where 1 = disagree and 7 = agree.

Table 4.13. Business and free enterprise.

	Age			
	17–26	*27–40*	*41–65*	
This community is a better place to	3.69	4.52	5.34	Male
live because of this company	4.00	4.90	5.57	Female
This company is essential to the	4.87	5.26	6.00	
local economy	4.90	5.65	6.13	
If this company closed down,	4.16	4.42	4.77	
many people would have to move	4.34	4.83	5.18	

Note: 7-point scales where 1 = disagree and 7 = agree

69

Table 4.14. Company loyalty and commitment.

	Age			
	17–26	*27–40*	*41–65*	
My company is just a place to work and is separate from my personal interests	4.24	3.40	3.20	Male
	4.10	3.68	3.47	Female
The needs of the company are more important than my own personal interests	2.81	2.97	3.66	
	2.61	2.88	3.54	
It would be unfair to the company for me to look for another job or change jobs for personal gain	2.46	2.53	3.28	
	2.64	2.86	3.28	

Note: 7-point scales where 1 = disagree and 7 = agree.

Table 4.15. Job satisfaction.

	Age			
	17–26	*27–40*	*41–65*	
Me at work: appreciated/ unappreciated	4.63	5.00	5.24	Male
	4.98	5.33	5.29	Female
Me at work: satisfied and dissatisfied	4.53	4.87	5.20	
	4.82	5.09	5.23	
My job: attractive/repulsive	4.74	5.30	5.61	
	4.95	5.49	5.51	
My job: exciting/dull	3.86	4.80	5.01	
	4.15	4.76	4.79	
My job: interesting/boring	4.33	5.23	5.56	
	4.62	5.30	5.45	

Note: 7-point semantic differential scales where 1 = unfavorable adjective and 7 = favorable adjective.

Table 4.16. Company satisfaction.

	Age			
	17–26	*27–40*	*41–65*	
Considering everything about the company, I am very well satisfied with it	4.30	4.79	5.27	Male
	4.81	5.13	5.47	Female
People in top management respect my personal rghts	4.08	4.41	5.06	
	4.37	4.75	5.15	
I have a lot of confidence in the business judgment of top management	3.94	4.48	4.87	
	4.54	4.73	5.17	
The company tries to take unfair advantage of its employees	3.65	3.05	2.76	
	3.00	2.81	2.59	
This company is a good one for a person trying to get ahead	3.66	4.26	4.48	
	3.98	4.23	4.34	
This company is a better place to work than most companies around here	4.64	5.11	5.43	
	5.04	5.31	5.61	

Note: 7-point scales where 1 = disagree and 7 = agree.

Table 4.17. Job enrichment.

	Age			
	17–26	*27–40*	*41–65*	
How much responsibility do you have in your job?	4.58	5.12	5.17	Male
	4.04	4.51	4.38	Female
How much responsibility would you like to have?	5.59	5.82	5.51	
	5.10	5.32	5.04	
How independent (versus closely supervised) are you in your job?	4.87	5.44	5.41	
	4.63	5.08	4.92	
How independent (versus closely supervised) would you like to be?	5.79	5.84	5.57	
	5.21	5.62	5.20	
How much opportunity do you now have to participate in the decision making of the company?	2.28	3.26	3.05	
	2.13	2.53	2.54	
How much opportunity would you like to have to participate in the decision making of the company?	5.11	5.52	4.94	
	4.17	4.53	4.26	

Note: 7-point scales where 7 represented the high end of each scale

Table 4.18. Beta coefficients showing effects of age on work values and attitudes.

Dependent Variables	Age	Sex	Occupational Status Level	Income	Seniority	Education
Moral importance of work	.305	.014	–.020	.006	–.018	–.031
Pride in craftsmanship	.167	.109	.055	.018	–.010	–.013
Acceptability of welfare	–.141	–.043	–.061	–.056	.022	–.069
Job satisfaction	.238	.016	.251	.035	.000	–.009
Company satisfaction	.272	.089	.148	.048	–.096	–.090
Company commitment	.186	.024	.162	.068	.009	–.146
Community involvement	.242	–.038	.036	–.018	.027	.075
Business and free enterprise	.356	.053	.012	–.091	.037	.044

5

THE GENERATION GAP
IN WORK VALUES

Surveys of worker opinions clearly indicate that younger workers are significantly less work-oriented than older workers. Many younger workers do not accept the traditional work ethic as enthusiastically as older workers. The survey presented in Chapter 4 found that, as a group, younger workers differed from older workers in many of their attitudes and values. This chapter examines the differences between the age groups and considers their implications. No doubt there are many contributing factors. But conversations with numerous workers suggest that the following three hypotheses best explain the generation gap: maturity, historical events, and values training.

MATURITY

The first hypothesis suggests that the differences in work values result from the process of growing older. As people pass through different stages in life, their frame of reference changes. Perhaps the importance of work increases as age forces a person to reexamine the meaning of life. A stronger relationship between personal effort and accomplishment is apparent. Personal integrity demands that people assume responsibility for their own well-being and provide for themselves. Often, as people mature, they realize more clearly that ethically they cannot shift the responsibility of providing for themselves onto society, and that a society cannot survive when it is forced to support increasing percentages of the population.

Because their range of experience is narrower, younger workers are more self-centered; they focus on what is fun and interesting for them. Older workers base many of their values on what is good for society. The perspective that comes from seeing life for more than one generation is especially profound. The consequences of bad decisions, wasted time, and other errors of judgment are meaningful learning experiences. The effects of maturity on an individual's working values is well illustrated by the comments of a man in his forties:

Case of the 36-Year-Old Grandfather

I didn't think much about life and work and what it was all about until I was 35. Then my daughter told me she was going to have a baby and it really woke me up. I wanted to tell her she was too young. She just wasn't grown-up enough. But she was two years older than I was when I had my first child, so what could I say? It made me realize how stupid I was when I was younger.

When I learned I was going to be a grandpa at 36, I said, "Hell, I'm not old enough to be a grandfather yet. I haven't even learned how to be a father." It made me do a lot of thinking. I decided I hadn't done much to teach my daughter some of the important things in life. You know, one generation has to teach the next generation so they can teach their kids. And I know I did a poor job teaching her. Now it seems like I'm always thinking of little sermons I'm going to tell her next time we're together. I have to be careful not to come on too strong. But I don't want her to make all the dumb mistakes raising her kid that I made with her.

I remember when I was 18 I thought I would live forever and the world owed me a living. I figured I could do what I wanted. That was the big reason my wife left me—because I wasn't responsible. Now I realize that

74

we're all responsible for ourselves; no one owes us anything. And the only way we're going to make it as a society is for everyone to pitch in and do their part.

Experience is a profound teacher, and the lessons this man learned from experience opened his eyes to ideas he had refused to see earlier.

HISTORICAL EVENTS

The second hypothesis suggests that the differences in values between older and younger workers are caused by the historical events they lived through. The Great Depression and World War II undoubtedly had a deep effect on the attitudes and values of older workers. When jobs were extremely scarce, almost any job was better than no job at all. The consequences of losing your job because of careless performance were serious. There was no reason for an employer to tolerate excessive absenteeism and tardiness when there was an abundant supply of job applicants. Working long and hard hours in your garden sometimes meant the difference between an adequate diet and intense hunger. The comments of a 65-year-old woman show that there are important lessons to be learned from a family garden besides how to grow food.

A Gardener During the Depression

I learned how to work when I was a young girl; it was during the Depression. Times were very difficult and our family didn't have much money. It took almost all our money just to make our house payments. But we had a big garden and that's how we ate.

It was my job to take care of the garden. The first year I got a lot of help, but after that I took full responsibility for it. I decided what we would plant and I was responsible for the weeding and watering. Sometimes I would get a little help during the planting and harvesting, but otherwise it was all up to me. If I needed help, I had to ask for it.

75

Father was a very proud man. He wouldn't accept government money. He always said, "We can make it on our own if we aren't afraid of a little work." It seems like he said that quite often.

We stored our food in a vegetable pit. I had it all rationed out in different sacks. I can still remember how proud I was one time. On the first day of February I brought up February's sacks and we still had some from January left over. I knew that my family had food on the table because I had done my job, and it made me feel very proud.

The pride this woman felt was evident from the tears that filled her eyes as she related her story.

The lessons of experience seemed to leave an indelible mark on those who lived through the Depression, because the lessons were learned in hard times. During the war, employees had an added incentive to raise productivity in order to support the war effort and maintain national security.

VALUES TRAINING

The third hypothesis suggests that the differences between the work values of older and younger workers arise from the training and learning experiences of each group. Older workers were taught the character ethic in their homes and schools, whereas younger workers were not. The evidence summarized in the remainder of this chapter, especially a review of the popular literature from 1900 to 1975, supports this hypothesis—that the importance of hard work, perseverance, and industry has not been propagated in society as frequently or as enthusiastically in recent years as it was in the past.

These three hypotheses for explaining the data have dramatically different implications. According to the maturity hypothesis, there is no reason to be concerned about the differences between older and younger workers. Even though young workers have less favorable attitudes toward the importance of work, satisfaction with the company, and the role of business in society, they can be expected to acquire more work-oriented values as they mature.

According to the historical events hypothesis, concern about the character ethic would be justified only if the future were stable, secure, and unchallenging—an unlikely prospect. Coupled with the uncertainty in international economics and politics is the problem of an energy shortage. Even without a severe shortage, frugality and conservation could become as socially acceptable today as they were two centuries ago.

According to the values-training hypothesis, however, there is a legitimate reason to be concerned. If the survival of the character ethic depends on whether it is taught to succeeding generations, then we must decide how to perpetuate that ethic—if, indeed, we want to do so. If all or part of the character ethic is to be rejected, what should replace it? Adults, who have a powerful influence on children, can teach the character ethic. Similarly, managers can influence employees' values by creating more explicit expectations about the quality of performance and by evaluating performance more frequently and carefully. In the past, the character ethic was taught with tremendous clarity, enthusiasm, and conviction. The sounding of the modern trumpet, however, is not so certain. Perhaps we ought to be more certain of who the preachers are and what they are preaching.

DECLINE IN WORK ETHIC TRAINING

The three hypotheses presented above are all plausible explanations for the differences in work values of older and younger workers. Each of these explanations contributes to our understanding of the changing work values, and none of them should be ignored. But since the last explanation has some serious implications for parents and managers, it is important to examine it in greater depth. To what extent has the teaching of the work ethic declined in our society?

There is good evidence showing that the work ethic was not

taught in America as frequently or as enthusiastically after 1950 as before 1950. The teaching of the work ethic was carefully documented in a study of the articles that appeared in the popular literature between 1900 and 1975.[1] This study made three important assumptions. The first was that the work ethic is acquired through a developmental process that involves teaching work values. This teaching includes such activities as telling learners what is expected of them, emphasizing the importance of work and the dignity of labor, helping and encouraging people as they perform a task, providing feedback and reinforcement for performance, and explaining and reinforcing ideas about the importance of pride, craftsmanship, and task accomplishment.

The second assumption was that the importance of the work ethic and an indication of how aggressively it has been taught are related to what is written in the popular literature. The popular literature is primarily written to appeal to the middle socioeconomic class and reaches a large segment of society. The articles published in these journals generally reflect the attitudes of authors and editors and influence the attitudes and behavior of their readers.

The third assumption was that the best source for analyzing the content of the popular literature is the *Reader's Guide to Periodical Literature*. This index began in 1901, covering only 15 of the more popular periodicals at first, and gradually extended until it covered 180 periodicals in the 1970s. The *Reader's Guide* indexes U.S. periodicals of a broad and popular character, and provides a well-balanced selection of U.S. popular nontechnical magazines representing all the important scientific and subject fields. Thus the *Reader's Guide* was assumed to indicate the popularity and acceptance of the work ethic during different periods.[2]

If the hypothesis about the decline in teaching work values is correct, then we would expect to find this decline reflected in the popular literature. That is, fewer articles supporting the work ethic would have been published within the past two or three decades than in previous years. This hypothesis was tested quantitatively by examining the number of work ethic

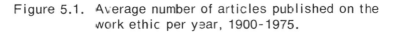

Figure 5.1. Average number of articles published on the work ethic per year, 1900-1975.

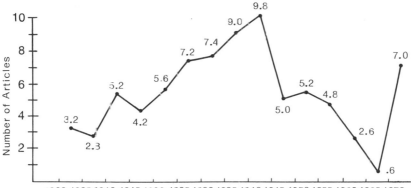

articles per year as well as qualitatively by examining the changes in the content of the articles as they discuss the work ethic.

Work Ethic Articles Per Year.   A count of the number of work ethic articles published in the popular literature was derived by examining the *Reader's Guide to Periodical Literature* from 1900 to 1975. Since leisure is usually considered the opposite of work, a count of the number of articles about leisure was also made. The key words "work" and "leisure" were used to find articles in the index, except for 1900 to 1904, when articles about work were indexed under "labor."[3]

Figure 5.1 shows the average number of articles on the work ethic and leisure during each five-year period. Since there were more journals in later years and the journals contained more articles, the relative frequency of work ethic and leisure articles was computed by dividing the average number of articles per year by the average number of pages in the *Reader's Guide* per year. This produced an index which partially compensated for the increase in the number of periodicals in later years and more accurately reflected the relative attention to the work ethic and leisure.

The evidence presented in Table 5.1 clearly demonstrates a

Table 5.1. Average frequency of articles over five-year periods.

Years	Average Number of Pages Per Year in Reader's Guide	Work		Leisure	
		Average Number of Articles Per Year	Average Number of Articles per Number of Pages	Average Number of Articles Per Year	Average Number of Articles per Number of Pages
1900–1904	328	3.2	.0097	.4	.0012
1905–1909	498	2.8	.0056	2.4	.0048
1910–1914	573	5.2	.0091	2.2	.0038
1915–1919	560	4.2	.0075	1.6	.0028
1920–1924	624	5.6	.0090	5.6	.0089
1925–1929	703	7.2	.0108	13.6	.0193
1930–1934	779	7.4	.0096	35.4	.0466
1935–1939	982	9.0	.0092	11.4	.0116
1940–1944	1,097	9.8	.0089	2.8	.0025
1945–1949	1,106	5.0	.0045	1.8	.0016
1950–1954	1,186	5.2	.0044	5.4	.0045
1955–1959	1,256	4.8	.0038	9.4	.0075
1960–1964	1,071	2.6	.0024	11.8	.0110
1965–1969	1,316	.6	.0004	7.4	.0056
1970–1974	1,286	7.0	.0054	7.2	.0056

high frequency of work ethic articles from 1900 to 1945. During this time, the average number of work ethic articles per year was 6.05. There was a slight increasing trend over the period, with the peak years occurring in 1931, 1938, and 1942. From 1945 to 1970 there was a significant decline in the number of articles—to the point that no work ethic articles appeared in the popular literature from January 1963 to March 1967. Since 1970 there has been a resurgence in the number of articles; however, many of these articles ask, "What has happened to the work ethic?"

Work Versus Leisure.   A more complete understanding of the work ethic can be obtained by examining the content and frequency of the articles on leisure. If leisure is the opposite of work, then the frequency of articles on the work ethic should be inversely related to the frequency of articles on leisure. The relationship is more complex, however, because some leisure articles advocate work.

A review of the articles on leisure revealed that there were three major themes: (1) wise use of leisure, (2) shorter work hours, and (3) leisure ethic. The wise-use-of-leisure theme suggested that people should use their leisure time carefully to increase the quality of their lives, to make money, or to be of service to society. In most respects, the leisure articles that focused on this theme were similar to articles on the work ethic. A proportionately smaller number of leisure articles after 1940 discussed the wise use of leisure, whereas prior to 1925 almost all leisure articles focused either on this theme or on a related theme condemning the idle rich.

The shorter-work-hours theme was the major reason for the tremendous surge in the number of leisure articles from 1925 to 1935. Prior to 1914, the typical workday was 10 hours, usually six days a week. During the last half of the 1920s the average length of the workweek began to drop significantly. Under the New Deal, the 40-hour week came into effect for the greater part of industry and commerce. This drop in hours meant that workers would have more time to spend in recreational pursuits. Consequently, many articles described activities that could be used to fill leisure hours. Authors, perhaps with vested interests, were quick to note that greater leisure would allow for increased use of museums, the Y, parks, and libraries. Community and school programs in such areas as music, drama, and athletics were proposed to instruct people in the use of leisure time. Also, as large numbers of people were forced into unemployment during the Depression, several articles proposed leisure activities to fill their time. Although most of the articles related to this theme appeared from 1925 to 1940, many articles on the same theme have appeared since then owing to an even shorter workweek, increased technology, and the emergence of large-scale industries supporting hobbies, sports, recreation, and other leisure activities.

The leisure-ethic theme suggested that people should take

time to enjoy life and to pursue pleasure. This theme was scattered throughout the leisure articles but became especially popular after 1940 and was predominant from 1960 to 1975.

The relationship between work and leisure was examined by correlating the frequency of work ethic and leisure articles per year from 1940 to 1970. This period of time was considered most appropriate, since the majority of the leisure articles focused on the leisure ethic, which is essentially the opposite of the work ethic. The years after 1970 were not included in the correlation because many of the work ethic articles questioned the work ethic rather than supported it. The correlation coefficient between the number of work ethic and leisure articles per year between 1940 and 1970 was −.49. This negative correlation clearly suggests that the work ethic is inversely related to the leisure ethic. During periods when the work ethic was stressed, the leisure ethic was not; and as attention shifted to the leisure ethic, there was less discussion of and enthusiasm for the work ethic. Thus a quantitative assessment of the number of work ethic and leisure articles published per year since 1900 helps to explain why younger workers have different work values from older workers. Rather than stressing the importance of work and pride in craftsmanship, recent articles have tended to focus on the pursuit of leisure activities.

JUSTIFICATIONS FOR WORK

While the frequency of work ethic articles was changing, there was an even more dramatic change in their content. An examination of articles from 1900 to 1975 reveals that the work ethic was not only discussed more frequently prior to 1950; it was also discussed more enthusiastically and with greater conviction. Recent articles, especially since 1970, have questioned the relevance of the work ethic. Before 1950, however, the relevance of the work ethic was virtually unchallenged. At least six major justifications were used to support the work ethic.

Religious Principle.   The first justification for hard work was based on religious principle—the same theme that had been taught for centuries. Work was ordained by God and was considered to be basic to human nature and essential to society. Biblical references were frequently quoted, such as Exodus 20:9—"Six days shalt thou labor and do all thy work." The religious justification for hard work was emphasized by the titles of articles, such as "Greatest Delusion in the World: The Fool Idea That Work Is an Affliction," "The Christian and His Vocation," and "Blessing of Adam."[4]

During the early 1950s the ecumenical movement brought a small flurry of articles associating the work ethic and religion. The World Council of Churches appointed a labor committee to examine the meaning of work in Christianity. One of the products of the committee was a small booklet called *The Biblical Doctrine of Work*. This booklet reviewed the meaning of work and leisure in the Bible and stated quite emphatically that the work ethic was a central philosophy in both the Old and New Testaments.[5]

After 1954 very few articles attempted to justify diligence and hard work as a commandment of God. Those articles which did so were published in religious journals such as *Christianity Today* and *Christian Century*. Other articles treated the religious basis for the work ethic as a dated philosophy (loosely described as the Puritan ethic or Protestant work ethic) that had historical significance but was no longer viable.[6]

Work Brings Success.   The second justification for the work ethic was that hard, dedicated work was necessary for success. A prominent theme of graduation speeches and short editorials in educational journals was that success would follow diligence, honesty, perseverance, industry, and a lot of hard work. The experiences of people who started their careers in poverty and worked their way to wealth and status were frequently used to emphasize the rewards of hard work and diligence.[7]

Work Creates Character and Happiness. The third justification for the work ethic was that performing your job dependably and enthusiastically would develop your character and lead to greater happiness. This justification was clearly stated in several articles and implied in many others. For example, a counselor discussed the value of a part-time job in helping delinquent or maladjusted boys. He suggested that work could benefit youth in a therapy program. Other examples were given of how pleasant tasks were an effective treatment of mental patients.[8]

The idea that hard work would bring happiness and a feeling of accomplishment seemed to be a basic assumption in numerous articles. The relationship appeared to be accepted as common knowledge, with no need for explanation or evidence.[9]

Work Improves Health. The fourth justification for hard work was that it improved mental and physical health. In 1909 R. C. Cabot, a professor of medicine at Harvard University, wrote an article called "Work Cure" which suggested that work is the best of all psychotherapies. In a later book, *What Men Live By,* he discussed the relationship between work, play, love, and religion and called for a balance among them. His justification for work was greater physical and emotional health, although his evidence was only anecdotal. A noted psychologist, E. L. Thorndike, also stated that a job well suited to a person's abilities and interests was a source of satisfaction and emotional well-being.[10]

The relationship between a long life and active work, especially mental activity, was suggested in 1913. "Work and the interest which goes with it is undoubtedly a determining element in longevity." Many years later an empirical study by medical researchers supported a similar conclusion. The study found that the best predictor of longevity was job satisfaction.[11] Concern was expressed frequently that extremely long and hard work was unhealthful, particularly if it created stress. However, most articles suggested that stress could be avoided and that purposeful mental exertion as well as heavy physical labor were healthful.[12]

Work Improves Education.   The fifth justification for the work ethic was that learning to work improved the quality of education. Several articles argued that work experiences which taught students perseverance, diligence, and pride would enhance their ability to learn and their motivation to excel.[13]

A related theme was that the work ethic should be an integral part of the educational curriculum, especially in vocational schools Several articles argued that pride, craftsmanship, and the dignity of labor were the most vital subjects in vocational training. Many of these authors suggested that some form of work experience should be included in the school curriculum to help students acquire work values.[14]

Work Benefits Society.   The sixth justification for hard work was that it was necessary for the good of society—to bolster the economy or maintain national security. Most of the articles on this theme appeared during the Depression or during World War II. One article, titled "Constructive Citizenship: Trusteeship," argued that good workmanship was the foundation of good citizenship. Another article, "Helping Men to Be Happy," stated that the way to help people achieve happiness was to cooperate as a nation and find worthwhile work for them to do. The alternative was meaningless work to justify government welfare.[15]

One author suggested the formation of mandatory work and service groups among American youth to build moral fiber. His reasoning was that the work ethic was needed to preserve the nation. Without dedicated effort, society would disintegrate. A year later the same author called upon young people to support the war effort by joining the workforce. Again, he stated that hard work was necessary for the preservation of the nation. Some articles described the unusual efforts people made in support of the war: "Concert Pianist on the Production Line" and "Mrs. Profwife, in the Tomato Patch." Other articles described the effects of the war in teaching the importance of work, especially to youth.[16]

Four years after the war, one observer suggested that a general lethargy had set in among workers. He stated that the United States had been founded on the principle of hard work, and the country's prosperity stemmed from hard work. In order to survive, therefore, the country had to change its languor to a greater vigor in work.[17]

TEACHING CHILDREN TO WORK

One of the most frequently mentioned ideas in the work ethic literature from 1900 to 1975 was the need to teach children to work. Throughout the period, the articles repeated much the same theme. Children should be given opportunities to work; they should be taught to work; and parents should supervise them and work with them. Except for 1952, when three articles appeared, there was a fairly consistent pattern—every four to six years an article was published suggesting that children be taught to work. These articles emphasized teaching work values to youth in the home as well as on the job. Young workers needed to learn the dignity of labor and pride in craftsmanship.[18]

There were two slight changes in the tone of the articles, however, over the 75-year period. First, there was a shift in the assessed strength of young people's work values. In Chapter 4 it was noted that young workers today do not espouse the work ethic as strongly as older workers. In one respect, this condition is not a recent problem: articles complaining about the values of young workers appeared throughout the century. However, earlier articles seemed to suggest that young people accepted the work ethic and needed only a little encouragement and training. Later articles implied that the work ethic had been largely rejected.

Second, there has been a growing uncertainty about what to teach young people. Earlier articles did not hesitate to encourage parents to teach their children the dignity of labor. Recent articles admit that youth need to be taught to work, but they offer very little advice on how to deal with the problem. There appears to be a basic uncertainty in recent articles about what values should be taught.

THREE EXPLANATIONS

Three explanations have been proposed for why the work ethic was not discussed as much in the popular literature after 1950: (1) it was forgotten; (2) it was inappropriate for today's work; and (3) it was rejected along with other social values like sexual morality and religion.[19]

During the 1960s many exciting events captured the public's attention, including the war in Vietnam, urban riots, civil rights legislation, federal social programs, and a massive space program that influenced both industry and education. It has been suggested that these events were more exciting than the idea of hard work and thus captured the interests of authors, editors, and the public. The work ethic was simply overlooked or forgotten. However, the social changes during the 1960s probably did not create any more excitement than the Great Depression in the 1930s or World War II in the 1940s. Yet the work ethic was strong during the 1930s and 1940s and largely disregarded in the 1960s.

There is some evidence that the work ethic was judged to be inappropriate for today's work. Clearly, numerous changes have occurred in the work environment, especially in the hours of work, working conditions, and the extent of mechanization. Today's worker can produce more in a shorter time and with less effort than earlier generations. Consequently, some workers have asked, "Why should I work hard? I don't need to." Obviously, it is easier to provide for yourself today. But the opportunities to benefit society by hard work have not diminished, and the prognosis for the future is that opportunities for dedicated work will still abound.[20] Many of the dramatic changes in the nature of work, such as assembly lines and shorter work hours, occurred years before the frequency of work ethic articles began to decline. Likewise, the industrial revolution began decades before the decline in teaching the work ethic. Thus the idea that the work ethic is inappropriate for today's work does not seem to be an adequate explanation of the decline in articles about the work ethic.

The third possibility, that the work ethic deteriorated with other social values, is actually a description rather than an explanation of what happened. Clearly something did happen to the work ethic, as evidenced by the content and frequency of work ethic articles and questionnaire surveys. At the same time that the work ethic was changing, other social values were being challenged and changed. For example, prayers and other religious ceremonies were being eliminated in schools; racial integration was being legislated and enforced in schools, businesses, and neighborhoods; divorce laws were changing and divorce rates were increasing; church attendance was declining; and pornographic films and literature were becoming more publicly accessible.[21] The extent to which these changes were related to the change in the work ethic is not clear. Also, the extent to which the changes are thought to be socially desirable depends on one's personal values.

The best explanation for what happened to the work ethic is that it was not consistent with the changes occurring in other social values. During the 1960s it was probably as socially unpopular to call for perseverance and dedicated work as it was to call for fidelity in marriage, greater church attendance, and more restrictive divorce laws. It is uncomfortable for an author to swim against the tide of popular opinion, and it does not sell magazines. Proselyting for diligence, industry, and frugality was unfashionable and unpopular. Consequently, the work ethic was not taught or passed on to succeeding generations as enthusiastically as it had been in earlier years.

REFERENCES

1. The fully documented report of this study is in David J. Cherrington, "The Work Ethic's Struggle for Survival: As Reported in the *Reader's Guide to Periodic Literature*," Erteszek Working Paper

Series, Graduate School of Management, Brigham Young University, Provo, Utah, 1976. Also reported at the Annual Academy of Management Meetings, Orlando, Florida, August 1977.

2. See Constance M. Winchell, *Guide to Reference Books,* 8th ed. (Chicago: American Library Association, 1967), p. 145. The *Reader's Guide to Periodical Literature* absorbed the *Cumulative Index* (1896–1903) in 1903 and took over the *Annual Library Index* in 1911.

3. Some articles indexed under "work" were not related to the work ethic, such as articles about work accidents and workbenches. Only articles associated with some aspect of the work ethic were included in the count. In some instances the decision was slightly subjective, since the work ethic was not discussed directly in the article. Several articles were not available for review, and the decision to include them was based on their title. Fortunately, most titles were reasonably descriptive. When an article was reprinted in either the same or abridged form, it was counted each time it appeared, since it was essentially a new article each time and usually reached a larger audience. Furthermore, the fact that it was reprinted suggested that it was judged to be an important article.

4. F. Crane, "Greatest Delusion in the World: The Fool Idea That Work Is an Affliction," *American Magazine,* Vol. 89 (February 1920), p. 59; "The Christian and His Vocation," *Christian Century,* Vol. 71 (September 22, 1954), pp. 1153–1157; C. E. Montague, "Blessing of Adam," *Forum,* Vol. 83 (January 1930), pp. 28–31.

5. C. P. Hall, "Daily Work and Christian Vocation," *Christian Century,* Vol. 71 (July 28, 1954), pp. 896–897; Carl F. H. Henry, "Dignity of Work: The Christian Concept," *Vital Speeches,* Vol. 20 (August 15, 1954), pp. 665–671; Alan Richardson, *The Biblical Doctrine of Work* (London: SCM Press, 1952).

6. Compare Finley Eversole, "The Meaning of Work in Our Time," *Christian Century,* Vol. 78 (August 30, 1961), pp. 1024–1027, with Carl F. H. Henry, "Ailing World of Work," *Christianity Today,* Vol. 14 (January 2, 1970), pp. 22–23.

7. "Blessing of Work," *Industrial Arts and Vocational Education,* Vol. 20 (May 1931), p. 179; J. E. Morgan, "Your Usefulness in the Making," *National Education Association Journal,* Vol. 38 (May 1949), pp. 331–332; L. C. Hale, "What the Day's Work Means to Me," *Bookman,* Vol. 42 (December 1915), pp. 454–457; B. Sparkes, "Horatio Alger at the Bridge: Survey of Effects of Chores and Work in Youth upon Successful Men in Many Fields," *Saturday Evening Post,* Vol. 208 (May 2, 1936), pp. 20–21.

8. R. J. Fornwalt, "Part-Time Job Values for the Maladjusted Boy," *Occupations,* Vol. 26 (January 1948), pp. 221–223; "Work and Sanity," *Craftsman,* Vol. 25 (Feburary 1914), p. 499.

9. S. Crowther, "Henry Ford's Theory of Work and the Happiness of the Individual Who Finds His Work," *National Education Association* (1928), pp. 33–37; M. S. Jameson, "Joy of Work," *Forum*, Vol. 68 (November 1922), pp. 245–249; E. M. Stern, "There's Joy in Work," *Rotarian*, Vol. 57 (August 1940), pp. 12–14.

10. R. C. Cabot, "Work Cure," *Good Housekeeping*, Vol. 49 (September–October 1909), pp. 296–299; R. C. Cabot, *What Men Live By* (Boston: Houghton Mifflin, 1914); Edward L. Thorndike, "Psychology of Labor," *Harper*, Vol. 144 (May 1922), pp. 799–806.

11. "Work and Long Life," *Outlook*, Vol. 104 (August 2, 1913), p. 737; E. Palmore, "Physical, Mental, and Social Factors in Predicting Longevity," *The Gerontologist*, Vol. 9 (1969), pp. 103–108; E. Palmore, "Predicting Longevity: Controlling for Age," *The Gerontologist*, Vol. 9 (1969), pp. 247–250.

12. "Hard Work Does Kill," *Literary Digest*, Vol. 82 (November 29, 1924), pp. 25–26; "Physiology of Labor," *Scientific America*, Vol. 115 (September 30, 1916), p. 296; "Backbreaking Work as a Cure for Tired Feeling," *Literary Digest*, Vol. 82 (January 3, 1925), p. 48; "Is Hard Work Healthful?" *Literary Digest*, Vol. 52 (June 17, 1916), p. 1775; "Useful Employment as a Health Measure," *Science News Letter*, Vol. 33 (April 2, 1938), p. 220.

13. H. Feuerstein, "Teaching Practical Arts Pupils the Dignity of Work," *Industrial Education Magazine*, Vol. 29 (October 1927), pp. 122–123; W. H. Oxley, "Work as a Basis for Occupational Training," *School Life*, Vol. 26 (December 1940), pp. 82–83; N. E. Steele, "Work Your Way Through College? Yes," *Rotarian*, Vol. 57 (August 1940), pp. 27–28.

14. R. D. Howard, "They Also Serve: High Schools Should Furnish Direct Work and Service Experiences," *School and Society*, Vol. 56 (October 17, 1942), pp. 353–354; E. E. Ericson, "Hand of Man," *Industrial Education Magazine*, Vol. 30 (November 1928), p. 178; "Year of Work Between High School and College," *School Review*, Vol. 36 (April 1928), pp. 248–250.

15. L. P. Jacks, "Constructive Citizenship: Trusteeship," *National Education Association Journal*, Vol. 20 (March 1931), pp. 101–102; H. Braucher, "Helping Men to Be Happy," *Recreation*, Vol. 28 (August 1934), p. 217.

16. D. Thompson, "Discipline of Service," *Ladies' Home Journal*, Vol. 58 (February 1941), p. 6; D. Thompson, "Patriotism of Work," *Survey Guide*, Vol. 31 (May 1942), pp. 233–234; G. Maier, "Concert Pianist on the Production Line," *Etude*, Vol. 61 (June 1943), p. 367; J. C. Altrocchi, "Mrs. Profwife in the Tomato Patch," *Catholic World*, Vol. 156 (March 1943), pp. 691–696; W. C. Davis, "Youth and War Work: Value of Work Experiences," *School and Society*, Vol. 58 (November 20, 1943), pp. 410–412.

17. S. H. Adams, "It's an American Idea; Let's Not Give It Up," *Good Housekeeping*, Vol. 128 (March 1949), p. 33.

18. There were at least 19 articles that emphasized the importance of teaching children to work, such as the following from different time periods: A. D. Dean. "Child Labor or Work for Children," *Craftsman*, Vol. 25 (March 1914), pp. 515–521; K. Doyle, "Everybody Works at Our House," *Parents Magazine*, Vol. 27 (March 1952), pp. 43; E. J. Le Shan, "Chore War: Children vs. Parents," *Redbook*, Vol. 130 (March 1968), p. 65.

19. These explanations were proposed in Cherrington, "The Work Ethic's Struggle for Survival," *op. cit.*

20. D. F. Johnston, "The Future of Work: Three Possible Alternatives," *Monthly Labor Review*, Vol. 95 (1972), pp. 3–11.

21. For statistics on the decline in church attendance, see Constant H. Jacquet, Jr., *Yearbook of American and Canadian Churches* (Nashville: Abingdon Press, 1978), pp. 256–258.

6

SATISFACTION AND PRODUCTIVITY

In recent years the work ethic has not been propagated in society as a vital social norm as it was in earlier years. The dignity of labor and devotion to service are not the dominant social values they once were. But in this respect, the work ethic is not alone. We no longer advocate jousting or dueling as an acceptable way to resolve conflict and maintain honor. Dozens of other practices that once played a central role in our society have likewise been dropped. But what has been gained or lost in the change? This chapter examines the effects of the work ethic on a worker's behavior. The research evidence indicates that people who espouse the work ethic are more satisfied and more productive and report a higher quality of life.

COMMENTS OF OUTSTANDING WORKERS

During the data collection process described earlier, we not only obtained questionnaire responses but also interviewed many workers. The interview information was useful in identifying the characteristics of outstanding workers. Their comments illustrated how high performers were very work-oriented and derived enormous satisfaction from their work.

The major purpose of the interviews was to identify the

characteristics that distinguished outstanding from mediocre performers. Performance information was obtained on workers who completed the questionnaire by asking their immediate supervisors to evaluate them. The supervisors used a simple 7-point scale, and only the outstanding performers were to receive a rating of 7. As time permitted, many of these outstanding performers were interviewed. Some mediocre or poor performers were also interviewed to provide a basis for comparison. Approximately 50 outstanding workers were interviewed.

After the first 15 or 20 interviews, I was astonished at the consistency in the information I was obtaining. I had interviewed a heterogeneous sample of workers—both male and female employees of various ages with noticeably different jobs at different levels within their organizations. And yet they seemed to have several characteristics in common. Two of the most striking characteristics were their strong work orientation and their positive job attitudes. (Other characteristics relevant to the development of their work orientation will be discussed in the next chapter.)

The first question I asked each person was "How work-oriented are you?" All the outstanding performers replied without hesitation that they were very work-oriented; work was very important to them and was a major source of meaning and fulfillment in their lives. One woman said her work *was* her life. She was the executive assistant to the president of a small company, and the president claimed that she was really the one who managed the company. She said she was "about 70" years old but had no intention of retiring; she was active and alert and thought retirement was an absurd idea. She had no children and her husband had died several years earlier. Consequently, her life revolved around her work. She usually worked at least 12 hours a day, and frequently returned to work on the weekends. Employees in the company respected her as a competent and efficient administrator. She was paid less than the other two women in the office, but she set her own salary and did not see any reason why she should be paid more.

Most outstanding performers were not as immersed in their work as this woman. Even though they described themselves as very work-oriented, they were involved in other activities. Most of the younger workers were members of one or more athletic teams and actively competed in various sports. Two men coached Little League teams. One coached because his son was on the team; the other man was single and coached because he wanted to help the neighborhood. Numerous hobbies were also mentioned, such as painting, writing, and playing a musical instrument. The majority of outstanding performers were active church members and many held lay positions in their congregations. Several had been politically active, but usually as compaigners rather than as candidates. One of the outstanding performers had served on a city council.

In general, these outstanding performers were busy people who attacked numerous activities in life with the same aggressiveness that they brought to their work. They had a high energy level and an ability to be involved in many activities simultaneously. Their attention span also appeared to be greater than average, since they could focus on one project for long periods of time without a break.

Doing a "good job" was important to the outstanding performers, and many said that when they decided to do something they wanted to do it well. However, they did not consider themselves perfectionists who did everything exactly right. All the women reported that they were good housekeepers, but only a few said they could be considered immaculate. Most described their homes as clean and livable. One mother said, "A house is to live in and you have to allow for a certain amount of mess. That's just part of living." The men had much the same attitude about yardwork. Some had large yards, a garden, or even a pasture with horses and a barn, and said they spent a lot of time making them look nice. But most felt that there were more important things to do than "worry about the last couple of weeds in the corn." It was apparent that the outstanding performers did not really believe in doing everything perfectly. Only the important things were done exceptionally well; other things were done adequately.

All the outstanding performers said they thoroughly enjoyed their work. Many mediocre workers also said they enjoyed their work, but there were several subtle differences between the way each group described their jobs. The first difference was in their description of what made them satisfied. Mediocre performers usually mentioned general reasons that were not directly related to the content of their jobs, such as good pay, good hours, pleasant working conditions, freedom to pursue hobbies either on or off the job, and (in one case) the opportunity to operate a group gambling game on professional sports. Outstanding performers, by contrast, identified specific areas of work, usually numerous areas, in which they had contributed or excelled individually. For example, an airline reservations agent talked excitedly about group tours she had arranged. A leadman in a manufacturing company talked with pride about the co-workers he had trained. A sewing machine operator explained that the multicolor awards attached to her nameplate signified consistent high-quality performance. An operations vice president described the successful completion of numerous projects he had directed.

The second difference between the two groups was in the way they responded to problems in the company. Outstanding performers enjoyed their work, but their affection was not unqualified. They identified numerous problems with their jobs or with company procedures. However, they did not see these problems as insurmountable obstacles; rather, they viewed them as challenges to overcome, issues to be resolved, or constraints to live with. Mediocre workers were much more passive about organizational problems. They felt someone else was responsible for creating problems; therefore, someone else should solve them. Mediocre workers were less willing to get involved.

The third difference was in the way each group responded to unpleasant parts of the job. Almost every job has some unpleasant components: writing reports, reading reports, cleaning up, making repairs, and so on. Mediocre workers generally responded to unpleasant chores by postponing them until they absolutely had to be done. Then, after a little grumbling, they did the tasks in short stretches punctuated by rest pauses. Outstanding workers, on the other hand, generally did the unpleasant chores whenever it seemed like the most efficient time to do so. Sometimes they acted as soon as the job arose; sometimes they waited until several jobs accumulated and then worked on the tasks in a block for long periods of time.

In summary, the interviews with outstanding performers produced a profile of an employee who was extremely productive, very satisfied with his or her job and the company, and very work-oriented. The profile is considerably different from that described in the popular book *Working*.[1] To these outstanding performers, work was not an act of violence; nor was it a mind-numbing, soulless form of aggression. Rather, work was an important activity that brought meaning, satisfaction, and fulfillment to life. This profile is supported by research studies which indicate that work values are positively related to both job satisfaction and productivity.

WORK VALUES AND JOB SATISFACTION

Job satisfaction has normally been attributed to the nature of the job. Good jobs have been thought to increase satisfaction, while repetitive, menial work has been cited as the cause of boredom, alienation, and discontent. A recent survey revealed that managers believe there is a definite relationship between job satisfaction, motivation, and productivity. "Job dissatisfaction leads to high turnover, tardiness, loafing on the job, disruptions, poor workmanship, and indifference to customers or clients."[2]

The popular solution to the problem of job dissatisfaction has been to redesign the job. Satisfaction is expected to improve through job enrichment, improved compensation packages, and worker participation. Normally, it should. But where do these strategies recognize the role of the worker? How the worker chooses to respond to the job has been almost entirely disregarded, even though it is obvious that job satisfaction or dissatisfaction depends on a person's perception of the work environment.

Some excellent illustrations of this fact are games of chance, such as slot machines. Very few jobs in industry, even on assembly lines, have a work cycle as short as putting a coin in a slot and pulling a handle. Yet many people "play the slots" for hour after hour—and at their own expense. Clearly, repetitive activities are not necessarily boring. Boredom and alienation are psychological responses to the environment.

Research Evidence. One of the earliest examinations of the relationship between work values and job satisfaction was a study of 448 airmen and noncommissioned officers in the U.S. Air Force in 1969. Eight satisfaction measures were obtained from each person—five specific job attitude measures and three general satisfaction measures. Work values were also evaluated through:

1. A pro-Protestant-ethic scale measuring the importance of work. (*Examples:* "Hard work makes a man a better person." "A good indication of a man's worth is how well he does his job.")

2. A non-Protestant-ethic scale measuring the value of leisure and avoiding hard work. (*Examples:* "When the workday is finished, a person should forget his job and enjoy himself." "People who do things the easy way are the smart ones.")

The correlation coefficients between the pro-Protestant-ethic scale and job satisfaction measures were generally positive, but not very large. The largest correlation was only .28. The correlations with the non-Protestant-ethic scale were generally negative but again very small—the largest correlation was −.31.[3]

Several other studies have found positive correlations between measures of job satisfaction and belief in the work ethic. The correlation coefficients have not been very large, but the positive relationships are quite consistent.[4] The relationships between work values and job satisfaction were analyzed from the survey data described in Chapter 4 for 3,053 American

Table 6.1. Correlation coefficients between work values and job satisfaction for 3,053 American workers.

	Moral Importance of Work	*Pride in Craftsmanship*
General satisfaction at work	.20	.15
Job attractiveness	.23	.22
Company satisfaction	.29	.23
Pay satisfaction	.09	.15
Satisfaction with fellow workers	.04	.20
Supervisor consideration	.05	.21

workers. The correlations between two work values and six satisfaction measures are reported in Table 6.1. The first work value, called moral importance of work, was the average response to five statements about the importance of work in one's life. (*Examples:* "Working hard makes a man a better person." "Rich people should feel an obligation to work even if they do not need to.") The second work value, called pride in craftsmanship, was the average response to six statements about the value of doing a good job. (*Examples:* "A worker should do a decent job whether or not his supervisor is around." "A worker should feel a sense of pride in his work.") These two values were correlated with the following job satisfaction measures: general satisfaction at work, job attractiveness, company satisfaction, pay satisfaction, satisfaction with fellow workers, and supervisor consideration. The correlations for all six satisfaction variables were positive and ranged from .04 to .29. That is, workers who reported greater acceptance of these two work values also tended to report greater satisfaction, especially satisfaction with the company.[5]

Explanation. The positive correlations between work values and job satisfaction are not very strong, but they are strong enough and consistent enough to call for an explanation. Why do workers who place a higher value on work report greater job satisfaction?

The first explanation is quite obvious, especially for people who believe in work as a terminal value: work is its own reward. If you espouse the work ethic, work is a reinforcing behavior that contributes to your satisfaction. This does not mean that highly work-oriented people will work just for the joy of working (although some do). But in comparison to those who believe work is demeaning drudgery, people who believe work is important and meaningful will obtain added reinforcement from their jobs. Work behavior tends to be consistent with a personal value that such activity is desirable. As the Air Force researcher noted, "Someone who thinks that all work is an abomination to be undertaken only when all other strategies fail will likely be unhappy even in the most pleasant work situation. On the other hand, a person who feels that personal worth results only from self-sacrificing work or occupational achievement would likely derive some satisfaction even in a demanding menial position."[6]

This explanation was supported by a study examining the central life interests of 910 bank and telephone company employees. Central life interests were measured by asking employees whether they preferred a work or nonwork setting for various activities—for example, taking a vacation with family versus friends from work and borrowing money from friends versus co-workers. Employees with a work-oriented central life interest reported the highest job satisfaction, whereas nonwork-oriented employees reported the lowest job satisfaction. It was suggested that job-oriented people have an "affective orientation" to work—that is, work itself is invested with positive feelings "of pride in workmanship, autonomy, self-importance, and self-actualization." People with a non-work central life interest have an "instrumental orientation." For them, work is "viewed as the source of repetitive performance, boredom, physical weariness."[7] These orientations correspond to the terminal and specific instrumental values of work described in Chapter 2.

Another explanation for the positive relationship between work values and job satisfaction comes from the worker's inclination to selectively respond to positive or negative aspects of the job. The processes of selective perception have been well documented in the psychological literature. People selectively perceive their environment, seeing what they want to see and overlooking what they do not want to see. Thus a worker who believes work is desirable and important is more likely to perceive favorable aspects of the job, whereas a worker who thinks work is distasteful is more likely to observe undesirable working conditions.[8]

This explanation could be extended to the process of selective evaluation. People evaluate their environment consistent with their own beliefs and values. Certain factors in the job setting get weighted more heavily and play a greater role in the evaluation process. Consequently, someone who believes work is important evaluates such things as difficult work, tight production standards, and close supervisory control more positively than someone who believes work is demeaning. Both people might agree that these factors are undesirable, but the first person does not consider them to be as important in determining overall satisfaction.

All the above explanations suggest that work values "create" greater job satisfaction. Correlation coefficients, however, do not imply causal relationships. The positive correlations could be explained differently by making other assumptions. It is possible, for example, that the causal arrow goes in the opposite direction: job satisfaction creates greater work values. This explanation suggests that if people like their work and find satisfaction and fulfillment in it, they will come to believe that work is important and that doing a good job is desirable. This is a reasonable explanation according to cognitive dissonance theory. People are "rationalizing animals" and generally attempt to maintain cognitive consistency—that is, consistency in their beliefs and actions. If employees are working hard and doing a good job (for money, status, prestige, or whatever reason), it would be inconsistent for them to believe that work is useless and unimportant. To achieve cognitive consistency, these employees would have to either change their behavior by not working so hard or change their beliefs to think that hard work is important.[9]

Regardless of the explanation, the evidence indicates that work values are positively related to job satisfaction. Workers who espouse the work ethic generally report greater job satisfaction. Believing in hard work, pride in craftsmanship, and diligence does not mean living an ascetic life filled with pain and toil. Instead, the evidence suggests that a belief in the work ethic contributes to both job satisfaction and the quality of life, as illustrated by the earlier comments of outstanding performers as well as by research studies.

WORK VALUES AND INDIVIDUAL PERFORMANCE

It seems reasonable to expect work values to be positively associated with productivity. Employees who believe work is important and who think doing a good job is desirable should be better performers. Indeed, there is evidence supporting this relationship, but the evidence is surprisingly weak, largely because of the difficulty in measuring individual productivity.

One investigation showed that people who accept the work ethic are more productive. The Protestant Ethic Scale was administered to a class of 333 psychology students. Later in the semester 20 students with the highest scores and 20 students with the lowest scores were asked to participate in a study testing eye-hand coordination. The students were seated alone at a table with 100 sheets of paper and asked to draw an X in each circle on the paper with their nonpreferred hand. Each sheet had 250 circles on it, and the students were told to keep filling out the sheets until they became tired. The students with high Protestant ethic scores spent an average of 23.00 minutes at the task and completed 4.10 sheets, while students with low Protestant ethic scores spent only 16.85 minutes and completed 2.55 sheets. Students with high Protestant ethic scores not only worked longer and accomplished more work; they also worked at a faster rate of speed.[10]

Similar results were obtained in a study of 64 employees in

101

the accounting division of a large manufacturing company. Performance ratings were found to be positively correlated with the amount of satisfaction the employees derived from doing their jobs well. This work value, called internal motivation, was measured by six items, such as "I feel a great sense of personal satisfaction when I do this job well," and "Doing this job well increases my opinion of myself." These items were somewhat similar to the measures of pride in craftsmanship described in Chapter 4. The supervisors rated the performance of each employee on three 7-point scales: effort, quantity of work done, and quality of work done. Information about the number of days absent was also obtained. The results indicated that internal work motivation was positively correlated with work effort (.22), quantity of work (.22), and quality of work (.25), and negatively correlated with absenteeism (−.07). Thus performance levels can be predicted by an individual's motivation to do a job well.[11]

A study using similar instruments to measure the values and performance of 208 telephone employees also found that employees with high internal motivation had lower absenteeism (−.23) and higher performance (+.18 with "overall effectiveness" ratings).[12] These studies indicate that people who take pride in their work and feel bad when they do a poor job tend to perform noticeably better than others, as judged by their supervisors.

The relationship between work values and productivity was analyzed using the survey data from 53 companies, as described in Chapter 4. The same two work values mentioned above, moral importance of work and pride in craftsmanship, were correlated with seven performance measures. Supervisors were asked to rate each worker's quantity of work, quality of work, cooperativeness/initiative, and overall performance on simple 7-point scales. The supervisors were instructed to use 4 as an average rating and give 7 only to outstanding performers. Two others measures of performance —absenteeism and tardiness—were taken from company records when they were available. Absenteeism was the total

Table 6.2. Correlation coefficients between work values and performance.

Performance	Moral Importance of Work	Pride in Craftsmanship
Overall performance rating (N = 2,379)	.08[a]	.08[a]
Quantity of work (N = 817)	.04	.08
Quality of work (N = 815)	.06[c]	.10[b]
Cooperativeness/initiative (N = 784)	.05	.08[b]
Absenteeism (N = 870)	−.04	−.04
Tardiness (N = 292)	.01	−.05
Perceived performance rating (N = 3,053)	.23[a]	.34[a]

[a]Statistically significant at the .001 level of probability.
[b]Statistically significant at the .01 level of probability.
[c]Statistically significant at the .05 level of probability.

number of days the employee was absent the previous year for any reason except vacation. Tardiness was the percentage of days the employee came late to work. The final performance measure was a self-report in which each worker rated his or her performance on two 7-point items in the questionnaire: "How hard do you work on the job?" (As slowly as I can = 1, as fast as possible = 7) and "Compared to your fellow workers, how rapidly do you try to work?" (Much more slowly = 1, much faster = 7).

The correlation coefficients between the two work values and the seven performance measures are shown in Table 6.2. Half the correlation coefficients were statistically significant, but none of them were very large except the two correlations with the perceived performance rating. Employees who believed work was important and who felt pride in their work reported that they were significantly more productive than other workers. However, their supervisors rated them only slightly more productive. Thus it appears that work values are indeed related to individual productivity even though the association is not especially strong.

Explanation.   There are two major reasons why the performance data were only slightly related to work values. Both reasons have important implications for teaching work values, as will be discussed in Chapter 8. First, the performance information was not very reliable. Occasionally we tried to check the reliability of the supervisors' ratings by asking a supervisor to rate his or her subordinates a second time, or by asking a supervisor at the next level to rate them. Most supervisors could rate their subordinates quite consistently on a second round. But in some cases the agreement between supervisors was not very good. New supervisors and supervisors who were not considered very competent (by their superiors) seemed to have the greatest difficulty making judgments about the subordinates. These supervisors tended to give grossly inflated ratings or rate everyone the same.

Many supervisors took an unusually long time to decide on their ratings and admitted that they had never had to rate their people before. An unusual problem occurred in one company that had a formal performance appraisal procedure. We anticipated using the company's information until several managers confessed that the performance appraisal data reflected political finagling more than they measured individual performance. Another problem that arose in two companies was that some supervisors rated employees according to union membership and years of seniority. One supervisor insisted that everyone who had a journeyman's card and five years of service had to be rated outstanding; everyone else was rated average.

In general, we were quite disappointed at the difficulty in gathering supervisor evaluations. Absenteeism and tardiness information posed even more of a problem. Very few companies recorded absenteeism and tardiness in a way that could be retrieved and used. In many instances supervisors refused to report such data accurately (for a variety of reasons), and in other instances there were informal arrangements, like working late, coming in on weekends, and "covering" for a friend, which did not get recorded on personnel records.

The second major reason work values are only moderately related to performance is that productivity is influenced by numerous variables, and each variable has only a small influence. The behavioral science literature is filled with studies that show how performance is determined by dozens of variables. It is unlikely that any one of these variables, including the work ethic, would have a high correlation with performance.

One of the most useful models for understanding the determinants of performance is derived from expectancy theory. According to this model, job performance is determined by three variables: personal ability and knowledge, effort, and organizational design (and/or constraints). These three variables combine multiplicatively to determine the level of job performance. In other words, three numbers measuring the three variables could be multiplied together to represent numerically the level of job performance.

Personal ability and job knowledge refer to the physical skills, mental abilities, education, job training, and other knowledge necessary for the person to perform the job. Organizational design refers to the degree of efficiency that has been structured into each task, the adequacy of coordination among the tasks, and the possession of adequate resources, tools, and materials. Effort refers to the individual's motivation—how hard he or she is willing to work. According to expectancy theory, effort is determined by the individual's belief that effort will lead to positive job outcomes (like more money, promotion, and being of service) and avoid negative outcomes (like being fired or chewed out).

According to this model, work values are related to performance because they influence individual effort. Employees who accept the work ethic probably acquire greater job knowledge and try to make the organizational structure more efficient. But more important, work-oriented employees exert greater effort. Working hard and doing a good job are positive outcomes for those who espouse the work ethic, especially for those who value work in and of itself. On the other hand, workers who see little value in work as either a terminal or generalized instrumental value are motivated to exert effort only to the extent that it results in other valued outcomes, such as money, status, praise, social approval, and free time.

In summary, motivation theory helps to explain why workers who believe in hard work are more productive—because of their values, they are personally rewarded for their work. Thus both theory and research support the conclusion that work values are related to productivity. And both theory and research help to explain why the relationship is so weak: other rewards, personal limitations, and organizational constraints also influence productivity.

WORK VALUES AND NATIONAL PRODUCTIVITY

National productivity is a measure of the total goods and services produced in America divided by the employee-hours required to produce them. This measure, sometimes called output per employee-hour, is computed quarterly. The basic concept behind the measure is quite simple: it is the output of the economy (automobiles, houses, refrigerators, candy, medical operations, and so on) divided by the total employee-hours required to produce them. The computation of both the input and the output measures is quite complicated.

The labels "labor productivity" and "output per employee-hour" have confused some people into thinking that advances in productivity are attributable to labor. For many, the thought of increased productivity creates an image of an assembly line running faster and faster. While the energy, intelligence, and skill of labor are important to productivity, they are not the major factors responsible for increasing productivity. Of greater significance are the technological improvements and increased capital equipment. Better organization and management have also contributed.

Productivity Slowdown.   Productivity figures for the U.S. economy have been computed by the Bureau of Labor Statistics since 1946. During the first 20 years of measurement, from 1947 to 1967, productivity grew at an average annual rate of 3.3 percent. This average reflected a much sharper rate of gain during the first few years than in later years. During the first decade, from 1947 to 1957, the index of output per employee-hour for the private economy increased from 100 percent to 140.9 percent, an average annual increase of 3.5 percent. In recent years, the rate of productivity growth has been much lower. From 1967 to 1976, productivity growth averaged 1.6 percent annually. During this latter period, the productivity rates in 1974 and 1975 were actually less than in 1973.[13]

The decline in the rate of productivity growth has attracted a lot of attention and created a feeling of alarm because it is "below average." There is no consensus, however, about what an "average" or "reasonable" level of productivity growth is. During the "historical period"—the first 25 years when productivity was measured (1947–1972)—productivity increased 3 percent annually. Therefore, 3 percent is usually considered an acceptable rate of growth. The historical average for the past half century, however, appears to be a growth rate only somewhat in excess of 2 percent.[14] This time period includes both a major depression, when productivity was adversely affected, and a major world war, which stimulated productivity. Productivity growth rates during the 1950s and 1960s created the impression that a 3-to-3.5 percent annual growth rate was a realistic expectation. Recent projections suggest that productivity growth for 1980 to 1985 will average 2.7 percent annually.[15] This projection is probably overly optimistic, considering the recent slowdown in productivity growth and the factors which have contributed to it.

Role of the Work Ethic.   At the company level, the declining work ethic is rarely mentioned as the cause of productivity problems (except as it is related to absenteeism or tardiness). When companies run into serious labor problems, such

Table 6.3. Manufacturing productivity trends, selected countries: annual percentage increases.

	1960–1973	1973–1977
Canada	4.4	1.6
France	6.1	4.8
Italy	6.3	2.2
Japan	10.2	3.7
United Kingdom	4.0	0.1
United States	3.0	2.2
West Germany	5.5	5.6

Source: U.S. Bureau of Labor Statistics.

as wildcat strikes, absenteeism, turnover, declining productivity, and increasing costs, the cause of the problem is seldom attributed to the values or efforts of the workers. Instead, other causes are usually cited, such as management style, job alienation, and organizational climate. A survey of 563 members of the American Management Associations indicated that managers believed the key to improved productivity resided with management, not the workers. These managers identified the following five factors for improving performance: better planning, more effective management, improved job procedures, better communication, and more effective manpower and personnel policies.[16]

In the talks of business executives, however, the declining work ethic of American workers has frequently been cited as a major reason for the decline in national productivity.[17] Yet work values are only one of numerous variables which influence national productivity. The declining work ethic is probably less responsible than other variables for the unfavorable productivity comparisons of the United States versus other countries. The data in Table 6.3 show the average annual productivity increase for seven industrial nations. The results do not look especially favorable for American industry.[18]

The extremely high productivity growth in Japan has led to numerous comparisons of American and Japanese workers, which usually conclude that Americans should take a closer look at Japanese management. The chairman of a major U.S. company applauded the productivity growth rate of Japan: "The industriousness and hard work of the Japanese are a model for every other nation on earth." A group of personnel executives visited several Far Eastern countries and also praised their performance: "I came away with the strong impression that productivity is an integral part of life throughout the Far East. It is part of the individual's attitude toward his job, his role in the family, his citizenship." Japanese workers might have a stronger belief in hard work and greater loyalty to their companies than American workers. But the 10.2 percent increase in productivity from 1960 to 1973 was created more by imported technology than by increased dedication to work or management style. No amount of dedication or paternalistic management will maintain a 10 percent productivity growth rate without massive technological advances.[19]

Causes of Change in Productivity. Productivity changes are caused by several factors. During the decade from 1967 to 1976, when productivity increased only 1.6 percent annually, the economy experienced two recessions. The decline in productivity growth was attributable, in part, to cyclical fluctuations which created excess labor hours—managers were slow to lay off workers who were not needed. However, other long-term factors were also operating, which included the following: the decline in the work ethic, changes in the composition of the workforce, intersector shifts in employment, capital formation, and social legislation.

1. *Decline in the work ethic.* The decline in the work ethic has very likely contributed in a significant way to the slowdown in productivity over the past two or three decades. The growing tendency to work slower, take longer breaks, and socialize with fellow workers during work hours all contribute to a decline in productivity. This tendency is well illustrated in the construction industry. At the construction site of a large public utility, 32 observers were hired to record the behavior of the

workers. There were 20 observers from the utility company and 12 observers hired by the construction contractor. The construction workers were told that their work was being observed but they did not know if they were being observed at any specific time. The construction period lasted for two years at a cost of $3 million.

Eleven activities were identified and timed by the observers with the help of stopwatches and, in some instances, videotape equipment. The average percentage of time the workers spent performing each activity is shown below:[20]

Work-Related Activities	*Percentage of Time*
1. Direct work: time spent by the craftworker performing the craft	31%
2. Traveling	10
3. Transporting materials	4
4. Giving or receiving instructions	3
5. Obtaining tools or materials	2
6. Studying drawings or blueprints	1
Total	51%
Nonwork-Related Activities	
7. Idle/unexplained time	24
8. Waiting	13
9. Late starts/early quits	6
10. Personal time	5
11. Coffee breaks	1
Total	49%

Of these eleven activities, only the first six contributed to the actual construction of the public utility. The other activities, which accounted for approximately half the total time, did not contribute.

2. *Composition of the workforce.* The large growth in the number of new entrants to the workforce has also affected productivity. The rate of growth in the labor force rose sharply in the late 1960s due to the large increase in female employment and the "baby boom" of the 1940s. It has been estimated that

changes in the composition of the labor force have contributed .2 to .3 percent to the decline in productivity growth rates.[21] New entrants to the labor force are typically less productive because they lack the experience and skills of seasoned workers. Younger workers also tend to be less work-oriented, as indicated by the data in Chapter 4.

3. *Intersector shifts.* It has been suggested that intersector shifts in employment have contributed .3 to .4 percent to the decline in productivity growth rates. The most significant shift was from the farm to the factory. This shift was especially significant after World War II, when farm machinery forced many agricultural laborers to enter factory work. Because productivity is measured by gross domestic product in dollar values, the shift from low-paying farm jobs to higher-paying factory jobs increased productivity. The shift from farm to nonfarm was largely over by 1966, which partly explains why productivity increases have been lower since that time.

Shifts in employment in other sectors of the economy have both increased and decreased productivity. The number of personal-services jobs has greatly increased. This shift has frequently been cited as a major reason for reduced productivity. But since service jobs are paid on a fairly comparable basis with other jobs (and the productivity of service jobs is related to their pay), it appears that the shift to service work is, at best, only a minor source of the slowdown in the rate of productivity growth.

4 *Capital formation.* Increased capital expenditures in new plant and equipment, especially when accompanied by technological advances, have an enormous influence on the rate of growth of productivity. The slowdown in productivity growth, however, does not appear to have been caused by changes in the rate of capital formation. It is estimated that .1 percent, at most, can be attributed to decreases in the rate of capital investment. The growth rate in capital per employee-hour remained virtually the same from 1966 to 1973 as it was during the period from 1947 to 1966.

5. *Social legislation.* Social legislation and government

regulations have had a large impact on organizations. Many regulations have improved the environment and made plants safer. Other regulations have created confusion, indecision, and repeated delays which have slowed innovation, post-poned or prevented plant construction, and cost some com-panies billions of dollars.

Estimates by the Bureau of Labor Statistics indicate that expenditures for pollution abatement and health and safety measures have contributed only .1 to .2 percent to the recent decline in productivity growth. Business executives, however, generally claim that the effects of social legislation have been much greater. "Lawyers' briefs don't make more shoes," they argue. General Motors, which has kept a record since 1974, claims that it spends $1.1 billion a year on meeting government regulations—not including the costs to develop cars with better fuel economy or cleaner exhaust. That's the equivalent of 23,750 full-time employees, or 3 percent of its total workforce. The Environmental Protection Agency claims to have created an estimated 150,000 additional jobs at 25,000 companies in 1976 to operate and maintain water pollution control equip-ment. When the Occupational Safety and Health Act was passed, its supporters argued that the law would create 60,000 new jobs. Oregon has legislated a recycling program that creates 365 new jobs—not to produce new bottles, but to handle, collect, clean, and return used containers.[22]

Dow Chemical Company attempted to objectively measure the costs of federal regulations and determine which costs were necessary and which were unnecessary or excessive. Dow published the data in a short bulletin designed to inform the public, influence future legislation, and encourage other com-panies to measure the costs of regulation. Excessive costs were defined as "the costs resulting from unnecessary laws or regulations beyond what would be required by good scientific, manufacturing, business or personnel practices; or where such laws or regulations cause duplication among the requirements of several agencies." Appropriate regulatory costs were the costs of those activities resulting from or covered by regulations which Dow utilized in the normal course of business to provide for the protection of employees, stockholders, customers, and the general public. In 1975, Dow estimated that the appropriate costs were $87 million and the excessive costs were $50 million; another $10 million in costs were questionable. In 1977, the appropriate costs had grown to $139 million and the excessive costs had jumped to $115 million (with $14 million listed as questionable costs). This shocking increase of 130 percent in the costs of excessive regulation prompted Dow to disseminate the information to the public.[23]

Government regulation and the resulting creation of new jobs clearly add many employee-hours to the input index of productivity, but they do not add a corresponding increase to the output index. Consequently, labor productivity measures are adversely influenced by regulatory legislation. This is not necessarily all bad. It means we are increasing the number of higher-paying jobs, keeping the environment cleaner, providing a healthier work situation both physically and psychologically, and eliminating social injustices. It also means that we are concentrating more on the quality of life and less on the production of goods and services. Thus certain forces that adversely influence productivity have a positive effect on the quality of life. Nevertheless, these benefits are not free; they come at a price.

Effects of Stagnant Productivity. In the past the enormous advancement in the material wealth of Americans has largely resulted from productivity growth. The high standard of living enjoyed by most Americans is the result of the higher rate of productivity, which has reduced the number of labor hours required to produce most products. The average worker in the 1970s could produce as much in two hours as nineteenth-century workers produced in an average 12-hour day—and probably with less effort per hour. When productivity increases 3 percent annually, the productivity rate doubles every 25 years.

Continued advancements in productivity growth are seen

Table 6.4.   Indexes of productivity and related data (1967 = 100).

	Output per Hour	Compensation per Hour	Real Compensation per Hour
1950	61.0	42.4	58.9
1955	70.3	55.8	69.6
1960	78.7	71.9	81.1
1965	95.0	88.7	93.8
1970	104.2	123.1	105.8
1975	112.4	181.3	112.5
1979	118.1	252.8	116.3

Source: Monthly Labor Review, Vol. 103, No. 2 (February 1980), p. 107.

as a necessary condition in the campaign against poverty. Without productivity improvements, the real wealth in America will fail to expand, and continued increases in the standard of living will be curtailed. If the average standard of living is going to improve, productivity has to increase or workers must work longer hours. For the past century, workers have chosen to work fewer, not more, hours.

Without a gain in productivity, inflation is much more difficult to control. Table 6.4 illustrates the relationship between output per hour, average compensation per hour, and real compensation per hour. Compensation per hour in 1979 was six times as great as in 1950. Unfortunately, most of this gain was due to inflation; real compensation from 1950 to 1979 only doubled. Increases in real compensation are related to increases in productivity. When wage rates increase without a corresponding increase in productivity, inflation results. To increase real compensation per hour, there must be an increase in productivity. If productivity does not increase and inflation is to be brought under control, wage rates must remain constant.

Perhaps the most serious concern about stagnant productivity is America's inability to compete effectively in world markets. A slowdown in productivity means that other countries with higher productivity growth will be able to produce relatively less expensive products. By 1978, several industries had already been seriously influenced by foreign competition, especially shipping, steel production, television manufacturing, and footwear. During the 1980s, the auto, computer, and electronics industries are expected to confront enormous foreign competition that will result in the loss of many American jobs.[24] Business executives are very concerned about the productivity slump. "America's economic survival will depend on its ability to increase its rate of productivity advance to former levels," said the chairman of a major automobile company. "That is no exaggeration."[25]

Increasing Productivity. The solution to the problem of stagnant productivity depends on two popular slogans: working harder and working smarter. Several useful strategies contribute to working smarter. Perhaps the most important strategy is the development and application of new technology. New machines that perform the work of many people but take only one person to operate make enormous contributions to productivity The hosiery industry in America from 1972–1977 is an excellent example of how productivity can be increased through greater automation. During this five-year period, productivity in the hosiery industry grew at an average annual rate of 10.2 percent. This rapid growth resulted from advances in knitting machine speeds, automated drying techniques, and new packaging procedures.[26]

Other strategies for working smarter require more effective management practices. Careful planning to develop efficient job procedures is essential to productivity. Management frequently complains that employees spend too much time standing around, and managers think the employees should work harder. On the other hand, employees are critical of management for carelessness: workers' tasks are inadequately designed; the coordination between jobs is poor; time and effort are wasted waiting for someone else; and no amount of working harder will make much difference.

In summary, stagnant productivity is a serious and complex

115

problem. Achieving higher levels of productivity requires innovative production procedures, new technology, and a cooperative relationship between management and employees. The decline in the work ethic appears to be only a small part of the reason why national productivity has not maintained a 3 percent annual increase. But even though it has only a small effect on national productivity, the work ethic should not be overlooked. The research results summarized here clearly endorse the relevance of the work ethic. Employees with strong work values tend to be more productive and report greater job satisfaction. Greater individual productivity not only increases organizational effectiveness; it is also in the best interests of national productivity. Consequently, a strong work orientation is generally consistent with the interests of the individual, the company, and society.

REFERENCES

1. Studs Terkel, *Working* (New York: Avon Books, 1972).
2. Mildred E. Katzell, "Productivity: The Measure and the Myth," *AMA Survey Report,* 1975.
3. Milton R. Blood, "Work Values and Job Satisfaction" *Journal of Applied Psychology,* Vol. 53, No. 6 (1969), pp. 456–459.
4. Ramon I. Aldag and Arthur P. Brief, "Some Correlates of Work Values," *Journal of Applied Psychology,* Vol. 60, No. 6 (1975), pp. 757–760; Robert Dubin and Joseph E. Champoux, "Central Life Interests and Job Satisfaction" *Organizational Behavior and Human Performance,* Vol. 18 (1977), pp. 366–377.
5. This research is reported in greater detail in a technical report by David J. Cherrington and associates, "Relationship Between Work Values, Productivity, and Morale," Erteszek Working Paper Series, Graduate School of Management, Brigham Young University, Provo, Utah, 1976.
6. Blood, *op. cit.,* p. 456.
7. Dubin and Champoux, *op. cit.,* p. 375.
8. The effect of selective perception on a person's response to a work environment has been studied by Frank Friedlander and Newton Margulies, "Multiple Impacts of Organizational Climate and Individual Value Systems upon Job Satisfaction," *Personnel Psychology,* Vol. 22 (1969), pp. 171–183.
9. The process of cognitive dissonance reduction is well illustrated by

ELiot Aronson, "The Rationalizing Animal," *Psychology Today* (May 1973).

10. Matthew R. Merrens and James B. Garrett, "The Protestant Ethic Scale as a Predictor of Repetitive Work Performance," *Journal of Applied Psychology*, Vol. 60, No. 1 (1975), pp. 125–127.

11. Grey R. Oldham, "Job Characteristics and Internal Motivation: The Moderating Effect of Interpersonal and Individual Variables," *Human Relations*, Vol. 29, No. 6 (1976), pp. 559–569.

12. J. Richard Hackman and Edward E. Lawler, "Employee Reactions to Job Characteristics," *Journal of Applied Psychology*, Monograph, Vol. 55, No. 3 (1971), pp. 259–286.

13. The data come from the U.S. Bureau of Labor Statistics as reported in "Productivity Indexes for Selected Industries, 1967 Edition," and in Abraham L. Gitlow, *Economics* (New York: Oxford University Press, 1962), pp. 102–107.

14. This estimate is based on growth in GNP per employee-hour as reported in Gitlow, *op. cit.*, p. 104.

15. Ronald E. Krutscher, Jerome A. Mark, and John R. Norsworthy, "The Productivity Slowdown and the Outlook to 1985," *Monthly Labor Review*, Vol. 100, No. 5 (May 1977), pp. 3–8.

16. Katzell, *op. cit.*

17. R. Joseph Monsen and Borje O. Saxberg, "When Workers Won't Work and Managers Won't Manage," *Management Review*, Vol. 66 (August 1977), pp. 26–39.

18. Taken from the U.S. Bureau of Labor Statistics, "International Comparisons of Productivity and Unit Labor Cost Trends in Manufacturing." These are annual press releases since 1971. See also Keith Daly and Arthur Reef, "Productivity and Unit Labor Costs in 11 Industrial Countries: 1977," *Monthly Labor Review*, Vol. 101, No. 11 (November 1978), pp. 11–17.

19. An endorsement of the Japanese style of management was suggested in U.S. Department of Commerce, "Tips on Productivity Improvement: A Management Technique," *Situation Report*, Productivity Series Bulletin No. 2, 1976. Numerous other articles have discussed the adoption of Japanese management styles to American industries, such as Richard T. Johnson and William S. Ouchi, "Made in America (Under Japanese Management)," *Harvard Business Review*, Vol. 52, No. 5 (September–October 1974), pp. 61–69. The quotations are from Carl A. Gerstacker of Dow Chemical and James C. Toedman, editor of *The Personnel Administrator*, as found in James C. Toedman, "Needed: A New Emphasis on Productivity Improvement," *The Personnel Administrator*, Vol. 19, No. 7 (October 1974), pp. 24–27.

20. Personal correspondence from Remi C. Pattyn of Public Service In-

diana, "Report to Members of Coordinating Committee of the Indiana Construction Anti-Inflation Roundtable," December 13, 1974.

21. This and later explanations for the decline in productivity growth rates come from Krutscher, Mark, and Norsworthy, *op. cit.*

22. The quote and following data come from "Productivity's Price," *Forbes* (February 19, 1979), p. 123.

23. Bulletin distributed by Dow Chemical Public Relations Department, Midland, Michigan, 1979.

24. Jackson Grayson, Jr., "Why U.S. Workers Are Producing Less," *U.S. News and World Report* (May 1, 1978), pp. 95–96.

25. Comment by Thomas Murphy of General Motors, as quoted by Bradley Graham, "Productivity," *Washington Post* (September 10, 1978), F1, F5.

26. U.S. Bureau of Labor Statistics, "Productivity Indexes for Selected Industries, 1978 Edition."

7

THE DEVELOPMENT OF WORK VALUES

Previous chapters have shown that the work ethic was a dominant social philosophy in early America, but in recent times it has not been endorsed as enthusiastically. This change is not in the best interest of the individual, the organization, or society. There are many good reasons for advocating the work ethic and believing in the dignity of labor. A belief in the work ethic contributes to job satisfaction and a better quality of life. It also contributes to the productive efficiency of the organization and the material well-being of society.

The forces that cause some people to feel pride in craftsman-ship and internally rewarded for performing an excellent job are to be found both in the developmental experiences of early childhood and in the present work environment. This chapter focuses on early experiences that contribute to the develop-ment of a work ethic during childhood. The next chapter discusses the contribution of organizational and job-related factors.

The values of adults are largely shaped through childhood experiences. These include not just work values, but other values as well, such as honesty, compassion, and altruism. Children acquire a strong work ethic when their parents exert firm discipline, demand obedience, and expect children to accept personal responsibility for performing the tasks assigned to them. This style of child rearing sounds rather harsh and is not consistent with much of the "modern" advice to parents. But research evidence suggests that authoritative parenting develops children who not only believe in the importance of work but who are also independent, self-disciplined, and socially responsible. Furthermore, firm discipline does not mean lack of loving; parents can demand strict obedience and still be loving and empathetic.

CHARACTERISTICS OF OUTSTANDING PERFORMERS

The effects of early childhood experiences on work values were dramatically illustrated by the interviews with outstanding performers described in Chapter 4. The purpose of the interviews was to identify the characteristics of outstanding workers—what they were like and how they got to be that way. Several mediocre and poor workers were also interviewed to serve as a basis for comparison. The performance evaluations were obtained from immediate supervisors, and the identification of outstanding performers was usually confirmed by other managers in the company. Most of these outstanding performers were considered the "best workers in the company."

The first question asked in the interviews was "How work-oriented are you?" As noted in the last chapter, all the outstanding performers replied without hesitation that they were very work-oriented; work was an important part of their life and provided meaning, fulfillment, and satisfaction for them.

The second question asked was "How long have you been work-oriented?" All but three workers said they had been that way all their lives, at least back to their early childhood days. The three exceptions identified periods in young adulthood when they made a significant change in their environment. The case study of one of these three workers, Carol Blanchard, is presented in the next chapter.

The next question focused on the central purpose of the

interview: "How did you get to be so work-oriented?" All but three of the outstanding workers (the three exceptions to the previous question) said that they acquired their strong work orientation from their parents—"It was the way I was raised." Fathers were mentioned most frequently as the major source of work values. None of the outstanding workers could remember a specific learning experience when someone undertook to teach them the value of work. Instead, they reported numerous small episodes when they observed their parents at work, when they worked alongside their parents, or when their parents gave them a responsibility and supervised them as they performed it.

One worker described how he used to watch his father work. He remembered how important it was to his father to do things right. His father was a carpenter, and if the door he had hung did not swing right, he would rip it out and start over again. His motto was "If you do it right the first time, you won't have to come back and do it again," and he repeated it frequently, hoping to influence his children.

Another worker described how her experiences during the Depression shaped her philosophy about work. Her family was extremely poor, but they were determined to survive without government welfare. Her father repeatedly said, "We can make it on our own if we aren't afraid of a little work." Her responsibility as a young teenager was the vegetable garden. She solicited help from other family members, but it was ultimately her responsibility.

The experiences that these outstanding workers described were different in many respects, but they had several themes in common. The first and most significant theme was the importance of discipline and obedience. Almost all the outstanding workers indicated that their parents were loving and kind but believed in strict discipline and demanded obedience from their children. When told to do something, the children were expected to do it without a lot of complaining or whining.

A second theme was the importance of working. Everyone was expected to work. Even young children were assigned chores and were expected to do them. When unique situations occurred, such as family outings, everyone was expected to pitch in and help. If there was a job to be done, everyone was expected to help without being asked.

A third theme was the importance of religion. Most of the outstanding workers indicated that a belief in God and regular church attendance were fundamental parts of their early lives. Church attendance had decreased for some of them in their adult lives. But their early religious training was still the basis by which they made moral and ethical decisions about such things as divorce, abortion, bribery, and pornography.

A fourth theme was the importance of doing the "right" thing even if it was unpopular or hard. Several outstanding workers described experiences involving some form of self-denial where they did what they did because it was the right thing to do even if it was not pleasurable. In fact, certain activities such as heavy work and body conditioning were physically painful, but they did them because they were the right things to do. Some workers obviously derived great satisfaction in accomplishing difficult tasks that they thought would benefit them or others.

A fifth theme was frugality. Since many outstanding workers had been raised in poverty, frugality was a necessity. But even those who were not poor accepted thrift and conservation as important personal values. Turning off lights, fixing leaking water faucets, wearing clothes long after the first signs of wear, and avoiding impulse buying or the purchase of convenience items were well-ingrained characteristics.

The sixth theme was the importance of individual effort in achieving success. Outstanding performers rejected the idea that success is mainly determined by luck, chance, or who you know. Most believed that the major determinants of occupational success were the amount of skill and experience people had acquired and how much effort they put into their work.

These six characteristics seemed to be especially descriptive of outstanding performers. Mediocre and poor performers occasionally described themselves as possessing some of these

122

characteristics, but there was usually a dramatic difference in the frequency and intensity with which the characteristics were reported by outstanding performers.

REGRESSION ANALYSIS

To gain a better understanding of which variables contribute to the development of the work ethic, my associates and I analyzed the 3,632 responses to our survey questionnaire. (The data from 8 companies in the Far East, including Japan, Hong Kong, Indonesia, and the Philippines, were combined with the 53 U.S. companies in this analysis.) The information included two work values that measured the major components of the traditional work ethic: (1) the moral importance of work and (2) pride in craftsmanship. It also included various attitudinal measures toward the job, the company, and the community as well as demographic data and personal background information. The data were analyzed using a multiple regression equation to determine which variables were the most closely related to the two work values.

A multiple regression analysis indicates to what extent a set of independent variables predicts (in a statistical sense) a dependent variable. Stated differently, it indicates whether an individual's score on a dependent variable (such as the moral importance of work) can be predicted by knowing his or her scores on the independent variables (such as job satisfaction, company attitudes, community attitudes, and background information).

The statements measuring the two work values were listed earlier in Tables 4.2 and 4.3. The workers used a 7-point scale to indicate the extent to which they agreed or disagreed with each statement, and their responses were averaged to compute the two work value scores.

There were 43 independent variables: 5 variables for personal background, 4 variables for race, 6 variables for religion, 7 demographic variables, 3 variables measuring reinforcement contingencies, and 18 variables measuring attitudes toward the

123

Table 7.1. Multiple regression analysis predicting two work values.

Independent Variables	Moral Importance of Work		Pride in Craftsmanship	
	Beta	*F Ratio*	*Beta*	*F Ratio*
Personal Background				
Discipline in socialization	.233	128.5	.150	56.4
Importance of family life	.049	6.8	.070	14.9
Internal locus of control	.104	29.4	.181	94.2
Acceptability of individual initiative	.100	28.2	.129	50.3
Acceptability of welfare	−.049	6.4	−.120	40.6
Race				
Black	.038	2.0	−.032	1.5
Chicano	−.044	4.5	.010	.2
White	−.184	32.1	.085	7.4
Oriental	.008	.1	−.026	1.5
Religion				
Catholic	.038	.2	−.025	.1
Protestant	.049	.3	−.004	.0
Mormon	.130	4.8	−.015	.0
Oriental Christian	−.008	.0	−.043	1.6
Far East	.044	2.0	−.024	.6
No Religion	.013	.0	−.069	.8
Demographic Data				
Age	.161	56.4	.090	18.9
Educational level	−.024	1.4	a	
Father's education	.026	1.3	.001	.0
Mother's education	−.047	4.5	a	
Population of hometown	.012	.4	−.043	5.4
Occupation	−.034	2.2	.011	.2
Income	.017	.7	−.005	.1

job or company. The results of the regression analysis are summarized in Table 7.1. The F ratio in the table tests whether the beta coefficients are significantly greater than zero. The F value must exceed 2.0 to be significant at the .01 probability level.

The results clearly indicated that the best overall predictor of the work ethic was a variable labeled discipline in socialization, followed closely by variables labeled internal locus of

Table 7.1. (Continued)

Independent Variables	Moral Importance of Work		Pride in Craftsmanship	
	Beta	F Ratio	Beta	F Ratio
Job Attitudes				
Effort leads to performance	.028	2.3	.052	8.2
Performance leads to				
extrinsic rewards	.029	1.7	−.037	2.9
Performance avoids				
punishment	.011	.3	.018	1.1
General satisfaction	.003	.0	−.062	5.5
Personal skill	.018	.6	.070	10.1
Pay satisfaction	−.012	.3	.009	.1
Pay equity	a		−.012	.3
Pay adequacy	−.009	.1	−.025	1.2
Interpersonal attraction	−.036	2.3	.039	2.8
Satisfaction attributed				
to co-workers	.004	.0	−.065	7.2
Supervisor consideration	−.072	8.1	.049	4.0
Supervisor competence	.028	1.3	−.008	.1
Job attractiveness	a		.053	4.9
Job complexity	a		a	
Job security	−.012	.3	.015	.5
Satisfaction with company	.106	14.0	.086	9.9
Organizational effectiveness	−.005	.0	.058	6.0
Company commitment	.200	89.9	.015	.5
Job enrichment	.039	2.5	.061	6.1
Discrepancy in job				
expectations	.044	3.8	.137	39.1
Work group cohesiveness	−.015	.5	.040	3.5
Adjusted R^2	.32		.36	
Degrees of freedom	41; 2150		40; 2151	

[a]F level was too low for this variable to enter the equation.

control, the acceptability of individual initiative, and the acceptability of welfare. Another good predictor was a variable called importance of family life.

The best predictor of the work ethic, discipline in socialization, was computed by averaging the responses to the following five items:

1. "My family expects me to perform well on the job."
2. "While I was young I spent a lot of time working alongside my father (mother)."
3. "I came from a close-knit, happy family."
4. "Some young people are expected to do a lot of work (farm chores, yardwork, or part-time job), while others are expected to do very little. Compared with other youth, how much work would you say you were expected to do during your teen years?"
5. "How important is religion in your life?"

It is obvious from examining these five items that the development of the work ethic is strongly influenced by the experiences and expectations the individual has earlier in life. A strong belief in the moral importance of work would be predicted for people who come from a close-knit family in which children are expected to assume personal responsibilities and parents occasionally work with the children to make certain the jobs are done. The item asking about the importance of religion suggests that discipline and self-control are important personal characteristics accompanying family expectations in the development of the work ethic. It seems reasonable to conclude that the relationship between the work ethic and discipline in socialization is a causal one. Family expectations, early work experiences, and discipline are important factors in the development of a strong belief about the importance of hard work and the dignity of labor.

A commitment to pride in craftsmanship was predicted by a strong belief in individual initiative and responsibility. The internal locus of control variable, which predicted pride in craftsmanship, consisted of three statements about the determinants of success in an occupation: luck, effort, or how much you know. (*Example:* "Success in an occupation is mainly a matter of how much you know.") The acceptability of welfare score, which predicted *low* pride in craftsmanship, asked how acceptable government welfare, church welfare, or help from family and friends would be if one were not making enough money. Individualism and self-determination are apparently personal characteristics highly associated with pride in craftsmanship. Employees who take pride in their work and who are committed to doing a high-quality job believe strongly in individual initiative and personal responsibility.

Equally impressive as the significance of some variables was the lack of significance of others. While the importance of religion in one's life was a significant predictor of the work ethic, it did not seem to matter much which religion one professed. None of the religions were associated with pride in craftsmanship and only one was associated with the moral importance of work. The moral importance of work variable is similar to what has been called the Protestant work ethic. However, the Protestant religion was the thirty-fourth variable (of 43) to enter the regression equation, just ahead of the Catholic religion. Neither religion was a significant predictor of the work ethic. Mormonism was the only religion that slightly predicted the moral importance of work.

If the career counseling and professional preparation that students receive in later years of school effectively taught work values, there would be a significant relationship between years of education and work values. However, this was not the case. Workers with more education did not report stronger work values than those with less education. In other words, work ethic attitudes were not predicted by years of education. This suggests that the work ethic is not taught in the educational system. In fact, the work ethic slightly declined as the mother's educational level increased. The negative relationships for mother's education, along with the positive relationships for the importance of family life, suggest that the work ethic develops in more traditional families where mothers are in the home training their young children.

It has been suggested that employees would be more inclined to believe in the importance of work and pride in craftsmanship if they had more attractive jobs. However, the evidence clearly indicates that the work ethic is not associated with occupational status, monthly income, job attractiveness, job complexity, or job security. In fact, pride in craftsmanship is predicted by a larger rather than a smaller discrepancy between the amount of autonomy and decision making workers have compared with how much they would like to have.

The implications of these results are that while job enrichment, participative management, and job autonomy may be important factors for work-oriented employees, they do not *cause* the work ethic. Participation and loose supervision cannot simply be tossed to the worker and expected to *promote* an increase in work values. This does not mean that the work ethic of older employees cannot be influenced. But it does suggest that discipline and self-control are fundamental characteristics of the socialization process and very important elements in developing the work ethic.

DISCIPLINE AND SELF-CONTROL[2]

The comments of outstanding performers and the results of the regression analysis present a consistent description of the antecedents of the work ethic. Parental child-rearing practices which emphasize firm discipline, obedience to authority, close parental supervision, involvement with the child, and warm emotional support all contribute to the development of work values in children.

These conclusions raise two rather disturbing concerns. The first is whether close supervision and high parental demands create resistance and antagonism in children. Common wisdom suggests that firm rule enforcement in the home causes hostility in children. Rebelliousness and "running away from home" have frequently been attributed to excessive parental control. The second concern is whether strict discipline and rule enforcement create overly submissive children who suffer a loss of individuality and self-assertiveness. Blind obedience to rules and unquestioned compliance with authoritative commands have been attributed to the conditioning process by which children learn to obey parental authority. Some have suggested that children should be subjected to only limited amounts of parental authority or none at all.[3]

Numerous studies on the effects of child-rearing practices

do not support some of the popular notions about permissive parenting. The research indicates that firm discipline does not necessarily create either aggressive antagonism or submissive compliance. On the contrary, firm discipline has been shown to contribute to socially responsible and independent behavior in children.

Authoritative Parents.   Several significant contributions have been made in recent times to our understanding of effective child-rearing practices. The literature review and research of Diana Baumrind have been especially useful in explaining the effects of parental control, obedience to authority, and discipline on children's moral and social development. Her research has provided an alternative model of parental influence in addition to the typical dichotomy of permissive versus authoritarian control. She has described a third model, called authoritative control, and has provided evidence showing that it generates well-socialized behavior as well as willful and independent behavior in children.[4]

Baumrind reviewed the results of 12 studies on child-rearing practices and concluded that the evidence did not support some of the popular notions about child discipline. In each study, the data on the parents and children were independently collected through observations and interviews.[5]

One of the major myths that these studies failed to support was that rebelliousness in children, particularly adolescents, was caused by close parental supervision, high demands, and other manifestations of parental authority. On the contrary, the studies found that higher demands were made by the parents of children who were the *least* hostile or delinquent. Firm control was associated with responsible conscience development.[6] Baumrind suggested that affection and concern were important accompaniments to high parental demands. Parents who demanded that their children be orderly and assume household responsibilities also seemed to provide surroundings conducive to the children's well-being and to involve themselves conscientiously in the children's welfare. Perhaps that was why such demands were viewed by the children as reasonable, in most of the studies, and did not provoke rebellion. Additional studies have indicated that parental demands provoke rebellion only when the parents are also repressive, hostile, and restrictive.[7]

A second myth, that firm parental control generates passivity and dependence, was also not supported by the studies. Generally, the most self-reliant children came from parents who were rated highest in firm control. A similar myth, that parental restrictiveness decreases self-assertiveness and buoyancy, was also not supported. Delinquent boys, for example, tended to come from nonrestrictive homes where parents made few demands and were not highly controlling. Nondelinquent boys came from more restrictive homes where parents created explicit expectations for behavior, exerted firm discipline, and enforced rule compliance. The studies indicated that restrictiveness decreases self-assertiveness only when it is accompanied by parental hostility and overprotectiveness.[8]

Another myth Baumrind examined was that permissiveness frees the child from the authority of the parent. Permissiveness not only failed to generate individualism and self-reliant behavior; it also increased the incidence of aggression among nursery school boys. When parents did not discipline the child for aggressive behavior, their lack of response was interpreted by the child as condoning aggressiveness.[9]

These findings suggest that parental control and discipline do not produce the negative effects that common wisdom dictates. Simplistic notions, such as "permissiveness produces individuality," fail to consider the significant role that discipline and obedience to a rational authority play in the development process.

Commenting on a later study, Baumrind described authoritative parents and reported data on the value of this style of parenting:

> The authoritative parent attempts to direct the child's activities in a rational, issue-oriented manner. She encourages verbal give-and-take, shares with the child the reasoning behind her policy, and solicits his objections when he refuses

to conform. Both autonomous self-will and disciplined conformity are valued by the authoritative parent. Therefore, she
exerts firm control at points of parent-child divergence, but
does not hem the child in with restrictions. She enforces her
own perspective as an adult, but recognizes the child's individual interests and special ways. The authoritative parent
affirms the child's present qualities, but also sets standards for
future conduct. She uses reason, power, and shaping by
regime and reinforcement to achieve her objectives and does
not base her decisions on group consensus or the individual
child's desires.[10]

The behavioral differences between authoritative and authoritarian parents are rather small, but they produce a
significant difference in the behavior of children. Both kinds of
parents take an active role in shaping the child's behavior. Both
exercise power to obtain obedience, exert firm discipline and
rule enforcement, and disapprove of children's defiance. But
they differ in the extent to which they encourage independence
and individuality. Unlike authoritarian parents, authoritative
parents define the child's individuality clearly, encourage
intimate verbal contact, display empathetic understanding, and
give reasons with their directives.

In a series of studies, Baumrind and her associates observed
children at school while assessing their parents through structured interviews and home visits. The results indicated that
the children of authoritative parents were the most socially
responsible, self-reliant, self-controlled, explorative, and
content. The children of authoritarian parents were discontent,
withdrawn, and distrustful; they were also lacking in independence, but not lacking in social responsibility. Permissive
parents were noncontrolling, nondemanding, and relatively
warm, but they did not produce independent children. The
children of permissive parents were the least self-reliant, the
least explorative, and the least self-controlled. Furthermore,
the children of permissive parents were generally lacking in
social responsibility.

To explain why authoritative parental control produced
well-socialized and independent children, Baumrind reexam-

ined the concept of freedom. She rejected the notion that freedom means giving children the liberty to do as they please without interference from adult guardians. Instead, she defined freedom as the *appreciation of necessity*. That is, children gain freedom by understanding the nature of the outside world and controlling their reactions to it. This concept of freedom implies the power to act rather than the absence of external control. The implications of this distinction for child rearing are profound. It suggests that independence and individuality develop not by the absence of controls but by the presence of appropriate controls that help children master their environment.

Internalized Self-Discipline and Self-Control. Another interesting study, focusing on a much different problem, supported the value of discipline and parental control. Richard H. Blum and his associates wanted to discover why some children succumbed to environmental pressures and began using illicit drugs while other children successfully resisted these social pressures. Their research showed that family influences were the important factors governing the use of illicit drugs. Thus their study is really a study of family interactions and parental child-rearing practices.[11]

The study covered blue-collar white families, blue-collar black families, Mexican-American families, and "hippie families." But the largest and most extensively studied group consisted of 101 white middle-class families. These families all lived in the same area. Both mother and father lived at home, and they had at least one child in college and younger children in the home. In many respects, the researchers said, all 101 families could be considered solid, respectable middle-class American families.

These families were classified into high-, medium-, and low-risk categories according to the drug use of their children. A risk score was calculated for each child based on the frequency of drug use and the kind of drugs used. The risk score referred to both the present and potential danger accompanying the use of psychoactive drugs without medical approval or supervision. Thus high-risk families had one or more children who frequently used opiates, cocaine, LSD, and other illicit drugs. There was no use of illicit drugs in low-risk families.

Several major differences were found between the high- and low-risk families. Low-risk families were more likely to be politically conservative and to attend church regularly. High-risk families tended to reject all major political parties and did not attend church. Low-risk families were father-led or authoritative families in which the father supervised studies and had the last word on health practices, major purchases, and the like. There was less freedom of choice for younger children in low-risk families, but older children seemed to go about their activities without fuss, as though the choice were their own. In high-risk families, the concept of discipline was not emphasized as a required part of child rearing. Children were given greater freedom of choice at an earlier age on everything except their study habits.

The parents were given a list of ten child-rearing goals and asked to rank their importance. Low-risk parents emphasized teaching the child self-control, whereas high-risk parents emphasized expanding the child's creative potential and preparing the child for a world of change.

The children mirrored their parents' attitudes and values. When asked to rank a list of ten child-rearing goals, low-risk children gave high priority to turning the child into a respectable citizen, teaching self-control, and teaching obedience. High-risk children gave high priority to helping the child become a loving person and to expanding the child's creative capacity. When asked at what age they should be allowed to decide things for themselves, high-risk children set earlier ages than low-risk children for deciding about friends, bedtimes, church attendance, belief in God, how much liquor to drink, political activities, hairstyles, where to go for fun, whom to date, sexual intercourse, use of marijuana, and when to respect the police.

133

Differences were also reported in the work experiences of high- and low-risk families. Low-risk children began participating in family chores earlier than high-risk children. More than half of the low-risk families encouraged the child to begin chores before the age of six, whereas high-risk families frequently waited until the child was nine years old. Yardwork in particular was more often assigned to children in low-risk families.

To some people, the lifestyle of the low-risk families appears to combine the worst aspects of a military dictatorship and prison life. Some might argue that the fathers of low-risk families are much like "drill instructors." Nevertheless, low-risk families successfully immunized their children against the use of drugs, even though drugs abounded in neighborhoods and schools. But did these families do so by such strict discipline that it produced mindless submissiveness or a loss of individuality? Does the authoritative discipline of the low-risk family have any other redeeming value?

The final project undertaken by Blum and his associates was an intensive clinical investigation of 13 of the families that had been interviewed earlier. These families were observed by a researcher who visited them in their homes as a dinner guest. The families also participated in videotaped group discussions with a narcotics officer, a minister, and a girl with hippielike appearance and attitude. The topic of the discussion centered on what children should be taught about drugs. Two psychoanalytically trained professionals also observed the families and made independent evaluations of the quality of family interactions. The goal was to learn whether the drug risk scores determined earlier corresponded to the clinicians' rating of the excellence of family interactions.

In general, the families' drug risk scores were closely associated with the ratings of family interactions. For example, none of the families rated "superior" or "good" came from the high-risk group, whereas the families rated as "troubled" or "pathological" in their interactions were all high-risk families. Low-risk families tended to produce a climate that was conducive to the emotional growth of their children. The family circle was generally happy and family members enjoyed being together.

Perhaps the most profound paradox was the inability of high-risk children to participate in the group discussions. High-risk parents had indicated that they wanted their children to be creative and independent, yet high-risk children were generally incapable of participating openly in the group discussions. High-risk children were the least creative and the least able to think for themselves. They seemed to be easily influenced by the arguments of others and complained most about restrictions on their freedom.

The low-risk children participated most aggressively in the group discussions. They argued for their point of view and tried to persuade the hippie girl to their "straight" way of thinking. Low-risk parents had placed high values on discipline, self-control, respect for the rights of others, and obedience to God's commands. Once their children had internalized these values, they were free to develop their own individuality. They had learned the rules of the game and demonstrated to their parents that they had sufficient discipline and self-control to direct their own behavior. Their parents trusted them and approved of the decisions they made.

In my interviews with employees, I occasionally asked questions about family interactions and child-rearing practices. The purpose of the questions was to assess whether the characteristics of low-risk families, as described by Blum, also described outstanding performers. One forced-choice question involved two sets of child-rearing goals: becoming creative, independent, and thinking for oneself versus developing discipline, obedience, and respect for the rights of others. Mediocre performers frequently indicated that they thought their parents' child-rearing goals were the development of creativity and independent thinking. Outstanding workers said almost unanimously that developing discipline, obedience, and respect for the rights of others were the goals their parents espoused. This is not to say that their parents behaved like drill instructors; most said that the amount of discipline their parents exercised was reasonable and appropriate.

Other characteristics of low-risk families seemed to be equally descriptive of outstanding performers. For example, they were assigned various chores and household responsibilities at an early age. Most came from politically conservative homes where both parents expected children to learn obedience and respect for authority and age. A belief in God was generally quite important for all outstanding workers, especially during childhood. Church attendance for some had waned during later teenage years. But for many it revived after they became parents and had to decide about religion for their children. Until adolescence their parents made most of the decisions in their lives. But after the age of 16, they started to make their own decisions even though the decisions were about the same as the ones they thought their parents would make. Their family relationships were usually warm and friendly. Some said the relationships were not especially affectionate, but there was generally an absence of the bitter arguing and complaining that characterized the high-risk homes. Finally, the outstanding workers seemed unanimously opposed to the use of drugs, and many were opposed to the use of alcohol and tobacco.

The studies of Blum and his associates and the interviews with outstanding employees both demonstrate the significance of obedience and discipline within the home. These results are consistent with the multiple regression analysis presented earlier, which indicated that the work ethic is primarily developed through a process of child rearing that involves strong family expectations for good performance, work experiences in early childhood, religious commitments, and individual initiative.

Other studies have supported these findings. A study in 1948, for example, found that work adjustment was associated with family backgrounds characterized by a closely knit family group in which children had early work experiences and religious values and church attendance were stressed. Four other studies found, as did Blum, that the avoidance of drugs and alcohol is related to similar family characteristics.[12]

VALUE INTERNALIZATION

Parents can tell children that work is an important value and children can learn what their parents think about work. But this knowledge does not mean that children will think work is important. Children do not necessarily internalize their parents' values and accept them as their own.

The value internalization process has been examined in numerous studies on moral behavior.[13] Moral behaviors are actions considered intrinsically desirable, valued, or good because of their contribution to society. Most of the research on moral development has focused on three moral behaviors: aggression, honesty, and prosocial behavior, especially altruism. Work values have not been investigated in moral development research. Nevertheless, the internalization of work values would seem to follow a similar process.

There are two major steps in the development of the work ethic. First, work-related activities acquire the properties of a learned reinforcer and become intrinsic rewards. Second, the person learns to delay gratification.

Intrinsic Rewards.   The feeling of pride in craftsmanship that comes from doing high-quality work is a learned intrinsic reward. The good feeling that comes from being of service to others is also a learned reward. People are not born with a need to work or an instinct to be of service. Work-related activities acquire their positive properties through past experience and through their association with other rewards.

The comments of outstanding performers indicated that their parents exerted an enormous influence in making work a positive experience for them through expressions of approval and recognition. In the same way, comments by peers or expressions of appreciation by those who have been helped can make charitable service a positive reward for the donor. When

137

people see that their efforts please others, they gradually begin to accept work as a useful and worthwhile activity.

Work can also acquire positively reinforcing properties if it is consistent with a strongly held religious or political ideology. If you believe that God expects you to use your time carefully and be a wise steward, then working long hours and accomplishing difficult tasks are positive rewards. If you believe that the economic stability of your country depends on high worker productivity, then working faster and being more careful are rewarding experiences.

Delayed Gratification.   Believing that work is important is not sufficient to produce the diligence, perseverance, and high-quality craftsmanship characteristic of outstanding performers. Even if work is an intrinsic reward, it competes with other rewards for the control of the individual's behavior. The person must have the discipline to pursue an activity, perhaps for an extended period of time, without having to receive an immediate reward.

The capacity to delay gratification—to work for a long time without being rewarded—is important in developing the work ethic. Every work setting offers a choice of several behaviors, each with its own reward. For example, you can work hard and expend a lot of physical or mental energy; you can work slowly; you can avoid work altogether; or you can stay at the workplace but visit with co-workers. Each behavior has its own reward, and the behavior you select will be influenced by your ability to delay gratification. Some activities, such as scientific research, require a long period of dedicated effort. Some community service projects take a long time to complete, and their benefits are not reaped until years later. The real payoff on the time and energy spent in helping teenagers get their lives straightened out comes a generation later when they are raising socially responsible families. Obviously, many useful and worthwhile activities require a long period of diligent perseverance before they are rewarded.

Unless a person has the self-discipline to delay gratification, activities that are not immediately rewarding will not be pursued. Hard work, which may take a lot of energy and be physically uncomfortable, is often an immediate punisher. It is not likely that the person will work hard unless there are other rewards, either intrinsic or extrinsic, to offset the discomfort. Pride in craftsmanship and joy in service are intrinsic rewards that are extremely meaningful to some, but meaningless to others. People who are motivated by such rewards do not have to wait for others to reward them. When they have completed a significant project, they immediately feel joy in service or pride in craftsmanship. People who are not motivated by intrinsic rewards for dedicated work generally lack the persistence to accomplish long-term projects. Money, praise, and recognition are positive rewards for working, but they are not immediate and not necessarily dependent on doing a good job. Mediocre performance often results in just as much money and recognition as outstanding performance.

Leisure activities often compete with work for control of a person's behavior. Even though the rewards of leisure are usually small and temporary, they have a significant impact on behavior because they are immediate. Watching television is probably the most common leisure activity for Americans. It has been estimated that adult males spend an average of 25 hours per week watching television and adult females watch an average of 30 hours per week.[14] The television industry spends millions of dollars trying to make television viewing immediately rewarding. The networks compete intensely for the attention of the viewing audience; programs that receive low ratings are dropped. Even the commercials have to be appealing and entertaining.

Another immediately rewarding activity that competes with work is visiting with co-workers. Social conversations provide an immediate reward in the form of friendly interpersonal interaction. They also help people escape from the less pleasant activity of working. Furthermore, visiting seems even more legitimate if everyone is doing it.

The ability to delay gratification depends primarily on the

individual's past history of reinforcement. People who were rewarded frequently in the past for forgoing immediate pleasures find it easier to postpone immediate satisfactions in the future. Parents who emphasize self-control and self-discipline help children learn to delay gratification. Research on moral development has identified two important techniques by which work becomes an intrinsic reward and children learn to delay gratification. These techniques are induction and modeling.

1. *Induction.* Induction is perhaps the most significant process by which work becomes an intrinsic reward. Induction refers to all forms of verbal explanation, such as reasoning, preaching, and teaching. Induction includes cognitive information describing appropriate behaviors and a justification of why it is appropriate. It also includes the various verbal reinforcements for prosocial behaviors. ("Thank you for helping." "You're a good worker." "I couldn't have done it without you.") There is abundant evidence showing that induction is a useful, if not necessary, technique in moral development. Parents who use induction frequently to explain the implications of behavior on others generally have children who show more consideration for others, more resistance to temptation, and less aggression. Laboratory studies have demonstrated that induction techniques tend to increase altruistic behaviors.[15]

An important consequence of induction is that it contributes to the internalization of moral standards. Unlike other influence techniques, such as physical rewards and punishment, induction reinforces the perception that you are the source of your own moral standards. Induction directs your attention to the consequences of your behavior for others and the logical demands of the situation. It provides you with a cognitive understanding of your actions and allows you sufficient freedom to process this information for yourself. You thereby control your own behavior, and the basis for your moral standards is internal.[16] Therefore, logical explanations about the importance of dependable performance and high-quality workmanship contribute to the internalization of work values.

2. *Modeling*. Another technique that has a significant impact on the development of moral behavior is modeling.[17] Modeling refers to the example parents and other significant individuals set for children. Parents are usually influential models whether they want to be or not. They can use induction or physical punishment, but it is difficult for them to not be models. In early childhood, parents are usually the most influential models; in later adolescence, peers and significant others also become important models.

Modeling has a major impact on the development of numerous personal behaviors, values, and attitudes. Children pattern their communication after their parents, adopting a similar vocabulary and sentence structure and similar hand motions. If parents spit on the ground, children often spit on the ground. If parents smoke children are more likely to smoke, and they will even model the way their parents hold a cigarette and blow the smoke in the air. If parents get upset with children and slap them, it is likely that children will strike siblings when they become angry or frustrated. If parents respond to insults or criticism in a calm and open manner, children are more likely to respond calmly. And children are more likely to appreciate the arts if they have seen their parents appreciate them.

Developing an intrinsic value for work and learning to delay gratification are greatly influenced by modeling. Children first learn that a house should be clean by seeing their own house clean. What they see and experience becomes their standard of excellence. Although it is subtle, the most powerful influence on children's perceptions of expected behavior comes from what they see their parents do. "If my parents do_____ (make their bed, clear their dishes from the table, clean spills on the floor, wipe their feet), I'm expected to do_____." A mother who cleans the house rapidly and efficiently sets a pattern of behavior for her children to follow. Even if they do not adopt that pattern immediately, they are likely to imitate the parent as their own behavior is formed.

Research on the development of moral behavior has shown that the effects of modeling become more significant and pronounced as the model becomes more attractive. Well-liked models have a larger impact on behavior than disliked models. In one study well-liked fathers who provided a model of responsibility and self-control tended to have sons who were responsible and nonaggressive. Aggressive boys lacked such a paternal model of inner control. They were influenced relatively less by their fathers and relatively more by factors outside the home, especially neighborhood groups.[18] In another study of child-rearing practices among fathers of delinquent adolescents and normal adolescents, it was found that a far greater number of delinquents perceived their fathers as ineffective, irresponsible, and emotionally unstable.[19] Fathers who were perceived as effective, responsible, and stable were influential models for their children.

CONCLUSIONS

The following conclusions about the development of work values are supported by the results of questionnaire analysis, interviews, and research on moral development and child-rearing practices.

1. Outstanding workers have a strong work orientation that is generally acquired during early childhood and adolescence.

2. Children develop a strong work ethic when parents exert firm discipline, delegate work assignments, encourage personal responsibility, establish standards of personal conduct, and encourage religious commitments.

3. Authoritative parents who emphasize discipline and self-control tend to have children who are socially responsible, self-reliant, and well behaved. Authoritarian parents tend to produce children who are withdrawn, discontent, and dependent. Permissive parents tend to produce children who are lacking in self-reliance, self-control, and social responsibility.

4. Two essential processes in the internalization of work values are acquiring the positive properties of work activities (work becomes an intrinsic reward) and developing the capacity to delay gratification.

5. Two of the most influential techniques in the develop-

ment of the work ethic are induction and modeling—teaching
by precept and example.

REFERENCES

1. These results are reported more fully in David J. Cherrington, "Development of a Work Ethic," *Proceedings of the Nineteenth Annual Southwest Academy of Management,* Tulsa, Oklahoma, 1977, pp. 164–169.
2. The remainder of this chapter is a brief summary of another work by the author which examines popular child-rearing advice, the history of child-rearing practices, disciplinary techniques, and moral development See "And Johnny Can't Work, Either: Teaching Children to Work," Unpublished Monograph, Graduate School of Management, Brigham Young University, Provo, Utah, 1979.
3. The abuses of blind obedience are illustrated in Stanley Milgram, *Obedience to Authority* (New York: Harper & Row, 1974).
4. The research of Diana Baumrind is presented in four major publications: "Effects of Authoritative Parental Control on Child Behavior," *Child Development,* Vol. 37 (1966), pp. 887–907; "Child Care Practices Anteceding Three Patterns of Preschool Behavior," *Genetic Psychology Monographs,* Vol. 75 (1967), pp. 43–88; "Current Patterns of Parental Control," *Developmental Psychology Monographs,* Vol. 4, No. 1, Pt. 2 (1971), pp. 1–103; and Diana Baumrind and A. E. Black, "Socialization Practices Associated with Dimensions of Competence in Preschool Boys and Girls," *Child Development,* Vol. 38 (1967), pp. 291–327.
5. The review appeared in Baumrind, "Effects of Authoritative Parental Control on Child Behavior," *op. cit.*
6. The conclusion primarily came from studies by A. Bandura and R. H. Walters, *Adolescent Aggression* (New York: Ronald Press, 1959); S. Glueck and Eleanor Glueck, *Unraveling Juvenile Delinquency* (New York: Commonwealth Fund, 1950); and William McCord, Joan McCord, and Alan Howard, "Familial Correlates of Aggression in Nondelinquent Male Children," *Journal of Abnormal Social Psychology,* Vol. 62 (1961), pp. 79–93.
7. The studies supporting this conclusion include Lois Hoffman, S. Rosen, and Ronald Lippitt, "Parental Coerciveness, Child Autonomy, and the Child's Role at School," *Sociometry,* Vol. 23 (1960), pp. 15–22; R. Middleton and P. Snell, "Political Expression of Adolescent Rebellion," *American Journal of Sociology,* Vol. 68 (1963), pp. 527–535; and A. Pikas, "Children's Attitudes Toward

Rational Versus Inhibiting Parental Authority," *Journal of Abnormal Social Psychology,* Vol. 62 (1961), pp. 315–321.

8. Bandura and Walters, *op. cit.*

9. Alberta E. Siegal and Lynette G. Kohn, "Permissiveness, Permission, and Aggression: The Effects of Adult Presence or Absence on Aggression in Children's Play," *Child Development,* Vol. 30 (1959), pp. 131–141.

10. Baumrind, "Effects of Authoritative Parental Control on Child Behavior," *op. cit.,* p. 891.

11. Richard H. Blum and associates, *Horatio Alger's Children* (San Francisco: Jossey-Bass, 1972).

12. J. G. Friend and E. A. Haggard, "Work Adjustment in Relation to Family Background," *Applied Psychology Monographs,* No. 16 (1948), pp. 1–150; Melvin Kuhn and Donald F. Klein, "Social Values and Drug Use Among Psychiatric Patients," *American Journal of Psychiatry,* Vol. 128 (1972), pp. 131–133; Donald W. Goodwin, James Johnson, Chauncey Maher, Allan Rappaport, and Samuel B. Guze, "Why People Do Not Drink: A Study of Teetotalers," *Comprehensive Psychiatry,* Vol. 10 (1969), pp. 209–214; John F. Kinnane and Martin W. Pable, "Family Background and Work Value Orientation," *Journal of Counseling Psychology,* Vol. 9 (1962), pp. 320–325; Joseph C. Pentecoste, "Occupational Level and Perceptions of the World of Work in the Inner City," *Journal of Counseling Psychology,* Vol. 22 (1975), pp. 437–439.

13. One of the best summaries of the moral development literature as it relates to value internalization is Larry C. Jensen, *What's Right? What's Wrong?* (Washington, D.C.: Public Affairs Press, 1975).

14. Statistics indicate that 97 percent of all U.S. households have a television set. The average hours per week spent viewing television are: adult women, 30 hours and 14 minutes; adult men, 24 hours and 25 minutes; teenagers 12 to 17, 22 hours and 36 minutes; and children 2 to 11, 25 hours and 38 minutes. See James Mann, "More Sex, Less Violence: TV's New Pitch," *U.S. News and World Report,* Vol. 83 (September 12, 1977), pp. 20–23.

15. W. McKinnon, "Violation of Prohibitions," in H. W. Murray (ed.), *Exploration in Personality* (London: Oxford University Press, 1938), pp. 491–501; J. Philippe Rushton, "Generosity in Children: Immediate and Long-Term Effects of Modeling, Preaching, and Moral Judgment," *Journal of Personality and Social Psychology,* Vol. 31, No. 3 (1975), pp. 459–466; Hugh Hartshorne and Mark May, *Studies in the Nature of Character Education,* Vol. 1, *Studies in Deceit* (New York: Macmillan, 1928).

16. See Martin L. Hoffman, "Moral Internalization, Parental Power, and the Nature of the Parent-Child Interaction," *Developmental Psychology,* Vol. 11, No. 2 (1975), pp. 228–239.

17. Reviewed by J. Philippe Rushton, "Socialization and the Altruistic Behavior of Children," *Psychological Bulletin,* Vol. 83, No. 5 (1976), pp. 893–913.
18. William McCord, Joan McCord, and Alan Howard, *op. cit.*
19. B. Mia Musunda Milebamne, "Perception des Attitudes et Pratiques Educatives du Pères par les Délinquants et les Normaux," *Canadian Psychiatric Association Journal,* Vol. 20 (1975), pp. 299–303.

145

8

TEACHING WORK VALUES ON THE JOB

Today's managers face a constant influx of new entrants to the workforce. Some new employees are outstanding workers—the answer to the prayers of every beleaguered supervisor. They are bright, aggressive, and well educated. From previous experience they have developed personal initiative and special job skills. Because of their high achievement orientation, they are committed to personal accomplishment and organizational success. Managers wish every new employee fit this description.

Most employees, however, do not fit the description. The consensus among managers is that about a third of the new entrants are dependable, work-oriented, motivated individuals; another third are apathetic and can be swayed by the situation; and the other third are unreliable, careless, and lacking in the self-discipline and motivation needed to perform well. Many in the last group are bright and well educated, but they have not developed the work habits required to make them outstanding employees.

Many new employees have had very little previous work experience. There are several reasons for this. Fewer children are raised on farms, where work is an unending part of life. Household chores and yardwork have become increasingly unpopular for children raised in suburban areas. Teenage employment has become increasingly temporary and separated from the adult workforce, where youth acquire adult work habits. Large and impersonal corporations have decreased the likelihood that new employees will feel a personal commitment to the success of the company.

The previous chapter described the tremendous influence of parental discipline and early socialization experiences in developing work values. Realizing that the home environment has such a pervasive influence on work values has caused many managers to feel intense despair. "These kids don't know how to work, and they don't want to learn. All they want is more money and more time off. It seems like their values have all gone soft and there is nothing I can do about it."

It is true that early developmental experiences have an enormous influence on personal values, but there *is* something supervisors and managers can do. This chapter examines how a supervisor can teach an adult employee the value of work. Believing in the dignity of labor and taking pride in one's work are not inherited characteristics; they are values an individual learns. While the work values of most people are developed in youth, they can also be influenced on the job. Most people who play the piano learned when they were between the ages of 6 and 16. But that does not mean an adult cannot learn to play the piano. Just as adults can learn new skills, so they can develop new values. People who have not developed positive work values in their youth can go through a similar developmental experience to learn initiative, responsibility, commitment, and perseverance as an adult. These values can be taught through sound principles of management that contribute to the development of work values.

THE CAROL BLANCHARD STORY: AN ILLUSTRATION

Before managers throw up their hands in despair, they should consider the story of Carol Blanchard. I interviewed Carol at her job in much the same way I interviewed other outstanding performers. She had worked for an electronics company for 10 years as the manager of inventory control. Several members of top management had identified her as an extremely competent worker who was very productive and highly efficient.

Like all the other outstanding performers, Carol was extremely work-oriented. Her work was an important part of her life, and doing her job competently was a major source of satisfaction. She enjoyed her work and enjoyed most of her co-workers. She identified various company problems, but it was obvious that she was determined to continue working to solve them and make the organization more effective. Unlike most of the outstanding performers, however, Carol developed a strong work ethic as an adult. She had been work-oriented for about 12 years. Before that, she said, she disliked work and avoided doing anything she disliked.

I had been so accustomed to hearing the outstanding performers describe how their parents taught them to work that I was surprised to hear Carol's story. She had not learned to work when she was young. Indeed, she claimed her parents taught her very little; she was raised in the neighborhood, not in the home. She was not expected to help with the housework or work in the yard. She did not clean her own room, and apparently no one else did either. She described both her physical environment and personal character as sloppy, unkempt, and careless.

She finished high school and one year at a community college but did very poorly because of erratic study habits and lack of interest. At the age of 19 she was married. For the next five years, she said, she and her husband led sloppy, unkempt, careless lives, with one job after another. Their employment records indicated that they were not dependable employees and their credit records indicated that they could not manage their personal finances.

After their new television set was repossessed, they moved to California, where both she and her husband were able to find employment. They had only one car and were fortunate to find jobs where he could drop her off at work en route to his job.

This was a fortunate situation in other ways, since it motivated her to keep her job rather than quit. Over the next two years there were many times when she wanted to quit.

They were in California for only four years, but during that time a tremendous change occurred in her work orientation. At the end of the four years, Carol was an extremely competent employee. She took pride in her work, which was well organized and meticulously accurate. She was in charge of the entire inventory control system in a small manufacturing company and had responsibility for ordering all parts and purchasing all supplies. The system she used for inventory control was one she had designed herself. She was an outstanding employee and the organization depended heavily on her to operate efficiently.

Carol's description of how she "learned to work" largely revolved around her supervisor. She described him as a "patient teacher" who was always willing to help and encourage her and never willing to accept errors or careless work. Initially, she had been hired as a file clerk and was expected to perform only a limited number of elementary tasks. During the first year, making a lot of errors did not bother her, but it did bother her supervisor, who repeatedly asked her to correct her mistakes. What began to bother Carol was the way her supervisor would not accept careless work. When he found an error, he would show it to her and politely ask her to take care of it. He was never punitive or threatening, but he was very persistent. Carol did not like her job and there were many times when she wanted to quit.

During the second year Carol began doing her job right. At first it was not because she wanted to do it right; it was because her supervisor would not accept work that was wrong. As she improved, he recognized her improvement and frequently expressed appreciation for her work. Gradually she began to see how pleased he was with her performance and how much happier she felt about her work.

Occasionally her supervisor made subtle comments about the importance of work and the value of dedicated effort. These comments began to make sense to her and she started to internalize the ideas. One particular phrase he used, "If it's worth doing, it's worth doing right," changed from a criticism of her work to a guiding philosophy for other aspects of her life.

By the end of the second year, her orientation toward work had changed. Rather than "putting in time," she was finishing a job. She began to explore the relationship between her job and other jobs. She started to look for things that kept her from performing her job more effectively and examined what she could do to help others.

As she demonstrated greater competence, her supervisor began to allow her more freedom. Rather than checking everything she did, he made only periodic checks and finally left her with total responsibility for checking her own work. He was always receptive to new suggestions and would carefully evalute them. When she redesigned the inventory control system, he was very encouraging and offered to help in every way possible.

After four years in California, Carol accepted a job offer from another manufacturing company which hired her to implement her new inventory control system. During her 10 years with the new company she continued to exhibit the same outstanding dedication and pride in her work. The president of the company said that her tremendous capacity to get things done made her a valuable member of management. He stated that three average employees could not adequately replace her. I was aware of how carefully she organized her work when she took the pile of papers by her phone and "casually" sorted them during our conversation.

The change that occurred during Carol's first two years in California can be attributed to many factors, such as her economic status and need for money, the influence of her co-workers, comments by neighbors, and attitudes in the community. However, Carol attributed the change to her supervisor. And although she could not explain very thoroughly how he did it, she suggested several possibilities. While he refused to accept mediocre work, he was very expressive and complimentary when she did a job right. He seemed able to give her objective feedback, identifying her errors and communicating an expectation to do it right without condemning her. To help her improve her attention span, he frequently helped her set goals for accomplishing various jobs in a specified length of time. The most subtle but perhaps most important influence came from the many offhand comments he made that supported the values of hard work, pride, and initiative. These values were a part of his life, and he taught them by precept and example.

The story of Carol Blanchard questions many of the popular solutions of behavioral science. Behavioral scientists propose to restore the work ethic primarily by giving employees "what they want." This includes more challenging jobs, flexible work hours, more money, more benefits, and more vacation. According to this logic, if employees get what they want, they will feel a greater commitment to the company, and then management will get what it wants—motivated employees.

Employees have certainly appreciated these rewards. Why shouldn't they? But the rewards have not led to greater job commitment or to greater appreciation of the value of hard work. They do not strengthen work values for some very good reasons. These rewards do not teach the kind of discipline and self-control necessary for developing work values. Rather than focusing on the value of high-quality work and the satisfaction of having done one's best, these rewards often focus on leisure pursuits.

Carol Blanchard's story illustrates how managers can dramatically influence the work ethic. If Carol's analysis is correct, managers *can* teach work values. Their criticism of the work values of today's youth may be legitimate, but they should not despair and assume there is nothing they can do about the situation.

PRINCIPLES FOR TEACHING WORK VALUES

The work ethic is developed through good supervision. There is nothing mystical or magical about teaching the work ethic to new employees. Nor is the process faddish or popular. A commitment to high-quality craftsmanship is not created by a new management gimmick. Organizational changes, such as a new incentive system and flexible work hours, have very little to do with the acceptance of work as a terminal value. The principles of teaching work values on the job are simply good principles of supervision. To stimulate greater acceptance of the work ethic, managers do not need a new model of human behavior or another novel theory of motivation. They need to manage more effectively. The development of the work ethic does not occur in a day or a week. But over a period of time high-quality work experiences can have a dramatic impact on work values.

Principle No. 1. Establish an organizational climate that fosters positive work values and a commitment to excellence.

Organizational climate refers to the overall conditions of a company, both physical and psychological. It includes the expectations and feelings employees have about the goals of the organization and their perceptions of what occurs within the organization. Organizational climate has a major impact on employee behavior. The climate can contribute either positively or negatively to the development of work attitudes and values. Therefore, the proper climate should be carefully created to elicit the kinds of attitudes and values that management desires.

To illustrate, managers have realized for many years that their style of leadership shapes the climate of the organization. Some organizational climates promote intense competition and conflict. Other climates foster a supportive environment of friendly interdependence. A climate of efficiency and concern for productive service contributes to the development of good work values and habits.

One aspect of organizational climate that has been extensively studied is the creation and operation of group norms. Group norms have a profound influence on the members of the group, especially among cohesive groups. As group cohesiveness increases, the pressure to conform to the informal norms of the group also increases. This increased conformity can be either good or bad. If group norms are consistent with the goals of the organization, a cohesive group is more productive and contributes to organizational effectiveness. But if the goals are inconsistent, a cohesive group can disrupt the efficient functioning of the organization.

Many studies have illustrated how group norms that run counter to the organization can create serious problems. Group norms restricting productivity have been observed among workers who are paid on individual piece rates. Even though members of the group know that higher performance will increase their pay, they still conform to a norm setting an arbitrarily low level of output.[1]

Group norms can create a climate that is either favorable or unfavorable to the development of the work ethic. They can have a destructive influence on the value of work and pride in craftsmanship by creating pressures to be uncooperative, take long rest breaks, come late to work, work slowly, disregard quality, and refuse promotions. On the other hand, group norms can facilitate the development of work values by helping employees set personal goals, encouraging them to achieve goals, recognizing dedicated effort, praising outstanding accomplishment, and providing informative feedback.

To create an organizational climate that contributes to the development of the work ethic, managers need to set a good example in (1) their own behavior and (2) the functioning of the organization. Supervisors normally exert a much greater influence on subordinates through their personal behavior than through the things they say. Company policies about quality, service, punctuality, or pride are just so many words if supervisors disregard them in their actions. Many workers justify their apathy to work with this comment: "Why should I care about my work when my supervisor doesn't give a damn?"

Modeling is a powerful form of social influence. If supervisors expect subordinates to be punctual, supervisors should be punctual. If supervisors expect subordinates to take pride in their work, supervisors should take pride in their work. Modeling is especially effective in ambiguous and novel situations. For example, new employees have not had a lot of experience receiving formal performance feedback. Consequently, they do not know whether they should act defensive, sorrowful, offended, honored, chastised, or indifferent. If supervisors expect subordinates to respond openly to criticism and performance feedback, supervisors ought to respond openly and nondefensively to the comments they receive.

Work values are also influenced by the way the organization functions. If work is to become either a generalized instrumental value or a terminal value, and if employees are to display the positive work habits most managers say they want, the organization must foster a climate that promotes work values. To begin with, the organization should have a purpose that legitimates its reason for existence and justifies the personal commitment of its members. All employees should feel that the company is producing some useful product or service for society, the community, and the employees. It is inconsistent for people to work hard for an organization that has no sense of mission. If employees do not think the organization is doing anything worthwhile, they will not be highly motivated to perform. Furthermore, if employees think the goals and operations of the organization are inconsistent with their own goals, they will not show much dedication in their work.

Individual jobs need to be carefully designed and the operations of the company must be analyzed thoroughly. Waste, corruption, and inefficiency create an organizational climate that has a destructive influence on the work ethic. It is inconsistent for a company to produce inferior products and expect employees to take pride in their work. It is also inconsistent to have an inefficient organizational structure and expect employees to feel that work is an important part of their lives. A poorly designed job that lacks coordination and integration implicitly says to the jobholder, "This work is worthless."

An example of a company that has created an organizational climate favorable to the development of work values is ServiceMaster Industries, Inc. The company fosters a climate of dedication, service, and efficiency by setting explicit company goals. These goals are stated in the company's annual report and prominently displayed within the building. The four company goals, in order of importance as listed in the annual reports, are:

1. To honor God in all we do.
2. To help people develop.
3. To pursue excellence.
4. To grow profitably.

Once exclusively a carpet-cleaning business, ServiceMaster expanded into hospital housekeeping. In 1979 it handled the operations of 742 hospitals. Its unique personnel policies and organizational goals have been cited as the major reason for the company's efficiency and profitability. The general feeling is that the climate of dedication, service, and efficiency has a positive influence on ServiceMaster s style of management and the performance of its employees.[2]

Principle No. 2. Communicate clear expectations about productivity and high-quality craftsmanship.

Several research studies have shown that the expectations of others have a profound influence on an employee's behavior. The process has become so well accepted that it has been labeled the ''self-fulfilling prophecy'' or the ''Pygmalion effect'' (after George Bernard Shaw's play *Pygmalion,* which was the basis for the musical hit *My Fair Lady*).

The self-fulfilling prophecy has been impressively illustrated in several studies of schoolchildren. In a series of well-designed experiments, Robert Rosenthal demonstrated that a teacher's expectations about his or her pupils' intellectual competence served as a self-fulfilling prophecy. The teachers were told to expect certain students to show remarkable academic improvement. The expectations given to the teachers, however, were strictly arbitrary—the "early bloom-ers" were selected totally at random. The teachers did not know the selection was random and assumed that the early bloomers had been identified by a reliable test. Because the teachers had been led to expect greater performance from certain students, they somehow treated these students differ-ently. During the course of the school year, the academic achievement and intelligence scores of students expected to do well improved significantly more than those of students who had been randomly labeled average. The results were surpris-ing to the teachers, since they thought they had treated each student alike. The only difference between the two groups was in the expectations of the teachers. Certain students were expected to do well; and these expectations became a self-fufilling prophecy.[3]

The self-fulfilling prophecy also occurs with managers. Managerial expectations have been identified as a major factor in the success or failure of new managers' careers. During their early years in a business organization, young managers are strongly influenced by managerial expectations, which are critical in determining their future performance and career progress.[4]

Numerous research studies have shown how the expecta-tions of supervisors significantly influence the performance of subordinates. In one study, supervisors were told to communi-cate either high performance standards, low performance standards, or no performance standards (and let the groups set their own goals). The highest performance rates were achieved by the groups whose supervisors expected high performance. The results dramatically illustrate how a supervisor's expecta-tions can significantly increase performance, especially when there are other rewards for achieving the supervisor's goals.[5]

Other studies have shown that the expectations of em-ployees other than supervisors can also influence performance. Peer group norms and expectations can significantly change behavior, even when the peer group is not present. In one study, people performed creative tasks (such as thinking of different ways to attract tourists to the United States). Each person was told that other people had performed the task and had then decided what they considered to be an appropriate level of performance. Some individuals were given high performance expectations and others were given low expectations. The results indicated that the expectations of peers influenced the number of creative ideas each group produced. People who were told that they should produce more ideas did in fact produce more solutions. Numerous other studies have confirmed the finding that peer group norms exert a powerful influence on individual behavior. Members of a group tend to adhere to group norms regardless of whether the norms are consistent with the goals of the company.[6]

The expectations of others influence behavior through two major psychological processes: goal setting and changing the self-concept. Before engaging in any activity, workers usually establish a goal of some sort. Often the goal is not firmly or consciously established; it is only a loosely held level of aspiration. Past successes or failures tend to raise or lower the aspiration level on future trials. Influential others can also significantly alter aspiration: both supervisors and peers can influence an employee's self-set goals and thereby change behavior. People feel an internal commitment to achieve their goals and derive satisfaction from goal accomplishment.[7]

People behave consistent with their own self-concept. Numerous research studies have shown that academic performance, school attendance, juvenile delinquency, choosing an occupational career, and many other behaviors are consistent with one's self-image.[8]

At any given time, the self-concept is influenced by three factors. The first factor is the chronic level of self-esteem a person has developed over time through daily experiences and interactions. People who have a history of successful experiences develop a self-image of competence. Those who have a history of failures develop a self-concept of incompetence. The second factor influencing self-concept is the task-specific or situation-specific activity. Here the self-concept is influenced by a person's history of success or failure in performing a specific task. The third factor is the person's perceptions of the expectations of others about his or her performance. These expectations exert a large influence on the immediate present, and over a longer period of time they help to define the chronic level of self-esteem.

In a work environment, expectations about performance are communicated in innumerable ways—in recruiting, in assigning jobs, in evaluating performance, and in compensating performance. Expectations can be communicated through direct comments as well as through subtle inferences. Often the failure to explicitly state high expectations is perceived as a lack of concern about performance. Therefore, saying nothing may be interpreted as accepting low performance standards.

The orientation of a new employee is probably the most overlooked opportunity for clearly communicating perform-ance expectations. The first few days after new employees join a company, they are particularly susceptible to social influences. Clear statements of the company's policies can be presented along with expectations about the company's stan-dard of excellence. For example, new employees ought to be told the company policy about attendance, including absen-teeism and tardiness. They should know the expectations for their performance, including such considerations as quality, cost, time constraints, and service. Expectations about hon-esty and integrity, fair and impartial treatment of others, and personal development and training can also be communicated. These standards can have a profound influence on behavior if they are reinforced by subsequent experiences.

The value of new employee orientation in creating perform-ance standards is illustrated by the experience of a small automotive repair shop. Employee theft was a serious problem facing the shop. Most of the employees had a private business moonlighting at home fixing cars. The employees did not consider themselves thieves; they were only "borrowing" tools. Almost everyone did it. To curb the loss of tools, the owner called the police on three or four occasions to file a theft report. But before the police arrived, the missing items would magically reappear. Management knew what was happening to the tools, but new rules and threats only seemed to create management–worker conflict. The owner decided to discuss employee theft with new employees as part of their orientation. The entire crew of present employees was invited to attend the orientation, ostensibly to welcome the new employees. Everyone heard the company policy forbidding the use of company tools away from work and listened to management's justification for the policy. The policy was reiterated a short time later when another employee was hired. After this second session, the problem of employee theft was essentially solved.

The information presented to new employees at the orientation session should be carefully screened. Employees can retain only a limited amount of information at one time. Lengthy descriptions of company policies and benefit plans will not be remembered well and ought to be written in an employee handbook. Written policies have several advantages. They help managers clarify what standards of behavior they expect from employees and help them treat employees consistently. Employees can review written policies to gain a better understanding.

Employees will probably not remember many of the details presented at orientation, but they are likely to remember the standard of excellence expected of them. They may forget that the long-term disability rate is 66.7 percent and that it begins six months after the disability occurs. But they will remember that management feels strongly committed to producing a high-quality product for society, that the company makes an important contribution to the community, and that personal growth and development are highly encouraged in the company.

Principle No. 3. Teach and explain the value of work, the dignity of labor, and the joy of service.

This teaching process is called induction and was discussed in the previous chapter. Induction includes explanations of the value of work, comments about the pride that accompanies good-quality workmanship, discussions about the rewards that follow diligence, and other statements encouraging the work ethic. The values of workers can be significantly influenced by a carefully designed induction procedure.

Induction should not involve a lecture or sermon. Preaching about the work ethic accomplishes very little, no matter how well prepared the sermon is. Studies on moral development have shown that prepared lessons have only a small influence on behavior, whereas spontaneous comments made during a "teaching moment" can have a significant impact on behavior.[9] A teaching moment is a time when the learner is particularly receptive to an idea. This time usually comes when the learner's mind has been stimulated by something—a challenge, a dilemma, a personal problem, a social inequity. Many teaching moments arise naturally in the course of a working relationship. Teaching moments can also be created by structuring the situation around issues and problems that facilitate a discussion of work habits.

In spite of its limitations, a well-prepared lesson on the work ethic can accomplish some worthwhile objectives. It can raise social awareness about an issue and can provide a sound rationale for belief. It can also prepare the teacher for taking advantage of a teaching moment when it occurs. Unless it is combined with other motivational forces, however, a lecture will not usually influence the learner's behavior. Often the learner is not ready to listen to the message. Sometimes a lecture even creates an antagonistic or resistant response because the learner becomes defensive about the teacher's intention to exert influence. Therefore, induction attempts need to be tactful and light—suggestive and encouraging rather than heavy-handed or demanding.

The shaping of values through induction is a very sensitive process. Induction does not usually influence behavior directly. People can be taught a new idea, but they must adopt the insight for themselves and incorporate it into their own value system. This process rarely occurs through an intentional teaching effort. Instead, the behavior usually occurs first; then the individual looks for a rational justification for what he or she has done. The relationship between attitudes and behavior is an interactive one. Attitudes can influence behavior. For example, insights learned from a lecture on the importance of work can change a person's work habits. But behavior also influences attitudes and values. For example, working hard to complete an important project can change a person's opinion about the value of perseverance.[10] Consequently, induction should not only be suggestive and enlightening; it should also be persistent. A frequently heard comment that immediately comes to mind can influence the formation of a new value. For example, if an employee is behind schedule in the morning and is likely to be late for work, it makes a big difference whether the employee thinks "Ah, who cares?" or remembers a supervisor's earlier comment: "Punctuality shows respect for other people."

Principle No. 4. Establish individual accountability through effective delegation.

The value of work and pride in craftsmanship tend to increase as people develop a greater sense of accountability and responsibility for their actions. The regression analysis reported in the last chapter indicated that the internal locus of control variable was a significant predictor of pride in craftsmanship. That is, people who have strong feelings of pride in craftsmanship tend to report greater control over their lives. To them, success is primarily determined by individual effort and knowledge rather than by luck or chance.

Another line of research examined the role of personal responsibility in the development of an achievement orientation. David C. McClelland studied the characteristics of business executives and attempted to explain how the entrepreneurial spirit developed.[11] He found that entrepreneurs had a very strong motive for achievement. The three major characteristics of "high need" achievers were a desire for personal responsibility over the success or failure of an activity, a preference for conditions of moderate risk, and a desire for immediate feedback on performance.

McClelland made a distinction between the efficient, conscientious hard worker and the high need achiever. The first type works hard and efficiently at everything more or less indiscriminately. High need achievers work hard only at those things that are sufficiently challenging to give them a sense of personal accomplishment. While these two types of people are conceptually different, McClelland found that they were positively associated among American business executives: high need achievers were also efficient, conscientious, hardworking entrepreneurs.

Several attempts have been made to teach the achievement motive to managers. The training methods focus on four objectives. First, managers are encouraged to set personal goals and to keep a record of their performance. Second, they are taught the language of achievement—to think, talk, and act like people with a high achievement motive. Third, managers are given cognitive or intellectual support—they are taught rational justifications for believing that the achievement motive is important to success. Fourth, they are provided with group support—a group of budding entrepreneurs is organized and meets periodically to share success stories. In short, the managers are taught how to behave as entrepreneurs with a high achievement motive. Their new success-oriented behavior is reinforced verbally, intellectually, and through peer influence. The evidence suggests that personal responsibility and high achievement needs can be taught through a training program. McClelland investigated a training program for 52 business executives in Hyderabad, India. Six to ten months after the course, these executives appeared to double their natural rate of entrepreneurial activity.[12]

Delegation and follow-through on task assignments contribute significantly to personal accountability. Personal responsibility is developed through delegating assignments, providing encouragement and assistance, evaluating performance, and rewarding effective behavior.

There are three major steps in delegating a task. The first step consists in establishing the contract—the agreement between the supervisor and the subordinate. The second step is follow-through—providing clarification and assistance in periodic reviews. The third step is the final accountability report.

Before an assignment is delegated, two important issues need to be considered: (1) what needs to be done, and (2) who the most competent person is to do it. The supervisor should have a clear understanding of the assignment he or she plans to delegate. Many times task assignments are not done properly because the supervisor fails to understand and explain what needs to be done. If the assignment is not clear in the supervisor's mind, it's almost certain not to be clear in the subordinate's mind. This does not mean that supervisors must always know exactly what subordinates should do. Sometimes supervisors delegate problems and have their subordinates decide what to do. Regardless of the assignment, the supervisor should be able to explain the result to be achieved or the problem to be solved with sufficient clarity to direct the subordinate's efforts.

In delegating an assignment, the supervisor should select a person who possesses the requisite skills. For special projects and assignments, it is important to select the most competent person, taking into account technical and interpersonal skills, aptitudes, achievements, experience, and motivational potential. This selection process can be crucial, since the success or failure of major projects often depends on the competence of the project director. But for most assignments the issue is not so much finding the most competent person as making sure the person selected has sufficient competence. Many people can do an acceptable job. In recent years a new twist to this problem has emerged. Some employees are overqualified for the work they are asked to do. They have more academic skills and job preparation than they need to perform their job. Here, the employee has the skill but lacks the motivation. Either problem makes a person unfit for the assignment.

In general, the result or outcome should be delegated rather than the activities involved. If people are told to perform certain activities, they will feel responsible only for the ac-

GUIDELINES FOR EFFECTIVE DELEGATION

To be effective, delegation should occur only when the leader has decided what needs to be done, and who the most competent person is to do the job. Delegation is a three-part procedure: (1) establishing the contract, (2) providing clarification and assistance in periodic reviews, and (3) following up.

1. *Establishing the contract*
This step in the delegation procedure consists in outlining the task: what is to be done, how, when, where, who, and why. Authority should be commensurate with responsibility. In general, delegate the outcome or result, not the activities or processes involved.
 Leader roles:
- Describe precisely what is to be accomplished.
- Ask subordinates if they are willing to do the task, and get a commitment.
- Suggest a date when the task is to be completed.
- Ask subordinates what help they will need and build a *contract* or *agreement* to assist them if necessary. Build in review and follow-up sessions.
- Give the delegated employees appropriate authority and freedom to act; then let them do what they have agreed to do.

2. *Providing clarification and assistance in periodic reviews*
Many leaders have difficulty giving assistance without restricting the freedom of the person to whom a task has been delegated. Yet assistance is often needed in order to accomplish the task. How to assist is the question.
 Leader roles:
- Ask, "What can I do?" or "Do you need additional help?" Or say, "I can do _____ if you need me."
- Schedule a conference to discuss the progress of the assignment. Give encouragement.
- During the conference ask questions for information and inquiry. Each subordinate should be expected to evaluate his or her progress.
- Generally, don't make suggestions unless they are asked for.
- Forget about the task and leave it up to the person with the responsibility.

3. *Accountability report*
Follow-up begins with the act of delegation. It should be built in from the outset. Identifying a due date and providing clarification

and assistance are part of effective follow-up. There is, in addition, a final accountability report.

Leader roles:

- Assess the progress made to accomplish the task.
- Clarify any details remaining and *personally* convey appreciation for the work done.
- Ask subordinates how they want to be involved in reporting their assignments to others.
- Ask subordinates how their assignments fit into the general organization's goals.
- Examine the causes of failure to determine if the problem was a lack of ability, resources, motivation, and so on.

---

tivities, not necessarily for the outcome. The difference becomes significant when something unexpected occurs. The person who feels responsible for the outcome is more likely to adopt new activities to achieve results. The person who feels responsible for activities is likely to either continue to perform useless activities or do nothing until new instructions are received.

Effective delegation also requires that authority be delegated commensurate with responsibility. Employees should have the authority to reorganize and redesign their departments or alter their jobs, if necessary, to achieve the delegated results. Whenever employees have responsibility for results, they should also have responsibility for planning ahead to prevent crises that may arise. If a decision becomes necessary that subordinates are unable to make, they should have the responsibility for analyzing the problem and recommending a solution.

At the time the results are delegated, a "contract" should be established between the superior and the subordinate. The contract does not need to be formal or "legal," but it generally should be written. The contract should specify clearly what is expected of the subordinate so that both superior and subordinate will be able to agree on the adequacy of the results. If special assistance will be needed, it should be noted at the outset. The contract should also include provisions for periodic reviews to monitor the subordinate's progress and for a final accountability report.

It is unrealistic to expect subordinates to accomplish a delegated assignment without any assistance or periodic reviews. However, the assistance offered should not lead subordinates to feel that they have been released from the responsibility for achieving the result. The periodic reviews need to be expected, so that subordinates have no reason to think a review was necessitated by poor performance. This problem can be avoided if the reviews are clearly provided for in the initial contract.

Subordinates should assume responsibility for evaluating their own progress. The role of the superior is to ask questions when needed to guide subordinates in assessing their progress. When significant differences of opinion occur over the progress being made, these differences need to be resolved, even if the contract must be revised. Again, responsibility for asking for assistance, accepting ideas, or making a choice should remain with subordinates to ensure that they retain responsibility for the final result.

The periodic reviews and informal discussions should be held often enough to demonstrate interest and provide needed assistance. However the reviews should not be held so often that subordinates feel that they are constantly being monitored. Written feedback in the form of budget reports and other performance indicators can also be provided as long as the results are meaningful and are not too costly to prepare. The major purpose of the reports is to help employees monitor their own performance. Reports also serve as a valuable reinforcement.

If the contract between the superior and the subordinate was carefully constructed and periodic reviews were held, the final evaluation should be a pleasant time of accountability. The previous steps have been designed so that subordinates will be able to report the successful accomplishment of their assignments.

If subordinates have not achieved the expected results, the final evaluation should not be an unpleasant experience filled with anxiety and conflict. The atmosphere should be one of mutual problem solving. The discussion should focus, not on reprimanding the subordinate, but on trying to determine the causes of the failure and possible solutions. The failure might be due to unrealistic objectives, inadequate resources, or a lack of effort or skill on the part of the subordinate. If the superior chooses to retain the subordinate, a new contract is written. This contract, like the previous one, specifies the results to be achieved by a certain date with periodic reviews; it might also provide for additional resources, greater opportunities for training, or whatever else is necessary for the subordinate to achieve success.

Delegating task assignments helps develop individual accountability and personal responsibility. These characteristics are not acquired rapidly; they develop over a period of time. The process is effective only in an atmosphere that supplements personal choice, with effective performance evaluation and appropriate reinforcement.

Principle No. 5. Develop personal commitment and involvement through individual choice and participation.

Every employer wants employees who are "committed" to the company, even though commitment is not easy to define. To most employers, commitment is associated with loyalty and other desirable behaviors: committed employees are better performers, they have better attendance records, and they are more likely to stay with the company. Consequently, most employers think that commitment and loyalty, whatever they are, should be cultivated in the workforce as positive social values.

Research evidence shows that commitment is indeed related to work values and job performance. Commitment has been defined in several different ways, but most definitions are similar. Organizational commitment generally refers to the strength of an individual's identification with and involvement in a particular organization. One of the best definitions of organizational commitment comes from the Organizational Commitment Questionnaire, a research instrument developed

167

to measure it. According to this definition, commitment is characterized by three factors: (1) a strong acceptance of the organization's goals and values, (2) a willingness to exert considerable effort in behalf of the organization, and (3) a strong desire to maintain membership in the organization. The Organizational Commitment Questionnaire has been found to correlate with several work values and attitudes. People with high organizational commitment scores tend to have high intrinsic motivation scores ("Doing my job well gives me a good feeling"). Their life interests are generally focused on work-related (as opposed to nonwork-related) activities, and they report a greater motivation to perform and a greater intent to remain with the organization.[13]

Research on organizational commitment suggests that it is more than a passive expression of loyalty to the organization. Organizational commitment involves not only positive beliefs and attitudes about the organization but also a willingness to give of yourself in order to contribute to the organization's well-being. This does not mean that people will not be committed to other aspects of their environment, such as family, church, and politics. It means that those who are committed to an organization accept its goals, work hard to achieve those goals, and strive to maintain organizational membership, regardless of other commitments. The interviews with outstanding performers suggested that people who are committed to their work organization also have relatively strong commitments to other organizations, especially family and church.

One research study focused directly on the relationship between organizational commitment and work values. Two different kinds of commitment, calculative and moral, were identified and measured. Calculative commitment refers to the individual's willingness to remain with a particular organization. It was measured by four questions which asked whether the employee would leave the organization for another job offering slightly more pay, higher status, friendlier co-workers, or more interesting work. Moral commitment refers to the individual's incorporation of organizational values and goals. It was measured by nine questions asking about the extent to which the person identified with the goals of the organization. The results of the study showed that work values were associated with moral commitment but not with calculative commitment. Pragmatic considerations regarding salary, status, and co-workers were not related to the work ethic. However, people who identified with the goals of the organization tended to espouse the work ethic.[14]

While this study showed a relationship between moral commitment and the work ethic, it did not show whether the work ethic increased commitment or vice versa. The relationship is most likely an interactive one. As people's moral commitment increases through greater identification with the organization's goals, they probably acquire a stronger work ethic. Similarly, as people acquire a stronger work ethic and begin to value work as a generalized intrinsic reward, they probably develop a stronger commitment to the organization (but not if the organization's goals are illegal or contrary to societal norms). Thus it appears that the work ethic and commitment to organizational goals develop simultaneously as part of a general value orientation.

The development of organizational commitment is facilitated primarily by two factors. First, the goals of the organization have to be perceived as legitimate and worth pursuing. As discussed earlier, the purpose of the organization needs to be clearly established and employees need to have a rational justification for the organization's existence. Employers ought to continually note evidence of the organization's reason for being and communicate this information both to employees and to the public.

Second, commitment and involvement are facilitated by personal choice. When people are told what to do and implicitly forced to do it, either by threat of punishment or promise of reward, they feel little personal commitment. They do not "own" the task—that is, they do not feel responsible for how it is done or for the result.

When people agree to perform a task, however, they feel

169

more committed to it. They feel personally responsible for its success or failure. When people perceive themselves as the origin of their behavior, all their activities, including work, acquire added significance. It becomes important to them to perform competently, because the outcome will affect their sense of self-worth.

Personal choice can be involved at numerous points in employer–employee relationships. The most overlooked opportunity to allow employees personal choice is in the assignment of daily tasks. Supervisors often decide what to do and then tell subordinates to do it. Even though employees know they cannot really refuse without being fired, they would prefer to be asked rather than told.

Participation in redesigning one's job and in setting performance standards has been strongly advocated by several studies on participation. The evidence suggests that when employees participate in setting their own budgets and work standards, they accept them as their own plan of action. Participation decreases employee resistance to change and contributes to higher satisfaction and reduced turnover.

Semiautonomous work teams provide another level of participation and individual choice. Some organizations have been examining the success of work teams that manage themselves by group decision making. A supervisor is not appointed; instead, the members of the group make the decisions that a supervisor would normally make. Illustrations of these teams are presented in Chapter 11. The participative decision-making process seems to increase the degree of commitment members feel to the group.

Principle No. 6. Provide feedback on performance through performance appraisals.

Performance feedback contributes to the development of work values in several ways. First, providing continual feedback generally increases an employee's sense of personal accountability and responsibility. Second, performance feedback helps develop the employee's skills. Third, feedback is an

170

important source of positive reinforcement. As work becomes an intrinsically rewarding activity and people take pride in personal accomplishment, they want to know how well they have performed. Employees who have performed well will be greatly disappointed if their diligence and initiative go unnoticed.

Because performance appraisal has been severely criticized, many managers have abandoned it as a useless and perhaps dangerous practice. There are, indeed, numerous potential problems with performance appraisal. Some of the most frequently cited problems include:

1. The "halo effect"—one attitude about a person strongly influences all other attitudes.
2. The "leniency-strictness" effect—some evaluators give mostly favorable ratings to everyone while other evaluators rate employees more unfavorably.
3. The "central tendency" effect—raters avoid sticking out their necks to identify performance differences and give everyone average ratings.
4. "Interrater unreliability"—different raters do not agree in their evaluation of a behavior.
5. "Subjectivity"—performance has to be evaluated subjectively or indirectly because there are no visible products that can be counted.

These and other difficulties with appraisal have been examined extensively. However, they ought to be treated as problems to be solved, not as insurmountable obstacles. These areas are particularly troublesome to inexperienced supervisors. Experienced supervisors have usually overcome these problems as part of becoming proficient at their jobs. The ability to provide useful and accurate performance feedback is a critical supervisory activity.

An uncertainty in the minds of many supervisors is whether performance appraisals should be conducted at all. However, the ongoing demands to hire, fire, promote, and compensate all necessitate some form of evaluation. Supervisors have always evaluated their subordinates. It should be obvious that evaluations made in a random and unsystematic fashion, whether valid or not, have been just as important in influencing personnel actions as evaluations made in a more systematic and formal manner. Therefore, whether performance appraisals *should* be conducted is not the issue. The question is what should be evaluated, how and when it should be evaluated, and who should do it.

Some managers argue that since employees are hired to produce, only the quantity and quality of performance should be measured. Other factors, such as initiative, cooperation, work habits, and dependability, should not be considered. There is some merit to this argument to the extent that it eliminates inappropriate personality traits from being considered. Traits such as dominance, aggressiveness, sociability, and extroversion should not be included in the appraisal process if they have no relationship to performance on the job. Performance appraisals should focus on performance-related behaviors and outcomes.

There is more to effective performance, however, than quantity and quality considerations. It has been suggested that there are three important requirements of performance for effective organizational functioning. The first requirement is joining and staying with the organization. Attendance, punctuality, and length of service are important components of performance. The second requirement is dependable role performance—producing an acceptable quantity and quality of work. The third requirement is spontaneous and innovative behaviors. These include cooperative acts between fellow workers, acts that protect the organization, sharing constructive ideas and creative suggestions, self-training to make a greater contribution, and promoting favorable attitudes about the company in society.

An organization is considerably more effective when its members engage in these spontaneous and innovative behaviors. Since employees tend to do what they are rewarded for doing, recognition of their spontaneous and innovative behaviors should be part of the performance appraisal system.[15]

Performance appraisal systems should include three kinds of data: personnel data, production data, and the judgments of others. Personnel data include measures of absenteeism, tardiness, and other information that might be placed in an employee's personnel file (for example, letters of commendation, lists of training courses completed, and notes from a supervisor summarizing performance). Production data include measures of the quantity and quality of performance. In some jobs, especially white-collar jobs, production is difficult to measure, since it is not readily observable. However, such behaviors can always be described in essay form. The judgments of others are subjective evaluations of performance. The fact that the process is subjective should not dissuade managers from using it. The entire appraisal system is subjective, reflecting the values of those who designed it and defined effective performance. Furthermore, subjective judgment is usually the best way to assess an employee's spontaneous and innovative behaviors. The judgments of others can be obtained through rating scales, ranking procedures, or written descriptions of behaviors.

Most performance appraisal systems place responsibility for the evaluation process on the immediate supervisor. This arrangement is consistent with the hierarchical authority relationships in most corporations. However, supervisors are not always in the best position to make an informed evaluation. Depending on circumstances, supervisors may need to collect information from several other sources, including peers, clients, and subordinates, and especially a self-evaluation from the employee. It is the supervisor's responsibility to summarize this information and share it with employees.

Most evaluation procedures assume that employees play a passive role—they simply wait while the jury is out and then listen to the verdict. The process is much more effective, however, when employees take an active part in the evaluation process. Employees can assume some of the responsibility for measuring their performance and for collecting and organizing the information. They can also assume responsibility for scheduling the feedback session and can take the lead in the meeting by presenting the data they have collected. Self-evaluation is particularly important in the development of work values. When employees are involved in the evaluation of their own behavior, they feel greater control over and responsibility for their actions.

Research on the achievement motive indicates that performance feedback is especially desirable for people who have a high need for achievement. These people prefer activities that give them immediate and accurate feedback on their performance. Other research suggests that performance feedback contributes to the stability of a person's self-esteem, particularly in ambiguous situations. On a novel task, for example, where employees do not know whether their performance is above or below average, they will often turn a neutral situation into a competitive contest just to assess their personal competence.[16]

Because performance evaluation is used for several purposes, two different types of appraisal are needed: a contributions analysis and a personal development review. These two types of appraisal have different objectives and focus on different aspects of behavior. Therefore, they should be conducted differently and be separated in time. The contributions analysis focuses on the employee's contribution to the organization. The emphasis is on past performance, usually with the intent to reward employees for what they have done. The superior's role is to judge and evaluate, while the employee's role is to present and possibly defend his or her actions. The personal development review is developmental rather than evaluative. It focuses on the improvement of performance through self-learning and growth. The supervisor's role is to offer guidance, help, and counsel along with accurate performance feedback. The employee's role is active self-analysis and learning. Both supervisor and employee should have a clear understanding of the nature of these two types of evaluation.

Principle No. 7. Reward effective performance with pay and other social reinforcers.

In general, employees do what they are reinforced for doing. And if supervisors want employees to acquire good work habits, they should consistently and repeatedly reinforce such behavior. It is almost impossible to overuse sincere social approval. Verbal praise, recognition in company newsletters, employee-of-the-month awards, and dozens of other social reinforcements contribute significantly to the development of work values. Supervisors should generously use social reinforcement to reward desired behaviors as frequently as possible.

Money is not the most important form of reinforcement, especially for people who believe strongly in the terminal value of work. Nevertheless, pay and other financial incentives are essential to all workers and play an important role in the development of work values. In the American free enterprise system, workers exchange their labor for pay. Money is an essential outcome of the exchange: workers must be paid to support themselves and their families. Consequently, everyone works in part for money. A job that does not pay adequately may not attract capable workers even if it offers interesting work. Employees may be forced to seek other employment because of a need for greater income.

Perhaps the most important function of money in the development of work values is the feedback it provides about personal accomplishment. Merit increases, piece-rate incentives, year-end bonuses, sales commissions, and other reward systems that associate pay with performance provide employees with information about their effectiveness. Research on the achievement motive suggests that low need achievers are highly motivated by financial incentives, whereas high need achievers are motivated primarily by a desire for personal accomplishments. Nevertheless, pay is an important form of performance feedback for high need achievers and is a necessary part of the employment exchange. In one study involving simple laboratory tasks, low need achievers obtained high performance scores when monetary incentives were offered but low performance scores when there were no financial incentives. High need achievers had high performance scores regardless of the presence of monetary incentives.[17]

Like high need achievers, people who have a strong work

orientation are motivated primarily by nonfinancial rewards. Compliments by supervisors and recognition from peers are highly valued rewards. One line of research in recent years has examined the relative effectiveness of intrinsic and extrinsic rewards. Some research suggests that extrinsic rewards, especially money, inhibit the expression of intrinsic motivation. For example, piece-rate monetary incentives were thought to destroy the positive feelings an employee might otherwise feel for doing good work.

A classic illustration of this phenomenon is the neighborhood boy who is asked to mow the lawn of the widow next door. After mowing it the first time, he overhears two neighbors comment on how thoughtful and unselfish his charitable act is. These favorable comments, combined with his awareness of the valuable service he is providing, motivate him to continue mowing the lawn each week. Midway through the summer, the widow's son learns that the boy is mowing the lawn and insists that he accept money for his service. The boy is paid for several weeks, but then the widow's son moves out of town and the boy is no longer paid. The critical question now is whether the boy will continue to mow the widow's lawn and will continue to feel the same intrinsic satisfaction as before. Did the money increase, decrease, or have no effect on the boy's feelings of joy in service?

The original research which generated this controversy concluded that extrinsic rewards that are contingent on performance, especially money, tend to destroy the intrinsic motivation to perform an interesting task. In a series of experiments, students were asked to assemble four puzzles—supposedly interesting tasks. At the end of the session each student was asked to remain in the room for a few minutes and had the option of reading magazines, doing more puzzles, or just sitting. The amount of time spent doing more puzzles was assumed to measure the degree of intrinsic motivation. Some students were paid a dollar for each of the first four puzzles they solved; others were paid nothing. The results indicated that students who were paid did not spend as many minutes solving more puzzles after the session ended as students who were not paid.[18] It was concluded that extrinsic rewards inhibit intrinsic rewards because they focus people's attention on the external causes of their behavior. When extrinsic rewards are offered, people do not control their own behavior. It is controlled by someone else—the person who is paying them.

Generalizing from the results of the study, the researchers argued that pay should be based not on performance but on a fixed salary. To be intrinsically motivated, people have to feel that they are in control of their own actions. According to this reasoning, paying the neighborhood boy to mow the lawn will cause him to lose the intrinsic feeling of joy in service he initially felt. Now he is mowing the lawn because he is being paid to do it. His behavior is controlled by the person who pays him. When the pay ends, he will probably stop mowing the lawn.

The original studies have been extensively criticized for their methodology, interpretation, and generalizability. Their conclusions contradict the conclusions derived from the major theories of motivation—reinforcement theory, expectancy theory, goal-setting theory, and social comparison theory. These theories suggest that the effects of extrinsic and intrinsic rewards are additive, not inhibitory. Extrinsic rewards supplement intrinsic rewards in their effects on behavior. Thus the neighborhood boy will have the greatest motivation when he is being paid, because then he is receiving both extrinsic and intrinsic rewards. But after the pay is terminated, he will continue to mow the lawn for the intrinsic satisfaction of being of service—*maybe*.

Research on this issue suggests that there are two conditions when extrinsic rewards can destroy intrinsic rewards: when the external rewards are inappropriate or when they run counter to situational norms. For example, when pay is overtly used as a bribe to manipulate people's behavior or when pay is capricious and grossly inequitable, people's sense of honesty, decency, self-esteem, and self-determination may be so violated that their feelings of pride or joy in service are destroyed.[19]

These findings suggest that pride in craftsmanship and joy in service have to be centered in an employment exchange that is perceived as equitable and fair. Workers need to be appropriately reinforced. They should be paid according to their performance. In other words, outstanding performers should be paid more than mediocre performers. Excessive overpayment and excessive underpayment should be avoided.

For several years the effect of rewards on attitude change was the subject of an intense debate in social psychology. The controversy concerned two theories that predicted opposite results: incentive theory and cognitive dissonance theory. Incentive theory claimed that attitude change increased when larger rewards were offered to induce a change. Cognitive dissonance theory argued that small rewards created the greatest attitude change. This controversy is relevant to the question of how much to pay an executive who accepts a special assignment to serve on a community improvement project. Will the executive's attitudes about community service be more positive with high or low financial compensation?

Since the implications of the two theories were exactly opposite, the battlelines were formed. Research studies were conducted, the results were published, and each side discredited the conclusions of the other. Finally, the results were integrated into a consistent theory combining both positions. It was concluded that the predictions of incentive theory were generally correct—greater rewards do produce greater attitude change—except when cognitive dissonance is created by (1) inducing people to do something inconsistent with their personal values or (2) providing insufficient justification for their behavior (such as inadequate pay for what they did). When cognitive dissonance is created, the predictions of dissonance theory are most accurate—smaller rewards produce greater attitude change.

To illustrate, the research studies found that if people were asked to perform an undesirable activity, their attitudes were more favorable when they were offered a larger reward, as long as the reward was seen as fair and equitable and the behavior was socially acceptable. But if people experienced cognitive dissonance because they were bribed into doing something unreasonable or socially inappropriate, a smaller reward created greater attitude change. With a large reward there is little dissonance: people know why they did the undesirable task—they were paid to do it. But with a small reward, there is insufficient justification for having done the act. Therefore, people reevaluate the act and conclude that their initial attitude may have been wrong.

Cognitive dissonance is well illustrated by one of the earliest and most popular studies of rewards and attitude change. Students performed an extremely boring task for one hour and then were asked to tell the next student that the task was very interesting, intriguing, and enjoyable. The students were paid either $1.00 or $20.00 to tell the next student and be on call to do it again if needed. Then their attitudes about the task were reassessed. Students who were paid only $1.00 reported more favorable attitudes about the task than students paid $20.00. It was reasoned that students who received $20.00 did not feel any dissonance about saying the task was enjoyable—they were being paid to lie. But a $1.00 payment was insufficient justification for being dishonest. Therefore, students who received only $1.00 had to change their feelings about the task to make them more consistent with what they told the next student.[20]

In the development of work values, pay should be based on performance and used primarily as a form of performance feedback. This means that little attention should be focused on money per se, since it tends to be overly associated with nonwork-related objectives—material wealth, social status, leisure pursuits, physical comforts, and so on. The best approach to financial compensation is to base pay on performance, making certain that the pay is equitable and fair. Discussions about pay should focus on performance and signal to workers that the work they are doing is important to the employer and society. Pay communicates a message: "This activity is important, and if you do a better job you deserve a greater reward." Money is an indication of the quality of performance and should accompany other forms of social reinforcement, especially praise and social recognition.

Principle No. 8. Continually encourage employees in their personal growth and skill development. Workers should be encouraged to develop and follow their own self-improvement program.

Each employee should identify specific areas of development and set personal achievement goals. Working hard to achieve challenging personal goals is a meaningful and satisfying experience. Among earlier generations, Benjamin Franklin was one of the most eloquent advocates of self-development. He formulated his most well-known project for self-improvement at the age of 22. Franklin identified 13 virtues and focused on one virtue each week. In a small notebook he constructed a chart with seven columns for the days of the week and 13 rows for the 13 virtues. At the end of each day, Franklin would examine his behavior and give himself a black mark in the appropriate square if he had not achieved his standard of excellence.[21]

The benefits of personal growth and skill development accrue to both the employee and the organization. Employees are constantly interacting with people who have different personalities and backgrounds from their own. Many employees respond to such encounters with a rather rigid style developed from past experience. Expansion of interpersonal skills is an important part of self-development. Managerial and technical skills also need to be continually refreshed and upgraded. Skills and knowledge that are not used occasionally become lost over time.

Employees should assume responsibility for their own career development. The motivation for the development of personal skills and abilities must come from within. The company can contribute to career development through various programs (see Chapter 10), but the most useful approach for the organization is to encourage employees to develop their own skills and abilities.

Teaching Work Values on the Job

The eight principles for developing work values are summarized on the following pages.

PRINCIPLES FOR DEVELOPING WORK VALUES

Principle No. 1. Establish an organizational climate that fosters positive work values and a commitment to excellence.

A commitment to excellence is stimulated by:
—Group norms that encourage and support excellence.
—The example of supervisors who display excellence in their own work.
—An organizational mission which explains how the organization serves society.
—Organizational efficiency which maximizes the social benefits derived from the efforts of the workforce.

Principle No. 2. Communicate clear expectations about productivity and high-quality craftsmanship.

—Performance and expectations can be communicated by supervisors, peers, and even subordinates.
—Performance expectations often become a self-fulfilling prophecy.
—Expectations influence performance by changing workers' self-concepts, personal aspirations, and goals.
—Performance expectations can be effectively communicated during the assignment of regular tasks and especially during the orientation of new employees.

Principle No. 3. Teach and explain the value of work, the dignity of labor, and the joy of service.

—Insightful comments made during a teaching moment are more effective than prepared instructions.
—Enlightening and suggestive comments are more useful teaching tools than detailed discourses.
—Relevant comments should be made patiently but per-

Principle No. 4. Establish individual accountability through effective delegation.

Effective delegation involves three steps:
—Establishing an agreement about the results to be achieved.
—Conducting periodic reviews to evaluate progress.
—Preparing a final accountability report.

181

Principle No. 5. Develop personal commitment and involvement through individual choice and participation.

Commitment and involvement can be increased by:
—Explaining the legitimacy of the organization's goals. The goals should be ethical, socially worthwhile, and personally meaningful.
—Asking rather than telling employees to perform their tasks.
—Encouraging individual participation in job redesign and goal setting.

Principle No. 6. Provide feedback on performance through effective performance appraisals.

Three aspects of performance should be evaluated:
—Personnel data (attendance, punctuality, and length of service).
—Production data, (quantity and quality of work).
—Judgments of others regarding spontaneous and innovative behaviors beyond the normal job requirements.

Two separate performance appraisals are needed:
—A contributions appraisal for evaluating and rewarding past performance.
—A personal development appraisal to evaluate strengths and weaknesses and to encourage growth and learning.

Principle No. 7. Reward effective performance with pay and other social reinforcers.

—Effective performance should be highly rewarded with praise and recognition.
—Pay should be an appropriate reinforcement—that is, the amount should be adequate and equitable. High performers should receive more pay than low performers.
—Money should be an important form of feedback about individual performance.
—Money should be used to reinforce the significance and social usefulness of performing a job.

Principle No. 8. Continually encourage employees in their personal growth and skill development.

Workers should be encouraged to develop and follow their own self-improvement plan in the following areas:
—Physical exercise, to improve their health.

—Social development, to increase their interpersonal skills.

—Emotional development, to build greater self-awareness and emotional stability.

—Intellectual development, to further their knowledge, wisdom, and practical skills.

—Character development, to further their ethical and moral behavior.

—Spiritual development, to foster a greater awareness of the meaning of life.

The Developmental Process

The developmental process Carol Blanchard experienced was consistent with the preceding principles of management. Her supervisor patiently and persistently delegated assignments to her, obtained her commitment, provided feedback and assistance, praised her good performance, and taught her the importance of high-quality workmanship by precept and example. This case also illustrates the sequential process of starting with job assignments that entail elementary learning objectives and advancing to more responsible job assignments with higher learning objectives.

A well-designed program for teaching positive work values and attitudes was developed and successfully implemented at Berea College in Berea, Kentucky. The students at Berea come primarily from lower-income families. Every student is required to work part time to supplement the low tuition. The students receive a modest wage for their work and are expected to make a reliable contribution to the program. Each student's work performance is evaluated and a work report is included in his or her academic file. Some jobs are directly associated with the college, such as computer programming. Other jobs are indirectly associated with the college, such as operating a hotel. Still other jobs involve student-run businesses, such as broom manufacturing. The program has been highly praised by educators, employers, and alumni.[22]

Students at Berea progress through five job levels, each with its own learning objectives. Advancement depends on successful work performance.

Beginning Level—Grade 1.   The beginning-level jobs, assigned to entering freshmen, consist of unskilled work under the direction of a supervisor. The jobs are usually repetitive and routine with limited judgment required.

The learning objectives for this level are "basic work habits and attitudes." These include (1) meeting a schedule; (2) meeting specified standards of performance; (3) using time efficiently; (4) developing healthy attitudes toward work and supervision; (5) working cooperatively with others; (6) sharing responsibility for achieving results; (7) recognizing the importance of work; and (8) learning the basic skills and information needed to do the task. These eight objectives are considered to be the basic habits and attitudes a worker must acquire as the first step in learning to work. It is interesting to note that only the last objective is usually addressed in most industrial training programs.

Intermediate Level—Grade 2.   The intermediate-level jobs are classified as semiskilled work. There is less direct supervision than at the beginning level. These jobs entail some work variety and require some independent judgment and independent knowledge of the job.

The learning objectives for the intermediate level are "responsibility and skill development." They include (1) taking personal responsibility for your own results; (2) learning to apply your knowledge to the situation; (3) identifying your skills, talents, interests, and limitations; (4) learning and developing confidence in skill or program knowledge; and (5) developing an appreciation of work as a process as well as a product.

Journeyman Level—Grade 3.   The journeyman level consists of skilled work with little direct supervision. The job involves variety and depth and requires independent judgment about procedures. The journeyman also helps to train others and contributes to the improvement of the organizational unit.

The learning objectives for the journeyman level are

184

"creativity and awareness." They include (1) realizing the importance of initiative; (2) acquiring an awareness of program needs; (3) learning how to identify problems; (4) developing analytical ability; (5) developing problem-solving ability; and (6) realizing the importance of performance standards and proper leadership.

Supervisory or Management Level—Grade 4. At the supervisory level, the job entails being able to perform the work of a journeyman as well as provide supervision to others. Supervisors or managers are responsible for programs requiring a high level of administrative competence. They make independent judgments on the application of policy and receive only general supervision from a director.

The learning objectives for the supervisory or management level are "understanding and commitment." They include (1) understanding relationships between people, institutions, and processes; (2) comprehending work values, realities, and goals; (3) developing a commitment to service; and (4) developing the ability to articulate and interpret observations and experiences. These learning objectives comprise the technical and interpersonal skills necessary for supervising others.

Leadership or Directive Level—Grade 5. At the leadership level, an individual assumes the role of directing a major program. The job entails substantial supervisory responsibility over other supervisors; managerial responsibility for planning, organizing, directing, and controlling; and a high degree of independence.

The learning objectives for the director level are "leadership and autonomy." They include (1) acquiring an understanding of leadership in the context of the larger community; (2) developing responsible autonomy; (3) developing the ability to interpret and transmit values to others; and (4) obtaining confidence in one's knowledge and ethics. These learning objectives are the skills needed to be an effective manager. They enable the manager to integrate the goals and activities of the program into the larger community.

A fundamental assumption of this learning process is that people should progress from the beginning level to the director level. The learning objectives at each level are assumed to build on the objectives of previous levels. Thus the efficient use of time, meeting a schedule, and recognizing the importance of work at the beginning level are fundamental values and habits necessary for effective performance at all five levels.

The learning objectives at the beginning level are similar to the values measured by the moral importance of work scale. Some of the learning objectives at the intermediate and journeyman levels are similar to the values measured by the pride in craftsmanship scale. Many company training programs and college business classes attempt to teach the learning objectives at the three highest levels—problem solving, supervision, and leadership. Work values are generally not included in either company training programs or college business courses—an unfortunate oversight. If the learning objectives of the first three levels are indeed prerequisites for the effective development of higher-level objectives, work-values training should be included in these programs (unless work values have already been acquired).

REFERENCES

1. Two classic examples of the influence of peer group norms are described in Lester Coch and John R. P. French, "Overcoming Resistance to Change," *Human Relations,* Vol. 2 (1948), pp. 512–532; and Fritz J. Rothlesberger and William J. Dickson, *Management and the Worker* (Cambridge, Mass.: Harvard University Press, 1939).
2. "ServiceMaster: The Protestant Ethic Helps Clean Hospitals Better," *Business Week* (February 19, 1979), p. 58.
3. Robert Rosenthal and Lenore Jacobson, *Pygmalion in the Classroom* (New York: Holt, Rinehart & Winston, 1968).
4. J. Sterling Livingston, "Pygmalion in Management," *Harvard Business Review,* Vol. 47 (July–August 1969), pp. 81–89.
5. David J. Cherrington and J. Owen Cherrington, "Appropriate Reinforcement Contingencies in the Budgeting Process," *Empirical Research in Accounting: Selected Studies* (1973), pp. 225–253.

6. Abraham K. Korman, "Expectancies as Determinants of Performance," *Journal of Applied Psychology*, Vol. 55, No. 3 (1971), pp. 218–222.

7. Andrew Stedry and E. Kay, "The Effects of Goal Difficulty on Performance," *Behavioral Science*, Vol. 11 (1966), pp. 459–470; Edwin Locke, "Toward a Theory of Task Motivation and Incentives," *Organizational Behavior and Human Performance*, Vol. 3 (1968), pp. 157–189.

8. Abraham K. Korman, "Toward an Hypothesis of Work Behavior," *Journal of Applied Psychology*, Vol. 54, No. 1 (1970), pp. 31–41.

9. J. Philippe Rushton, "Generosity in Children: Immediate and Long-Term Effects of Modeling, Preaching, and Moral Judgment," *Journal of Personality and Social Psychology*, Vol. 31, No. 3 (1975), pp. 459–466.

10. A discussion of the relationships between attitudes and behavior is found in Martin Fishbein and Icek Ajzen, *Belief, Attitude, Intention, and Behavior: An Introduction to Theory and Research* (Reading, Mass.: Addison-Wesley, 1975).

11. David C. McClelland, *The Achieving Society* (New York: The Free Press, 1961), p. 228.

12. David C. McClelland, "Achievement Motivation Can Be Developed," *Harvard Business Review*, Vol. 43 (November–December 1965), pp. 6–24.

13. Richard T. Mowday, Richard M. Steers, and Lyman W. Porter, "The Measurement of Organizational Commitment: A Progress Report," Technical Report No. 15, Graduate School of Management, Eugene, Oregon, July 1978.

14. Aryeh Kidron, "Work Values and Organizational Commitment," *Academy of Management Journal*, Vol. 21, No. 2 (1978), pp. 239–247.

15. Daniel Katz and Robert Kahn, *The Social Psychology of Organizations* (New York: John Wiley & Sons, 1965), chap. 12.

16. David J. Cherrington, "Satisfaction in Competitive Conditions," *Organizational Behavior and Human Performance*, Vol. 10 (1973), pp. 47–71.

17. McClelland, *The Achieving Society, op. cit.*, pp. 234–235.

18. Edward L. Deci, "The Effects of Contingent and Noncontingent Rewards and Controls on Intrinsic Motivation," *Organizational Behavior and Human Performance*, Vol. 8 (1972), pp. 217–229; Edward L. Deci, "The Effects of Externally Mediated Rewards on Intrinsic Motivation," *Journal of Personality and Social Psychology*, Vol. 18 (1971), pp. 105–115.

19. See the review by W. Clay Hamner, Jerry Ross, and Barry M. Staw, "Motivation in Organizations: The Need for a New Direction," in Dennis W. Organ (ed.), *The Applied Psychology of Work Behavior: A Book of Readings* (Dallas: Business Publications, 1978), pp. 224–249.

187

20. This controversy is explained and the research studies are reported in Alan C. Elms, *Role Playing, Reward, and Attitude Change* (New York: Van Nostrand Reinhold, 1969).
21. *Benjamin Franklin: The Autobiography and Other Writings* (New York: Signet, 1961), pp. 64, 94–95.
22. The work program and developmental process designed at Berea College were presented by William Ramsey at the Third Annual Work and the College Student Conference in Denton, Texas, November 1977.

9

WORK THERAPY

One of the most persuasive arguments for having a job and developing strong work values comes from the success of work therapy programs. These programs are called "work therapy" because the most critical aspect of the therapy consists in having a job and producing a useful service or product for yourself and society. Work therapy programs have been used with varying degrees of success in prisons for the rehabilitation of convicts, in schools to reduce juvenile delinquency, in mental hospitals to treat various emotional disturbances, and in industry to treat alcoholism and drug abuse. All these programs seem to be based on an underlying assumption about the role of work in people's lives. They suggest that work is a fundamental human activity, that work helps to establish self-reliance and feelings of self-worth, and that work ties people into a world of reality.

EMPLOYEE ASSISTANCE PROGRAMS

During the 1970s, many organizations, both public and private, created "employee assistance programs" to help employees with alcoholism, drug abuse, and other financial, emotional, or behavioral problems. Most large organizations today have employee assistance programs, but the literature describing the results is not widely circulated. It appears that the following

189

considerations are important for the success of an employee assistance program: (1) employees need to be assured that all information will be treated confidentially; (2) competent social services within the community must be available; (3) the program needs to be widely advertised, since most referrals come from family members; and (4) good supervision must be provided so that reasonable performance can be demanded from employees who refuse to admit they have a problem.[1]

There are two major philosophies in the design of these programs: the "toaster" philosophy and the "inadequate performance" philosophy. According to the toaster philosophy, you wait until a problem "pops up" and then try to solve it. This philosophy requires employees to recognize they have a serious problem and request assistance. Unfortunately, most people wait until problems of alcoholism, drug abuse, divorce, and financial insolvency are extremely severe before they seek help.

The inadequate performance philosophy recognizes that employees are reluctant to admit they have a problem. Here the employee's performance is observed. If there is a noticeable deterioration in performance that persists over time, the employee is assumed to have a problem of some sort. The employee is confronted in a supportive climate with the deficiency in his or her performance. The purpose of the confrontation is to identify problems early and begin solving them. When employees realize that their performance has been judged to be inadequate and that the security of their jobs is in question, they have a strong incentive to honestly ask, "Do I have a problem?" and "How can I get help?" Some large organizations have their own professional counselors. Other organizations rely on services within the community.

Superior to either the toaster or inadequate performance philosophy is the "preventive" philosophy. According to this approach, an organization should establish an environment that prevents problems from developing. This is very idealistic, of course. There are limits to how much an organization can do to prevent personal problems. Substance abuse, for example, is both a physiological and a psychological problem and may have a hereditary component as well.

The interviews with outstanding employees described earlier produced some fascinating comparisons with the results of studies on drug abuse and alcoholism. There appears to be an inverse relationship between the factors that lead to substance abuse and the factors that lead to the development of work values. That is, the characteristics that distinguish substance abusers from non abusers are many of the same characteristics that distinguish people with work-oriented versus non-work-oriented values.[2] These characteristics included such things as the role of obedience, self-discipline, self-control, personal responsibility, the importance of religion, and the extent to which a person's life is guided by what is considered "right." They were discussed in Chapter 7.

These findings suggest that if an organization can improve work values, it will also reduce alcoholism, drug use, and other personal problems. This conclusion is based on assumptions that are probably true of many people but not necessarily all. The assumptions are that people who believe strongly in the moral importance of work will reject the excessive use of alcohol and illicit drugs for several reasons. First, workers who have a feeling of pride in craftsmanship and high self-esteem will not need to rely on alcohol or drugs to escape from the frustrations of life. Second, a dependency on alcohol and drugs and the loss of personal control that results are inconsistent with the strong feelings of responsibility and self-direction that work-oriented people possess. Third, the self-discipline of work-oriented employees is incompatible with the self-indulgence of drug use and excessive drinking. Finally, the religious beliefs of some work-oriented people are clearly inconsistent with the use of illicit drugs, and some religions even prohibit the use of alcohol and tobacco.

It has been suggested that drug addicts develop certain skills and abilities in support of their drug habit which are similar to the skills and abilities people acquire for success in the world of work. One study found that most heroin addicts want to be and can be successful on a job. Many addicts are forced to work hard to support their habit, even if the work involves an illegal activity.[3] To function successfully in the world of work, a former addict needs more than just the skills of a new trade and a job opportunity. He or she needs some basic training in social skills and sound work habits. Evidence has shown that work-values training can be very beneficial. At one hospital, several forms of therapy were used in combination to help alcoholics and drug addicts. The treatment included drug therapy, group and individual therapy, and work therapy. Teaching work values and providing patients with an opportunity to produce a useful service or product were important parts of rehabilitation.[4]

WORK THERAPY PROGRAMS

Work therapy has been useful for social and personal problems in addition to alcoholism and drug abuse. It has been used effectively in the treatment of mentally ill people, juvenile delinquents, prisoners, and chronically ill or retarded people. The effectiveness of a work therapy program was examined at a rehabilitation center for the mentally retarded. The patients who participated performed simple industrial benchwork, such as counting and packaging materials, under the direction of a supervisor and an occupational therapist. This training program attempted to develop several work habits in each worker: punctuality, reliability, perseverance, speed, accuracy, and cooperativeness. Fifty percent of the patients were successfully placed in outside employment, 25 percent were placed in sheltered workshops, and 25 percent returned to their homes, all feeling more self-worth and self-respect.[5]

In another study, psychiatric patients undergoing treatment for major mental illnesses participated in an in-hospital sheltered workshop beginning shortly after admission. A matched control group did not participate in the work therapy. All 387 patients were evaluated by a clinician 3 months and 12 months after they were discharged. Overall clinical ratings were higher for patients in the work therapy program. The patients also rated the value of the therapies, and work therapy was most frequently rated as "most beneficial." Ratings by staff members at the time of the patients' discharge revealed that work therapy patients tended to respond better to all forms of treatment than did the controls.[6]

A survey was made of work therapy programs in British psychiatric hospitals. This survey distinguished between occupational therapy (traditional employment of patients in hospital departments without pay) and industrial therapy (productive, useful, and satisfying work for which patients received remuneration). It suggested that more emphasis needed to be placed on industrial therapy, although both therapies were useful. The major problem for the hospitals was securing adequate industrial contracts.[7]

Another study examined the meaning of work to mentally retarded patients by depriving them of the opportunity to work. Thirty patients were randomly separated into an experimental group and a control group. Those in the experimental group were not allowed to work 13 days: their time was filled with games and pleasurable experiences. During and shortly after this period, observers noted the percentage of hedonistic, bored, or work-related comments and behaviors of both groups. It was found that people in the experimental group were strongly motivated to return to work. Work deprivation was a powerful incentive to mental patients: they preferred working to not working and derived meaning and satisfaction from their jobs.[8]

Work therapy programs have also been used effectively in the treatment of juvenile delinquents and prisoners. One study examined the effectiveness of a community-based work release or work furlough program which permitted selected inmates to work in the community during the day and return to the institution during their nonworking hours. The results indicated that inmates with work furloughs had fewer arrests and convictions after release. Furthermore, the prisoners paid some of the administrative costs of the program, repaid outstanding fines and debts, supported their families, and returned to society in better financial condition than inmates released from total incarceration. The work furlough program was especially beneficial to those having the highest risk of failure and the poorest work history.[9]

Allowing business organizations to take advantage of inexpensive prison labor has not been generally accepted in America. In other countries, however, it has been practiced with desirable results. A *Wall Street Journal* article described the controversy surrounding the use of prison labor in Colombia. The article noted that many Americans condemned the practice as slave labor. However, the prisoners in Colombia were anxious to work and competed intensely for the jobs that became available. Prison officials claimed that the work not only helped the employers, who were short on labor sources, but also helped the prisoners: there was less drug traffic, less violence in the prisons, more stability in the prisoners' families (since the inmates earned money and sent it home), and better adjustment after release from prison.[10]

There is also considerable evidence that work experiences can be beneficial to people who are chronically ill and people who are retired or have been unemployed for a long period of time.[11] In one project, productive remunerative work was provided to 44 chronically ill patients. The patients were given jobs compatible with their skills and limitations—for example, sewing linens and assembling or packaging novelty items. Eight beneficial effects were identified from the case studies: (1) financial security, (2) time-filling activities, (3) personal identity, (4) development of a pattern of associations with others, (5) creation of a set of meaningful life experiences, (6) creation of a displacement mechanism for life's frustrations and failures, (7) proof of personal worth, and (8) control over one's social environment by working at home.[12]

The work therapy programs described in the literature have usually reported favorable results, indicating that work therapy is beneficial and effective. But several studies have failed to demonstrate positive effects of work therapy. All these studies were unpublished dissertations,[13] suggesting that there may be a bias in the reporting wherein only effective programs are publicized. But it also indicates that we do not know what features of work therapy are essential for success. Is it simply having something to do and a schedule to follow? Is it the social interaction? Is it producing a useful product and getting paid for it? Or is it acquiring work values such as pride in craftsmanship? Most likely it is all of the above. Whatever the reason, the evidence on the whole strongly supports work therapy for a broad range of problems. Regular employment and good work habits appear to be desirable aspects of life in general.

REFERENCES

1. A survey of employee assistance programs was conducted jointly by the American Society of Personnel Administration and the Bureau of National Affairs, "Counseling Policies and Programs for Employees with Problems," *Bulletin to Management*, ASPA–BNA Survey No. 34, March 23, 1978.

2. This chapter is adapted from David J. Cherrington, "The Development of Work Values in the Prevention of Substance Abuse." Speech presented at the National Drug Abuse Conference, San Francisco, California, May 1977.

3. Stephen M. Pittel, "Addicts in Wonderland: Sketches for a Map of a Vocational Frontier," *Journal of Psychedelic Drugs*, Vol. 6, No. 2 (April–June 1974), pp. 231–241.

4. E. Rothstein, B. A. Norton, E. H. Lahage, and S. R. Mueller, "An Experimental Alcoholism Unit in a Psychiatric Hospital," *Quarterly Journal of Studies on Alcohol*, Vol. 27 (1966), pp. 513–516.

5. Donna Patrick, "Retardates in a Work Adjustment Program," *American Journal of Occupational Therapy*, Vol. 14 (1960), pp. 297–300.

6. Leo A. Micek and Donald G. Miles, "Perspectives on Work Therapy," *Current Psychiatric Therapies*, Vol. 9 (1969), pp. 202–208.

7. H. B. Kidd, "Industrial Units in Psychiatric Hospitals," *British Journal of Psychiatry*, Vol. 3 (1965), pp. 1,205–1,209.

8. Charles C. Clelland and Jon D. Swartz, "Work Deprivation as Motivation to Work," *American Journal of Mental Deficiency*, Vol. 73 (1969), pp. 703–712. See also Charles C. Clelland and Jon D. Swartz, "Deprivation, Reinforcement, and Peer Support as Work

Motivators: A Paradigm for Habilitation of Older Retardates,'' *Community Mental Health Journal,* Vol. 4 (1968), pp. 120–128.

9. Robert Jeffery and Stephen Woolpert, "Work Furlough as an Alternative to Incarceration: An Assessment of Its Effects on Recidivism and Social Cost," *The Journal of Criminal Law and Criminology,* Vol. 65 (1974), pp. 405–415.

10. Stephen J. Sansweet, "Captive Workers: Prisoners in Columbia Are Working for Units of U.S. Multinationals," *The Wall Street Journal* (June 20, 1975), p. 1.

11. David L. Ellison, "Work, Retirement, and the Sick Role," *Gerontologist,* Vol. 8 (1968), pp. 189–192; W. E. Thompson, G. F. Streib, and J. Kosa, "The Effect of Retirement on Personal Adjustments: A Panel Analysis," *Journal of Gerontology,* Vol. 15 (1960), pp. 165–169; Dorothy A. Evans and Forrest B. Tyler, "Is Work Competence Enhancing for the Poor?" *American Journal of Community Psychology,* Vol. 4 (1976), pp. 25–33; Donald J. Searls, G. N. Braucht, and R. W. Miskimins, "Work Values of the Chronically Unemployed," *Journal of Applied Psychology,* Vol. 59 (1974), pp. 93–95.

12. Donald Springer, "Remunerative Homework for the Homebound Chronically Ill: Observations on the Meaning of Work," *Personnel and Guidance Journal,* Vol. 40 (September 1961), pp. 51–57.

13. Francis L. Carney, "The Occupational Values of Delinquent Boys." Unpublished dissertation, The Catholic University of America, 1967, Order No. 67-15,439. Stanley E. Schneider, "The Effects of Work and Counseling on Chronic Psychiatric Patients with Differing Levels of Ego Strength." Unpublished dissertation, University of Maryland, 1969, Order No. 70-10,299.

10

CAREER DEVELOPMENT AND EDUCATION

Work and education have been structured as two separate worlds, and the gulf that separates them seems to grow wider each year. This separation promises to have undesirable results if it continues. Negative stereotypes have already emerged on both sides, and each side suffers from its nearsighted opinion. Some managers and production workers are very critical of education and what is taught in the schools. Likewise, some educators are very critical of industry and what business executives do.

These feelings surfaced in a recent meeting between a group of corporate executives and faculty members from a major university. The purpose of the meeting was to develop a program for liberal arts students to work in corporate advertising during the summer. At the conclusion of the meeting, the spokesman for the corporation said apologetically that the company would have to proceed slowly and carefully to overcome resistance from executives who were opposed to any association with universities and their "theoretical nonsense." The university representative confessed that the school too would have difficulty selling faculty members on the internship program. She said that other members of her department were accusing her of "prostituting her academic purity" by arranging for students to work in industry. For her to even be discussing the training needs of industry was considered an illegitimate concern.

The people who suffer from this sort of narrow-mindedness are students whose education lacks relevance and vitality and workers who are discouraged from pursuing further education. The purpose of this chapter is to discuss the need to integrate work and education. Several attempts at integration have had excellent results. These results support three major propositions:

1. Education improves the quality of work.
2. Work improves the quality of education.
3. Work and education are both facilitated by the development of positive work values—a belief in the moral importance of work, pride in craftsmanship, efficient use of time, and joy in service.

COMBATING OBSOLESCENCE

Obsolescence is a serious problem that is getting worse. Obsolescence refers to a reduction in effectiveness because of a lack of knowledge or skill. The lack is sometimes due to forgetfulness, but more often it results from the creation of new knowledge or technologies. Studies have documented the seriousness of obsolescence among managers, salespeople, and engineers. It is reasonable to assume that obsolescence is a problem in many other occupations as well, especially those occupations which require extensive educational preparation or the use of advanced technology. One observer, writing about obsolescence in the data processing field, estimated that the cost of executive incompetence in a single company exceeded $10 million a year.[1]

The erosion of applicable knowledge has been particularly steep in engineering. An analysis of course offerings in five engineering colleges from 1935 to 1964 indicated that for the class of 1935 the percentage of applicable knowledge 30 years later was only 6 percent.[2]

The concept of half-life, taken from nuclear physics, provides a useful measure of the extent of obsolescence in different occupations. The term refers to the length of time before a competent professional becomes roughly half as competent as he or she once was because of new developments. In engineering, the half-life of a 1940 graduate was estimated to be about 12 years. In 1965 the half-life of a well-trained college professor was estimated to be only 5 years.[3]

Professional obsolescence is thought to be the major reason for the decline in performance among older engineers. A study of six engineering firms found that the average performance level of engineers increased for the first 10 to 15 years, then decreased steadily until retirement. The peak performance was achieved by the 31–35 year olds. A similar performance curve was found for managers and engineering supervisors. Performance levels increased for the first few years, then decreased. The peak performance levels were obtained by the 36–40 year olds. The half-life of the supervisors' technical skills was thought to be considerably shorter than the half-life of their interpersonal and administrative skills.[4]

Obsolescence among professionals has become so serious that several states have required some professionals to return to school. In Minnesota, for example, lawyers must return to school for 45 hours of legal course work every three years. This order, issued by the Minnesota Supreme Court, was part of a national effort to require lawyers to keep up with their field. Lawyers who fail to comply receive a restricted status which limits them to representing only a full-time employer or members of their families.

Similar requirements for medical doctors have also been enacted. A number of medical boards require periodic recertification every six years. Several states, including Oregon, Pennsylvania, and New York, require physicians to take 50 to 60 hours of continuing education annually in order to maintain their license.[5]

The quantity of knowledge is expanding in virtually every

occupation. Furthermore, the creation of new knowledge is occurring at an accelerating pace, especially in occupations that disseminate or use new information, such as engineering and teaching. The accelerating creation of knowledge, however, does not necessarily mean that a person will become obsolete. Even though the study of engineering firms showed that the average performance of older engineers declined, the researchers were quick to note that some older engineers were extremely competent and productive. Through study, work assignments, and training, these older engineers were able to maintain high ratings of competence.

Organizational strategies for combating obsolescence should focus on two areas: (1) providing opportunities for learning to occur, and (2) creating the motivation to learn within the learner. Both of these areas are important, but proper motivation is essential. Many employees learn on their own and acquire new skills in spite of adverse learning conditions.

Numerous company actions have been proposed to combat obsolescence. Most of these suggestions are rather expensive. But they are usually cost-effective because the price of obsolescence and incompetence is so high.[6]

1. Continuing education can be used in numerous ways. The most popular form is evening classes at a local college or university. Tuition and other expenses, such as textbooks, are normally paid by the company, provided the course is relevant to the employee's job and the employee obtains a passing grade.

2. Training programs can be held at the company on company time or at some other site on weekends or evenings. These programs can be taught by competent members of the organization, outside consultants, or someone else, such as a service representative of a company selling a major piece of machinery.

3. Training materials can be purchased by the company and made available to employees. The materials might include reference books, professional periodicals, films, videotape

cassettes, and textbooks. These materials might be collected in a company library or sent directly to employees' offices to be kept on their bookshelves.

4. Seminars can be held periodically at which experts are invited to present information to a select group.

5. Sabbaticals can be arranged for managers and engineers similar to sabbaticals for college professors. Many executives feel that going to school full time for a semester is superior to going to evening school for much of their careers.

6. Job rotation and new project assignments can help employees obtain new skills and knowledge. There is almost always some lost time and frustration associated with beginning a new assignment. But the benefits of new learning usually outweigh the time and effort.

All these company actions are valuable, but they do not really focus on the root of the obsolescence problem: personal motivation. The motivation to learn and retain information must come from within. If people are motivated to learn, they will learn what they want in spite of the actions taken by the company. The company can facilitate the learning process by providing training materials and time to learn. But if the company does not create a learning opportunity, highly motivated employees will create it for themselves, even if it means leaving the company to do so.

In short, to foster employees' careers and combat obsolescence, a company should direct its primary efforts toward strengthening the meaning of work for employees and providing opportunities for them to be of service. Obsolescence is avoided more by promoting strong work values than by sponsoring company training programs.

The development of work values involves establishing high performance expectations, delegating task assignments and responsibility, evaluating and rewarding performance, and creating a climate of efficiency and usefulness for society. These strategies are based on the assumption that people who believe work is an important part of life will be highly motivated to learn new information and develop new skills. This assumption is supported by empirical research, although the evidence is limited.

Two of my colleagues collected data from 1,037 managers and engineers in a major corporation in the aerospace and electronics fields.[7] The questionnaire measured various attitudes about work and career development. The managers were asked to evaluate seven different methods for developing their knowledge and skills: taking formal courses, studying on their own, seeking career counseling, redesigning their current jobs, moving to a new job in the company, moving to a new organization, and changing their career occupation. Managers who selected self-study tended to be highly involved in their jobs. ("The major satisfaction in my life comes from my job." "I am very much involved personally in my work." "I live, eat, and breathe my job.") Furthermore, these managers tended to have jobs that encouraged learning—that is, jobs with greater variety, meaning, feedback, and responsibility. Those who selected self-study were also generally satisfied with their jobs and the company. In contrast, managers who said they would move to another company to develop new knowledge and skills were generally dissatisfied with their jobs and the company. They saw little opportunity for development in their present job.[8]

There is some question about the usefulness of formal courses in career development. The evidence is not very encouraging. In the study of six engineering firms described earlier, performance evaluations bore no relationship to the number of courses the person had taken. Furthermore, one of the six firms spent much more time and money than the others to provide continuing education for its engineers. In spite of this effort, the company's obsolescence problem was just as serious as that of the others.

A final observation helps to explain why formal courses have not shown impressive benefits for the development of new knowledge. In one engineering firm it was found that most of the engineers over 40 years of age who were taking the course were doing so because their performance ratings were low.

202

They had been pushed into the training by their supervisors because they were becoming obsolete. They apparently lacked the motivation to learn on their own and the pressure of taking a formal course was not having much effect. This suggests that formal courses are not necessarily ineffective. The problem stems from a lack of motivation rather than from a deficiency in the content of the course itself. If people are highly motivated to learn, a formal course could be a useful learning experience.

In a work environment, the major motivation to learn is to increase one's competence. This motivation stems not from a fear of becoming obsolete but from a desire to perform competently. For outstanding performers, new knowledge and skills are an opportunity to improve their performance. Coupled with this desire for competence is usually a strong belief in the value of diligent effort and a wish to be of service to the company and society. The desire to earn more money or to achieve public status or fame is a source of general motivation, but it has only a small impact on learning. Similarly, the motive to avoid becoming obsolete or to avoid being "chewed out" or fired does not really help the learning process. Indeed, if these concerns become intense, the learning process will be inhibited.

An Illustration. The career histories of two research scientists illustrate how the instrumental value of work and the motivation to serve help combat obsolescence. Both men were employed in the biology departments of major Ivy League universities for the major portion of their careers. During their thirties, both were highly respected teachers in the classroom and scientists in the laboratory. However, their professional careers followed quite different paths, largely because of their differing attitudes and commitments to work.

By his early forties, it was obvious that Professor B. was becoming obsolete in his technical skills. He did not exert enough effort to improve his competence because he lacked the desire to contribute to society or pursue professional excellence. He was unable to study and concentrate on difficult

203

information for long periods of time. He spent much of his time socializing with friends and pursuing leisure activities. Soon he was not able to conduct original research and in time he was not even capable of significantly contributing to the research projects of graduate students. His lectures became outdated and repetitive. His teaching was restricted to introductory courses. His time and interests had shifted to nonwork activities, especially to training and showing dogs. He was not motivated to regain his competence by any of the university's incentives, including money for research projects, complimentary textbooks, a well-supplied laboratory, travel money for professional conferences, subscriptions to major professional publications, and graduate students to serve as research assistants. In essence, he had retired himself in his early fifties. But since he had tenure, the university was unable to fire him.

The other man, Professor Robert H. Daines, avoided becoming obsolete and was productive throughout his professional career. To make research advances on new problems, he studied three new major fields of knowledge, often with the help of experts in the field. Even more important, he kept current in his own rapidly expanding field. During his career he authored over 250 research articles and numerous chapters in various texts. His contribution to the solution of plant diseases was so valuable that when he approached normal retirement age, a farmer's organization petitioned the state legislature for a special bill to extend his career. The bill was passed and provided money to support his research and fund the experimental station he directed for another five years. At the age of 70, he was forced by state law to retire from the university even though he was on the brink of a significant breakthrough in the treatment of a viral plant disease. He worked for a year on his own and then joined the faculty of a university in another state, where he is currently pursuing research as an adjunct professor.

When asked to explain the difference between his productive career and his colleague's "early retirement," he attributed

it to his belief in the importance of work and the value of
service:

> "I've always believed in hard work. I've always been
> a worker. And I've always believed in the value of
> service. All my life I've tried to prepare myself to be of
> service to my fellow men. When I was in graduate school
> I wanted to prepare myself so that I could help the
> farmers. Later, when the fruit growers or others had
> problems with their crops, I felt an obligation to help
> them. I don't think Professor B. ever felt the same
> satisfaction from helping. He wasn't doing things for
> others; he seemed to be doing them for himself.
>
> "I never studied to avoid becoming outdated. I always
> knew there was more to know than I'd ever learn. I
> learned because it was part of my work. I had to know
> more to solve the problems I was working on. I felt like
> there was always a new problem or two to work on and I
> wanted to get to them. Learning was a big part of my
> work. For example, I got into air pollution research
> because I found some plant damage that I thought could
> be explained in no other way. Then later I had to learn
> about animal physiology because we were looking at the
> effects of lead poisoning from auto exhaust on rabbits.
> Studying new ideas and gaining more knowledge are
> important parts of my life. I see life as a continuous
> process of learning."

The career history of Professor Daines is similar to the
histories of countless other outstanding scholars and workers
who have maintained currency and competence throughout
their careers. The motivation to learn comes from within, and
motivated people successfully pursue their own self-study and
learning programs.

Even if people study in groups, they must have initiative if
learning is to occur. While there are many things an organization can do to facilitate career development, the only viable
approach is to assume that people are responsible for training

205

themselves. Workers who are motivated to perform competently will pursue their own development and avoid obsolescence. The organization should focus on increasing the meaning of work and the opportunity to be of service. It should not try to solve the problem of obsolescence by pushing people into training programs.

If education is carefully structured, it will not interfere with work. In fact, education is likely to increase the employee's competence. Similar beneficial results are achieved when work supplements education. People who have argued for a combination of work and education have been lone voices crying in the wilderness. In general, they have gone unheard.[9] However, work is not a deterrent to academic achievement. Instead, the combination of work and education frequently produces several desirable results, including higher academic achievement.

FRUSTRATIONS AND JOYS OF PART-TIME WORK

An informal opinion survey at Brigham Young University found that some students thought part-time employment was a frustrating experience while others thought their work produced satisfaction and other advantages.[10] About 11,000 students from a total of 26,000 worked on campus during the school year, and roughly the same number held off-campus jobs. Consequently, a large percentage of the student body participated in part-time employment.

Some students would have preferred not to work but found it necessary to finance their education. They frequently described work as a "real drag" and student life as a "rat race." A freshman who worked in maintenance from 6:00 to 10:00 A.M. lamented, "There's no time to study. Everything's crammed together. I get home at 5:30 P.M., eat, and have three hours before I have to go to bed so I can be up by 5:00 A.M. to get ready for work." Another student complained that work interfered with school and social life: "If I didn't have to work, I would do better in school. I'm always tired and my body aches. This weekend I would have called a girl for a date, but I was too tired to do anything. When you get to bed by 7:30 on a Friday night, you know something's wrong." A student wife said that she did not get to see her husband because he left early for school and got home late from work. But she added, "I realize I have to sacrifice. You have to live. Because you have to work—everything else is sacrifice."

The majority of students had much more positive feelings about the work they were obliged to do, and many worked because they wanted to. One student said he chose to work because "it's an important physical release. It also makes me feel I'm on my own, since I live at home. I think it's immoral to take money from your parents if you can earn it. My grades have suffered a little, but they didn't have to. I just got a little lazy." Many students said that work gave them a feeling of independence and taught them self-reliance "You can have anything in life if you're willing to work for it. I've supported myself since the eighth grade, and though I haven't had a lot, I've never gone without."

Part-time employment forced many students to organize their time and plan their activities. "You have to set priorities. [My first year] I didn't work and I had a 2.8 GPA. Now I work and I have a 3.35. I just had to learn to plan my time wisely." "You can't just goof around. You've got to schedule time to have fun and learn to set priorities and place values."

One reason why some students responded so favorably to part-time employment was because they had a positive orientation toward work. "I was brought up to believe that work is desirable. Besides, I like the satisfaction that comes from completing a job."

There were other indirect benefits attributed to part-time employment. One student said it helped her develop a greater appreciation for her education and for money. "I've had higher grades since I started working because I'm paying for my education. If it's your money, you don't waste it. If you haven't put the work behind your money you spend it faster." Other students felt that student employment would help them get a better job after graduation. "It's always nice to have the references. One thing that impresses an employer is the fact that you've worked and gone to school." "You learn to push yourself and that will help out later. An employer wants someone who will work hard."

School officials agreed that work had positive effects on the quality of student life. The assistant dean of students encouraged part-time employment. "As a general rule, working students do as well as or better than those who don't—when they work within limits. They use their time more effectively because they know they don't have unlimited hours. Many have great learning experiences on the job." The dean cautioned, however, that when students exceed 20 hours per week (the limit set by the university for on-campus employment) their grades frequently suffer. The director of student health services also cautioned against working more than 20 hours per week while carrying a full academic load. "Students usually come down with a large number of colds and sore throats, complain of fatigue, weakness, and tiredness. . . . In extreme cases, some have had severe infections or gone into severe depressive reactions. Some have been unable to function and have had to drop out of school or quit their jobs."

The results of this informal survey were consistent with a 1966 survey of 2,000 undergraduates at Brooklyn College. In general, the students at Brooklyn reported that work was desirable because it provided money for education and leisure activities, gave them a feeling of independence, offered practical experience for postgraduate living, and provided valuable associations with businesspeople. They did not feel that work was detrimental to their grades, but some thought part-time work reduced their participation in extracurricular activities.[11]

WORK AND ACADEMIC ACHIEVEMENT

These opinion surveys have been supported by empirical studies at other universities. A study in 1941 of 332 students at Friends University expressed concern whether the number of hours students were working would affect their academic achievement. The data indicated that 39 percent worked over 22.5 hours per week and 10 percent held more than a full-time job (over 42.5 hours per week). The analysis found, however, that grades were not related to the number of hours worked. As outside workloads increased, students decreased their academic course work. The best predictor of grades was found to be a psychological rating of interest, motivation, and personal habits. Students with high grades were found to have "unusual ability, industriousness, and seriousness of purpose." Those with low grades tended to be "time wasters," students who were indifferent to school, or students who had difficulty mastering classwork.[12] Other surveys support the conclusion that the number of hours worked is not related to academic performance.[13]

A study at Kansas State University questioned the traditional advice that freshmen should not work their first semester because they needed time to adjust to college life. First-semester grades were compared for three groups of freshmen who were matched on sex, college entrance test scores, high school grades, and semester hours completed. The first group worked 10 to 15 hours per week and received financial aid. The second group received financial aid but did not work. The third group neither worked nor received aid. There were no differences in the grade-point averages of the three groups.[14] Similar results were obtained from a study of 202 students at Modesto Junior College. Grades were compared for matched groups of employed versus nonemployed students. The comparisons again showed no significant differences between the grades of students performing part-time work and the grades of students who did not work.[15]

In 1964, the Economic Opportunity Act established the federal work-study program. This program provided part-time employment (not to exceed 15 hours per week) for academically qualified students from low-income families. Analysis of the program indicated that part-time employment did not adversely affect the grades of low-income students and that in some instances the students performed better than their

209

high school averages and college entrance test scores would have predicted. One study reached the following conclusion:

> A well-supervised work program apparently does not interfere with the academic performance of first-semester freshmen. This is true for students of low ability as well as for those of high ability. . . . It would appear, on the basis of this and other studies, that financial aid officers and counselors can advise entering freshmen who need financial assistance to seek part-time employment up to 15 hours per week without fear of the students' sacrificing academic achievement. This evidence is in contradiction to much of the advice given to high school seniors.[16]

The studies reviewed above all concluded that part-time work does not adversely influence academic performance. The grades of students who worked were not lower than those who did not work. Other studies suggest that students with jobs (even those on academic probation) may sometimes achieve *better* grades than those without jobs. Separate investigations of students at Ohio State University, the University of South Carolina, Northern Illinois University, Southern Illinois University, and Pennsylvania State University–Ogontz all showed that the academic performance of working college students (usually freshmen) was *better* than the performance of a matched sample of nonworking peers. One study indicated that the number of hours worked should not exceed 15 hours per week and the work should be relevant to the student's major field of study. Another study suggested that the optimum amount of work for second-semester freshmen was 15 to 20 hours per week.[17]

These and other studies support the conclusion that part-time work (no more than 15 to 20 hours per week) can improve the academic performance of college students. Furthermore, there is evidence that reducing the employment hours for working students does not necessarily raise their grades.[18] All the evidence seems to suggest that work and education are not incompatible for college students and that students can be

210

encouraged to help finance their own education without fear that it will interfere with their studies.

Most research studies about the effects of work on education have examined college students. But part-time work probably has similar benefits for younger students as well. Over the past 14 years there has been a noticeable decline in the average SAT and ACT scores of high school students across the nation. However, there have been smaller than average declines in the scores of students who reported up to 15 hours of outside work each week. There were also smaller declines in the scores of students who participated in various extracurricular activities, such as athletics, social organizations, religious activities, student government, and various clubs. Thus both college and high school students can perform moderate amounts of work without having it interfere with their academic achievement, and many find that it improves their academic record.[19]

COOPERATIVE EDUCATION

There have been several attempts to formally combine work and education in America's past. The most successful attempt—in the sense that it has survived for many years and still exists in many colleges and universities—is called cooperative education. Loosely defined, cooperative education refers to a range of programs involving classroom study and off-campus work experience. Such programs are variously called field experiences, internship programs, interlude programs, professional practice programs, experiential work, and industry periods. In most institutions cooperative education follows a more traditional definition. This definition requires that four principles be observed:

1. The student's off-campus experience should be related as closely as possible to his or her field of study.
2. Employment should be a regular, continuing, and essential element in the educational process.
3. A minimum amount of employment and minimum stan-

211

dard of performance should be included in the requirement for the degree or certificate presented by the
school.
4. The work experience should increase in difficulty and
responsibility as the student progresses through the
academic curriculum and, in general, should parallel as
closely as possible the student's academic progress.[20]

Cooperative education began in 1906 at the University of
Cincinnati. The program consisted of two groups of engineering students who alternated each week between on-campus
study and off-campus employment in engineering-related jobs.
It was not long before the benefits of cooperative education
became evident. By 1919, there were cooperative education
programs in 10 universities. The number of programs grew, and
in 1970 there were 225 colleges and universities in the United
States offering some form of cooperative education.[21]

At first, cooperative education was thought to be useful
only because it was a realistic extension of the college laboratory. In time, however, it became increasingly clear that the
program offered valuable benefits to the student, the college,
the employer, and society. For the student, work experiences
have been found to contribute to a sense of identity and
self-worth, since the student relates to adults as an adult and
interacts with people from many different backgrounds. Students typically improve their academic performance because
of greater self-awareness and career planning; they organize
their time and studies better as a result of having to meet work
obligations; and they find greater relevance and greater
motivation for their studies. In addition, students often attain
greater emotional stability because they have a change of pace
from the lockstep routine of academic pursuits. Many find that
they have fewer financial worries to distract them from their
studies. Because cooperative education places the student in
new and challenging situations demanding new behavior, it
contributes to the student's personal, social, and career development.[22]

These advantages far outweigh the disadvantages for the

student, but the following disadvantages should not be disregarded: the course of study is generally lengthened by one year; students usually experience some confusion in shifting from school to work and back again; and some students complain about the lack of social life.

Cooperative education offers three major benefits to the employer. First, the employer has work that needs to be done. Cooperative students are usually capable and enthusiastic workers who are eager to learn. Second, cooperative education programs facilitate the recruitment and selection of new employees. During the work period the employer and the student can evaluate the desirability of a long-term employment commitment. On the average, 40 to 45 percent of all cooperative students (and 60 percent of students in professional programs) return to their cooperative employer as full-time employees after graduation. Studies of employment records consistently show that employees who worked as cooperative students remain longer and are better workers than those who had no prior connection with the company. Third, students who have been studying the latest developments in their courses usually bring new ideas to the company. These ideas can stimulate others and can help create an environment of continuing education.

The major benefit to the college or university is that students bring back to the campus current information on industrial and business practices and new technology. This feedback helps keep the academic curriculum current. It also ensures that students learn appropriate skills for their new profession and receive adequate training. Other advantages to the college include a more attractive curriculum for recruiting new students and a greater students–facilities ratio, since some students are away at work during the year. The biggest problem for the college or university is finding enough employing organizations to participate in the program.

The major benefit of cooperative education to society, in addition to the indirect benefits of helping the students, the colleges, and the employing companies, is the financial assistance provided to the cooperative student from working. This assistance reduces the need for educational support through government grants, fellowships, or loans and contributes to federal and state income through taxes paid on these earnings. Another benefit to society comes from the job mobility and flexibility cooperative education provides for minority and low-income students who may have never developed achievement-oriented attitudes and behaviors.

Below is a list of suggested ideas for companies, schools, and students to increase the usefulness of cooperative education.

Company

1. A company supervisor should be appointed to direct the new interns. The director should be carefully selected, since he or she will act as a mentor to the students and have a major influence on their attitudes and behavior. Since supervising new employees takes time, the workload of the supervisor should be reduced proportionately.

2. The work assignment should be carefully designed so that it can be explained, understood, and completed in the given time. The jobs do not need to be highly structured; some students can tackle very complex and loosely structured tasks. But for most students the jobs should be structured in the normal way for new employees. It is preferable to have a task or set of tasks that can be completed during the time the students will be employed. Completing a defined project gives them a sense of accomplishment and maximizes their contribution to the company.

3. The company should establish a fair wage based on what would be an equitable starting salary. As noted above, many interns return to the company for full-time employment after graduation and their internship salary is indeed their starting salary.

4. Physical arrangements, such as an office, phone, desk, calculator, and drafting table, should be provided for the intern just as for any new employee.

5. The intern should make a report on his or her work at the

end of the experience. This report could be a concise memo to the supervisor, a written dissertation defended orally before the management team, or some compromise between these two extremes. The primary purpose of the report is to encourage the student to think creatively, apply his or her academic training, and share this insight with others in the company.

School

1. The university should appoint a program director to interact and coordinate with companies. Some universities have a director of cooperative education who serves the entire university. However, more decentralized arrangements are preferable. For example, each division (school of business, school of education, school of engineering) or even each department might have its own director.

The cooperative education office functions much like a placement center for graduates. It lists internship opportunities, helps match opportunities with interested students, and assists in arranging interviews.

2. Even though the cooperative education office assists in placing students, it should be the student's responsibility to obtain an internship experience. At most schools, many of the best students find internships on their own initiative.

3. Since most students have not worked with professionals in a company environment, it is useful for the university to spend time preparing students for this experience. Training might include professional ethics, dress and grooming standards, attitudes about work and dedication, obtaining performance feedback, and responding to criticism. Such training could be included in a course or presented in separate seminars and lectures.

4. On-site visits by a faculty member are extremely informative for the student, faculty, and company. However, time constraints and travel expenses often make such visits impossible. Unless the company is located near the university or the faculty member has a consulting arrangement with the company, on-site visits are difficult.

5. The university should not give academic credit for the

work experience *itself*. This suggestion is inconsistent with most cooperative education programs but consistent with my own philosophy of education. Working in industry is indeed a valuable learning experience, but so are a lot of other things—such as getting married and raising children—that do not receive college credit.

Credit should be given, however, for an analysis of the experience. Students should be asked to prepare a report of their activities, carefully describing what they did, what they learned, what mistakes they made, what they could have done differently, and how their activities are related to their professional discipline. Such a report will make the work program a valuable learning experience.

Student

1. Assume responsibility for finding your own internship. Identify what activities you would like to do and what contributions you could make to an organization. Then prepare a résumé with an introductory letter and contact potential companies. Getting an internship is your responsibility. Any help you get from the school and companies is welcome, but do not wait for them.

2. Try to find a mentor who can help you learn "the ropes to skip and the ropes to know." A good mentor is an extremely valuable asset. He or she can help you understand what is important in the organization and what is acceptable and unacceptable behavior. A mentor can also help you obtain work experiences that will be valuable in your career development. A good mentor can act as a counselor in addition to representing you to upper levels of management.

Whether or not you find a mentor, you should still rely on your own initiative. Do not expect a mentor to carry you. You need to know your own job—what is expected of you—and you need to perform it competently.

3. Be inquisitive and do not hesitate to ask questions. If you think before you speak, you can usually avoid asking foolish questions. When you raise a question, listen carefully to the

answer. Do not hesitate to ask questions for fear of looking stupid. Such a fear can lead you to miss valuable learning experiences.

4. Explore applications of your academic training in your work experiences. This exploration often results in new insights, a desire for more knowledge, and useful innovations for the organization.

5. Try to develop interpersonal skills and a better understanding of others. Professional attitudes and behavior are best acquired through interaction with other professionals. Much can be learned by observing the behavior of your co-workers and understanding their values and attitudes. Being socially competent is as important as being technically competent.

6. Keep a personal journal of your significant experiences. Record the assignments that are delegated to you, the progress you make on them, your successes and failures, and other insights. Recording these experiences helps to make them more valuable because it forces you to analyze what occurred.

CONCLUSIONS

One of the popular myths of our time is that work and education should be separated. Our society has traditionally assumed that a student's job is to be a full-time student and a worker's job is to be a full-time worker. This separation is partly historical accident, resulting from years of trying to legislate against child labor. Starting in the 1850s, several states tried to forbid child labor by requiring children to attend school a minimum number of months. These early laws had little effect, however, because employers needed labor, parents wanted their children to work, and many children wanted the material benefits that work provided. The Fair Labor Standards Act of 1938 prohibited the full-time employment of children under the age of 16. Unfortunately, employers and educators were not able to achieve a compromise that combined work experiences and education.

Education has typically been viewed as something associated with youth—young people should go to school. In earlier years, children were encouraged to rush through their education to begin a career. When the life expectancy was only 40 to 45 years of age and people pursued only one career, this advice made a lot of sense. But today it makes much less sense, since the average life expectancy is over 70 years and many people make three or more major career changes. Increasingly, education is becoming relevant for both youth and adults. To pursue their goals and improve the quality of their lives, both young people and adults need continuing education— education that is geared to the needs of each group.

Work experiences for young people significantly contribute to the development of self-discipline and social maturity. This is not to suggest that children should again be placed in sweatshops for 12 hours a day. But one or two hours of part-time work daily, properly supervised and geared to young people's abilities, is valuable training. Some educators have said that vandalism and destruction of school property would be largely curtailed if students were responsible for the maintenance of school buildings. Maintenance assignments could be assigned, supervised, and graded just like English themes.

The three propositions stated at the beginning of the chapter have been supported by extensive research.

1. Education improves the quality of work. Continuing education is necessary to combat obsolescence. Career obsolescence is a particularly serious problem in technical occupations where new knowledge is expanding rapidly. But the erosion of applicable knowledge and the creation of new information are certain to have an impact on everyone. Continuing education is critical not only in an occupation but also in daily living—for example, in adapting to new developments in medicine, transportation, and consumer products. To perform their jobs skillfully, workers need to constantly learn new information and develop new skills. Continuing education is a necessary part of life for every worker.

2. Work improves the quality of education. Experience has demonstrated that part-time employment does not necessarily

keep students from obtaining a high-quality education. In fact, work experiences of 15 to 20 hours weekly often improve academic performance, especially for students with poor academic records. Work experiences help students set their priorities, schedule their time, organize their activities, and follow a schedule.

3. Both work and education are facilitated by the development of positive work values, such as the moral importance of work, pride in craftsmanship, efficient use of time, and joy in service. Personal initiative makes a good worker as well as a good student. Other characteristics common to productive workers and competent students include diligence, dedication, and perserverance. Feeling a sense of joy in being of service not only contributes to work performance but also motivates people to learn new information and develop new skills. Both workers and students need to develop the kinds of values that will make them more productive and competent.

These three propositions suggest that work and education should be integrated more extensively. Both the individuals and society benefit when students work part time and workers learn part time.

REFERENCES

1. Paul Armer, *Program on Technology and Society—A Final Review* (Cambridge, Mass.: Harvard University Press, 1972).
2. S. B. Zelikoff, "On the Obsolescence and Retraining of Engineering Personnel," *Training and Development Journal*, Vol. 23 (May 1969), pp. 3–15.
3. J. Lukasiewicz, "The Dynamics of Science and Engineering Education," *Engineering Education*. Vol. 61 (1971), pp. 880–882.
4. Gene W. Dalton and Paul H. Thompson, "Accelerating Obsolescence of Older Engineers," *Harvard Business Review* (September–October 1971), pp. 57–67.
5. J. B. Hickam, "Periodic Recertification," *Journal of the American Medical Association*, Vol. 213 (1970), pp. 1651–1657.
6. For a good recent book on career development, see Douglas T. Hall, *Careers in Organizations* (Pacific Palisades, Cal.: Goodyear, 1976).
7. I am grateful to my colleagues Gene W. Dalton and Paul H.

Thompson for sharing their data with me and allowing me to report their results.

8. Dalton and Thompson, *op. cit.*

9. See Jane Addams, *The Spirit of Youth and the City Streets* (New York: Macmillan, 1926), especially pp. 107–138.

10. This survey was conducted and reported by students in a communications class taught by Edwin O. Haroldsen. See "Students Who Work Find Frustration and Satisfaction," *The Daily Universe: Monday Magazine*, Brigham Young University, Vol. 31, No. 93 (January 30, 1978).

11. W. Archie MacGregor, "Part-Time Work—Good or Bad?" *Journal of College Placement*, Vol. 26, No. 3 (February–March 1966), pp. 127–132.

12. Harold B. Baker, "The Working Student and His Grades," *Journal of Educational Research*, Vol. 35 (1941), pp. 28–35.

13. Dennis L. Trueblood, "Effects of Employment on Academic Achievement," *Personnel and Guidance Journal*, Vol. 35 (1957), pp. 112–115.

14. Herbert E. Kaiser and Gerald Bergin, "Shall College Freshmen Work?" *The Journal of College Student Personnel*, Vol. 9 (1968), pp. 384–385.

15. Bert D. Anderson, "The Academic Load of the Employed Student," *The Journal of College Student Personnel*, Vol. 7 (January 1966), pp. 23–26.

16. Joe B. Henry, "Part-Time Employment and Academic Performance of Freshmen," *The Journal of College Student Personnel*, Vol. 8 (July 1967), pp. 257–260.

17. Charles E. McCombs, "What's Wrong with Working?" *Ohio State University Monthly*, September 1962; W. Boyd LeGrande, "The Effects of Holding a Work-Study Job on the Academic Achievement of First-Semester Freshmen at the University of South Carolina," Research Notes No. 9, May 21, 1960; Roland Keene, "Academic Achievement of Part-Time Workers at Southern Illinois University," Student Work Office, Southern Illinois University, December 1964, pp. 1–39; John E. Hay, "How Part-Time Work Affects Academic Performance," *Journal of College Placement*, Vol. 29, No. 4 (April–May 1969), p. 104; Jerry D. Augsburger, "An Analysis of Academic Performance of Working and Nonworking Students on Academic Probation at Northern Illinois University," *The Journal of Student Financial Aid*, Vol. 4, No. 2 (June 1974), pp. 30–39.

18. Anderson, *loc. cit.*, R. E. Silver, "The Effect of Self-Support upon Student Success in Walla Walla College," *Dissertation Abstracts*, Vol. 14 (1954), pp. 1819–1820.

19. Changes in the ACT and SAT scores of high school students are analyzed in *On Further Examination*, published by the College Entrance Examination Board, 1977. See especially pp. 39–41.
20. Defined by Stewart B. Collins, "Types of Programs," in A. S. Knowles and associates, *Handbook of Cooperative Education* (San Francisco: Jossey-Bass, 1971), pp. 29–36.
21. James W. Wilson, "Historical Development," in Knowles and associates, *op. cit.*, pp. 3–17.
22. Wanda Mosback, "Women Graduates of Cooperative Work-Study Programs on the College Level," *Personnel and Guidance Journal*, Vol. 35 (April 1957), pp. 508–511; Evelyn Murray, "Work: A Neglected Resource for Students," *Personnel and Guidance Journal*, Vol. 40 (November 1962), pp. 229–233; Leo F. Smith, "Cooperative Work Programs," *Journal of Higher Education*, Vol. 15 No. 4 (1944), pp. 207–212; Ralph W. Tyler, "Values and Objectives," in Knowles and associates, *op. cit.*, pp. 18–28.

11

JOB ENRICHMENT AND
JOB REDESIGN

The "latest thing" in management during the 1970s was job enrichment and other experiments in restructuring work. Job enrichment programs have been highly praised as the cure for low productivity, job discontent, lack of motivation, and the deterioration in the meaning of work. These programs involved such changes as giving workers the right to inspect their own work, flexible working hours, participation in business decision making, replacing the assembly line with semiautonomous work teams, and offering workers the chance to pursue personal hobbies and crafts after the required work was finished. Management journals are filled with descriptions of the successes and failures of job redesign experiments. Several books have summarized the major experiments in job enrichment. One of the best descriptions of these experiments around the world, especially in Europe and America, is Paul Dickson's *The Future of the Workplace*.[1] A few job enrichment programs will be discussed later, but only briefly. The purpose of this chapter is to examine job enrichment and job redesign as they are related to the work ethic. Four major questions will be discussed:

1. *Did mechanization destroy the work ethic, and will job enrichment restore it?* According to popular myth, the work ethic deteriorated because of the modern factory system of job

specialization and division of labor. Consequently, frustration, alienation, and a loss of personal identity have been attributed to highly specialized jobs. Many think job enrichment is the obvious solution to this problem. But if the diagnosis of the problem is wrong, the solution may also be wrong. Thus this question concerns the effects of job specialization on the meaning of work.

2. *Do all workers want greater job enrichment?* Early research found that the only workers who responded favorably to job enrichment were those who accepted the work ethic. Workers who rejected the middle-class ethic were found to respond negatively to job enrichment, with lower job satisfaction and productivity. Later research has not supported these conclusions. Thus this question asks whether work values influence ("moderate") the effects of job enrichment.

3. *Which redesign strategies enhance work values and which detract?* Some job enrichment programs build commitment, loyalty, initiative, and other values that contribute to the work ethic. Other job enrichment programs focus on leisure activities and work-avoidance strategies. This question concerns the enhancing versus deleterious effects of various job enrichment programs on the development of the work ethic.

4. *What factors in job redesign programs contribute to the development of general work values in addition to specific job attitudes?* Most job changes influence specific job attitudes, but they do not necessarily influence general work values. More variety makes a job more interesting, and flexible work hours reduce traffic problems and other frustrations in traveling to work. These changes create favorable job attitudes, but they do not necessarily enhance the meaning or importance of work. This question examines the factors that contribute to the development of general work values.

JOB SPECIALIZATION VERSUS JOB ENRICHMENT

The job specialization versus job enrichment controversy has had a long history. One of the major developments of the industrial revolution was increased task specialization: complex jobs were divided into separate tasks and assigned to individual workers. Indeed, the history of the industrial revolution was the history of task specialization. One of the earliest descriptions of the advantages of task specialization was Adam Smith's *The Wealth of Nations,* published in 1776. He described how one man could make 20 ordinary pins per day, but ten specialized workers could make 48,000 per day.

The modern factory system existed in America throughout most of the nineteenth century. But highly specialized and efficiently organized jobs did not become widespread until the scientific management movement at the end of the century. Under the leadership of Frederick Winslow Taylor, scientific management significantly changed the practices of management from traditional "handed down" methods to carefully analyzed tasks, methods, and piece-rate incentives.[2]

Through job specialization, a worker becomes more proficient in a narrow job and gives greater attention to the minute elements of the task. Training time is dramatically reduced, since the worker has to master only a small segment of the job. Specialized tools and machines can significantly increase performance. Less time is wasted going from one activity to the next. In many instances specialized tasks do not require highly skilled employees. Specialization also increases management's flexibility in making job assignments and gives workers greater mobility in changing jobs.

Taylor argued that scientific management was in the best interests of both the worker and the company. The worker's primary goal, he said, was high wages—which was particularly true then because of the massive influx of immigrants and generally poor living conditions. The company's goal, he said, was low labor cost—which is equally true today.

A popular myth today holds that job specialization has destroyed the work ethic. Numerous articles in recent management journals have blamed specialized jobs for the loss of meaning in work. Some authors have blamed the assembly line, with its repetitive tasks and loss of freedom to work at a self-determined pace. Other authors have blamed scientific management and its emphasis on time and motion studies, performance standards, efficiency, and piece-rate incentives. Other criticisms are more general, suggesting that the modern factory system deprives workers of their individuality and forces them to perform trivial, meaningless activities. These ideas constitute the central theme of Studs Terkel's bestselling book *Working*. From hundreds of recorded interviews, Terkel paints a scene of mind-numbing violence, alienation, and frustration arising from highly specialized work experiences.[3] The relationship, however, should be questioned: Why should increased efficiency make work less meaningful?

In our "modern" thinking, we have glorified the craftsmanship of the eighteenth-century cobbler, who took a piece of leather and fashioned a boot by himself. We think of him as a master craftsman because he had full responsibility for his labor. Each pair of boots was the product of his efforts, and when he sold them he could proudly say to the buyer, "I made these with my own hands." We also tend to think that every tailor was meticulous, because when he saw a prominent person wearing one of his suits he would point with pride and say, "I made that suit of clothes."

Today's workers do not make an entire pair of shoes or a complete suit. The sewing of even a simple pair of tennis shorts involves the coordinated efforts of more than 50 workers performing separate specialized tasks. How can a seamstress who makes 18 zippers per minute ever be expected to feel pride in her work or a sense of accomplishment? We assume that such repetitive activity is a form of violence to the individual. We long for the good old days of the true craftsman.

Unfortunately, the good old days were not so good. The more we learn about the work life of earlier generations, the more we realize that it was difficult and unpleasant. In the cottage system, or putting-out system, living conditions were not very pleasant and most workers had to supplement their meager incomes with farming and hunting. The work was long and hard and was probably motivated more by survival considerations than by the opportunity to say, "I made that myself.'' Much of the early factory work was done by apprentices who would be considered indentured servants by today's standards. They were not always treated well and sometimes ran away. ''Wanted'' posters promising a reward were advertised for their capture, much as is done for escaped criminals today. Such was the case of Benjamin Franklin, who escaped his apprenticeship and fled from Boston to Philadelphia at the age of 18.

The available evidence does not support the belief that the work ethic, so strong in early America, was sustained by enlarged jobs requiring a lot of skill and variety. Nor is there much reason to believe that task specialization was responsible for destroying the work ethic by creating meaningless, repetitive jobs. The work ethic was a moral belief consistent with societal norms and endorsed by religious principles. It was sustained by a consistent system of social and religious values.

If job specialization has indeed contributed to the deterioration of the work ethic, it is because it has made work *more productive* rather than more alienating. The scientific management movement, with its emphasis on standards, time and motion studies, and task analysis, made the efforts of workers more efficient: workers produced higher outputs with less effort and in a shorter time. At the close of the nineteenth century several businessmen and economists worried about the overabundance of some manufactured goods. Their only solution was to reduce the length of work, even though this seemed inconsistent with social norms about the importance of work. The overabundance of goods and services eliminated the obvious economic necessity of working hard. Material well-being challenged the logical imperative demanding that everyone contribute. Because we can survive today by doing less work, and think some people survive without doing any work at all, we are not as inclined to believe work is important or to teach work values to fellow workers or our children. Early Americans had to work hard to survive and it was logical for them to believe in the moral importance of work. If we had to work hard, we would probably believe in hard work, if for no other reason than to justify our behavior.

If job specialization was not the primary reason for the decline in the work ethic, one must question the value of job enrichment as a cure for negative work attitudes. When a worker's primary interests and rewards are outside the work environment, job enrichment may not lead to more positive work attitudes. The effects of job enrichment depend on the individual's values. If people's primary interests are in leisure activities, job enrichment will not be very beneficial. But people who are interested in benefiting society might gradually change their job attitudes and work values if they were taken off an assembly line and asked to assist with an environmental impact study or an economic education project in the community.

In short, job specialization did not necessarily destroy work values, nor will job enrichment necessarily reestablish the vitality of the work ethic. Workers performing simple repetitive jobs can feel as positive about work as workers performing highly enriched jobs. One of the significant observations that came from the interviews with outstanding workers (Chapters 5 and 6) was that the jobs they performed represented a variety of skill levels. Some outstanding workers were executives and skilled crafts workers with highly enriched jobs. But others performed very simple, repetitive tasks. It was obvious that those workers did not need to have enriched jobs to be productive, work-oriented employees.

Two important conclusions about the effects of job enrichment on work values need to be emphasized. First, even though job enrichment does not by itself restore the work ethic, it can still play an important role in the development of work values. Many of the principles for developing work values (presented in Chapter 8) could involve various forms of job redesign. For example, job enrichment might be involved in the following:

- Changing group norms (by letting the group manage itself).
- Developing a sense of mission (by having employees publish a company newsletter).

227

- Establishing expectations for high-quality performance (by letting employees participate in goal setting).
- Creating accountability for performance (by having supervisors delegate outcomes and letting employees have more authority and responsibility for the results).
- Developing commitment and involvement (by allowing employees to participate in directing the activities of the company).
- Providing performance feedback (by providing more information from the company's internal control system or from customers and clients external to the organization).
- Rewarding effective performance (by offering individual or group incentive plans and profit-sharing programs).

Thus some job redesign programs can be an integral part of a program to develop stronger work values.

The second conclusion is that job redesign strategies should be considered for humanitarian reasons. Even if some job redesign programs do not contribute to the work ethic, there may be other good reasons for them. Work has an enormous impact on the quality of life, and improving a worker's job can improve the quality of his or her life even if it does not increase productivity or enhance work values.

PERSONAL VALUES AND JOB ENRICHMENT

Early descriptions of job enrichment lauded it as a valuable motivational technique. A worker performing an enriched job was expected to feel increased motivation, which would result in greater satisfaction and productivity. Added motivation would compensate for any inefficiencies caused by the elimination of job specialization. No restrictions were placed on this new strategy of motivation. All workers were expected to respond favorably to an enriched job. It was assumed that all workers wanted more variety, greater autonomy, and increased responsibility.

In recent years, however, this assumption has been challenged. Investigations into how workers respond to various job characteristics revealed that some workers did not want job enrichment. The problem is determining which workers will respond favorably to job enrichment and which will not. How can a manager predict an employee's response to changes in the job? What individual variables moderate (influence) the effects of job enrichment on a worker's behavior?

Alienated Workers.   One of the earliest studies showing that some workers disliked enriched jobs was the work of Arthur Turner and Paul Lawrence in the early 1960s.[4] This study examined the influence of six job characteristics on job satisfaction and attendance: (1) variety, (2) autonomy, (3) required interaction, (4) optional interaction, (5) knowledge and skill required, and (6) responsibility. The initial hypothesis was that workers who had more favorable job characteristics would also have more favorable attitudes and better attendance. Turner and Lawrence collected data from 470 workers in 11 industries working on 47 different jobs. Each of the jobs was scored on the six attributes from field observations and interviews. Since the six characteristics were highly correlated, they were combined into one measure, called the Requisite Task Attribute Index (or RTA Index). Jobs with a high RTA Index were highly enriched jobs with a lot of variety, autonomy, interaction, skill, and responsibility.

Turner and Lawrence expected to find the RTA Index positively associated with satisfaction and attendance. Their hypothesis was only partially confirmed, however. Employees with high RTA scores had a better attendance record. But job satisfaction was not positively related to job level for all workers. The relationship held true only when the sample was limited to workers from factories in small rural towns. Workers in urban areas reported less satisfaction when their jobs were high on the RTA Index.

Why were city workers dissatisfied with supposedly desirable job characteristics, such as variety, and satisfied with such undesirable attributes as repetitiveness? Turner and Lawrence suggested that in large cities, where social cultures are extremely heterogenous, workers are more likely to feel anomie and to be alienated from group norms and middle-class social values. Thus they do not respond positively to more challenging and demanding attributes of high-level jobs.

The conclusions of Turner and Lawrence were supported by the investigations of Charles Hulin and Milton Blood.[5] They reviewed numerous studies of job enrichment and concluded that the results were ambiguous: job enrichment programs produced both increases and decreases in job satisfaction. They criticized most of the studies for failing to consider individual differences and for generalizing beyond the unique population studied. They claimed that individual values influenced the effects of job enrichment on behavior.

To resolve the contradictions, Hulin and Blood used a personal value—alienation from versus acceptance of middle-class values. They suggested that workers who are alienated from the middle-class norms of society do not want enriched jobs and respond to enrichment programs with decreased job satisfaction. However, workers who accept middle-class values desire more enriched jobs and respond with increased job satisfaction and motivation.

According to Hulin and Blood, there should be a positive enrichment–satisfaction relationship for workers who accept the middle-class work ethic.[6] These workers believe in the dignity and honor of work and supposedly desire more autonomy, responsibility, and variety in their jobs. However, the enrichment–satisfaction relationship should be negative for alienated workers who reject middle-class work values and prefer nonwork interests. Alienated workers supposedly dislike autonomy, responsibility, and variety and are dissatisfied when their jobs are enriched. ("Just let me put in my eight hours and then forget about work.")

Moderator Variables.   Numerous other research studies have examined whether work values or other individual differences influence the enrichment–satisfaction relationship. Later studies have focused on three types of moderator variables: urban versus rural location, the Protestant work ethic, and growth need strength.[7]

230

Most of the recent studies have not found any differences in the enrichment–satisfaction relationship among people who work in urban or rural locations. Job satisfaction is positively correlated with job level among workers in both locations. Thus urban versus rural location is not a significant moderator of the effects of job enrichment today, although it might have been several years ago. Modern transportation and communication systems, combined with extensive job mobility, have made urban and rural cultures increasingly similar.

The Protestant work ethic has also been proposed as a moderating variable of the enrichment–satisfaction relationship. People who believe work is important and who take pride in their work are expected to respond favorably to job enrichment—that is, to want important jobs where they can display initiative and dedication. In contrast, people who dislike work are expected to dislike having their jobs enriched. While this hypothesis seems reasonable, the opposite relationship has also been argued from much the same perspective. People with strong work values should be able to find greater than average satisfaction in performing menial, repetitive tasks, since they have more perseverance and are better able to provide their own meaning and contentment.

Neither hypothesis is supported well by the research evidence. Workers with enriched jobs tend to report higher satisfaction regardless of their work values. Both job enrichment and work values are positively related to job satisfaction. This suggests that if managers want to increase job satisfaction, they should both enrich the job and teach work values.

The third proposed moderator of the enrichment–satisfaction relationship is growth need strength. This variable refers to a person's desire for a job with opportunities to be creative and innovative, to make a lot of decisions, to control his or her own time, to have a lot of variety, and to use a number of personal skills (as opposed to a job with good pay, pleasant people to work with, vocational security, and a friendly supervisor). The research suggests that growth need strength is perhaps the best moderator of the enrichment–satisfaction relationship. The reason is quite obvious: people who are

231

interested in personal development should respond favorably to job enrichment, since most job enrichment programs provide growth opportunities. The only way to obtain a better moderator variable is to ask the worker directly: "How enriched would you like your job to be and what changes should be made?" The value of such an approach has been demonstrated in a study that asked workers how much responsibility and autonomy they wanted. This direct question was the best predictor of the effects of job enrichment on satisfaction.[8]

JOB CHARACTERISTICS MODEL

The best conceptual framework for examining the effects of job enrichment on work attitudes and behavior is the Job Characteristics Model.[9] This model explains the psychological impact of various job characteristics and predicts what effects these psychological states will have on work attitudes and performance. The usefulness of various job enrichment programs can be predicted from the model by analyzing how they change the core dimensions of a job and thereby influence the behavior of the worker. Questionnaires have been developed to measure each concept in the model. With these instruments, the model has been tested in numerous companies. The results indicate that the interactions specified in the model are generally correct, even though the measures are psychological perceptions rather than precise physical measures. The major outline of this model is shown in Figure 11.1.

Work Outcomes.   The model is explained best by starting at the outcome end and working backward. There are four important outcomes desired from each worker:

Figure 11.1. The Job Characteristics Model.

232

Figure 11.2. Relationship between psychological states
and work outcomes.

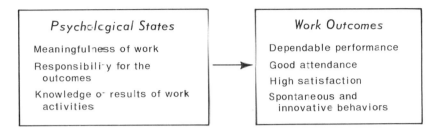

Psychological States	*Work Outcomes*
Meaningfulness of work	Dependable performance
Responsibility for the outcomes	Good attendance
	High satisfaction
Knowledge of results of work activities	Spontaneous and innovative behaviors

1. Dependable performance—high quantity and quality of work.
2. Good attendance—low absenteeism and low tardiness.
3. High satisfaction with work—positive feelings about the job, the company, and the treatment received at work.
4. Spontaneous and innovative behaviors—doing more than is called for in one's formal job description, such as showing initiative, making creative suggestions, cooperating with fellow workers, pursuing self-development and training, fostering a favorable public image, and performing acts that protect the physical and financial security of the company. These acts seem to be what many supervisors have in mind when they talk about an employee's "attitude." Showing a good attitude is important, they feel, even if they have a hard time defining what it means.[10]

These four outcomes are clearly in the organization's best interests: an organization that can elicit such behavior from its members will be more effective than an organization that cannot. Generally, these outcomes are also in the individual's best interests.

Psychological States. The desired work outcomes result from three psychological states, as shown in Figure 11.2. These three states represent the motivating force behind all activity (including nonwork activity, such as practicing a golf swing at a driving range).

233

Figure 11.3. Relationship between core job dimensions and psychological states.

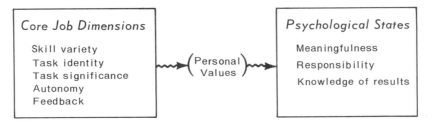

1. Meaningful—the activity must have a purpose and must be perceived as important and worthwhile by the employee.
2. Responsibility—employees must believe that they are personally accountable for results and that their efforts will influence the outcome.
3. Knowledge of results—employees need systematic and timely information about how well they are performing so they can make corrective adjustments if necessary.

Core Job Dimensions.   The three psychological states are created by five core job dimensions, as shown in Figure 11.3. The relationships between the core dimensions and the psychological states are moderated by the personal values of the worker (as indicated by the ragged arrows). The dimensions include:

1. Skill variety—the degree to which a job allows a worker to develop and use his or her skills and to avoid the monotony of performing the same task repeatedly.
2. Task identity—the degree to which a task consists of a whole or complete unit of work as opposed to a small, specialized, repetitive act.
3. Task significance—the degree to which a task has a significant impact on the organization, the community, or the lives of other people.
4. Autonomy—the degree to which a worker is free of the direct influence of a supervisor and has discretion in

scheduling his or her work and deciding how it will be done.

5. Feedback—the degree to which a worker obtains evaluative information on performance in the normal course of doing his or her job.

According to the model, skill variety, task identity, and task significance contribute to the meaningfulness of a job. Greater autonomy is expected to develop a greater feeling of personal responsibility. Feedback provides knowledge of results. The best form of feedback is usually from the job itself rather than from a supervisor. Letting workers know how well they produce is like letting chefs taste what they cook.

Job Redesign Concepts.   Numerous job enrichment programs have been proposed to establish optimal levels of each core job dimension, as shown in Figure 11.4. The following five concepts are recommended as guides to managers in redesigning jobs:

1. Combining tasks to eliminate highly specialized jobs and to make larger work modules.
2. Forming natural work units—teams of workers—in which each person feels a part of the team and certain jobs can be rotated among team members.
3. Establishing client relationships so workers know who uses the product or service they produce and how the client feels about their work.

Figure 11.4. Relationship between job redesign concepts and core job dimensions.

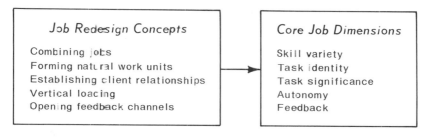

235

4. Giving workers greater authority and discretion by allowing them to perform functions previously reserved for higher levels of management (called vertical loading).
5. Opening feedback channels so that information about the quality of performance goes directly to the employee performing the job.

The Job Characteristics Model recognizes that job enrichment may not suit all workers. "Not everyone is able to become internally motivated in his work, even when the motivating potential of a job is very high indeed."[11]

Research studies have shown that growth need strength (GNS) influences the relationship between the core dimensions and the psychological states. For example, the moderating effects of GNS were tested in a study of 658 workers employed on 62 different jobs in 7 organizations.[12] The top fourth of these employees with the highest growth need strength were compared with the bottom fourth regarding the effects of the core dimensions on the psychological states. The results showed that the correlations were stronger for the high-GNS group than for the low-GNS group. For example, the correlation between skill variety and meaningfulness was .57 for the high-GNS group and .23 for the low-GNS group. This means that skill variety contributes significantly to the meaning of the task for people with strong growth needs but has only a small influence on meaningfulness for people with low growth needs.

Many other personal values influence work attitudes and behavior. These values can be examined by looking more closely at the concepts of meaningfulness and responsibility.

Meaningfulness. The meaningfulness of an activity depends on a person's value system. Something is meaningful to the extent that it is consistent with a framework of values in which certain actions or conditions are considered desirable and good. Acts are meaningful if they are perceived as a step in the direction of some larger and more enduring end state. As discussed in Chapter 2, work activities can be valued for many reasons, on either a temporary or general basis. But regardless of the reason, meaningfulness is determined by the person's value system.

To illustrate, preparing a lecture on the history of the early labor movement could be meaningful to you for many reasons: it increases your understanding of the past; it makes you a more knowledgeable scholar; it helps you become an excellent teacher; it contributes to the education of students; or it gives you valuable information to use in consulting with labor organizations. But if learning about the early labor movement is not consistent with your value system, then studying the life of Samuel Gompers will seem like a waste of time.

The same principle applies to assembly-line work. Sewing pockets inside the waistbands of tennis shorts is a meaningful activity if you perceive it as a necessary step in the production of a useful product and if you believe the production process contributes to the economic betterment of the company and the community. Furthermore, the work could be meaningful because the wages earned are necessary for other goals in life, such as buying your own home, paying for the educational expenses of a spouse or child, or simply supporting yourself. But you might perceive the same activity as meaningless if you thought tennis shorts were a worthless product consumed by a self-indulgent group of idlers in society.

In the Job Characteristics Model, meaningfulness of work refers to the degree to which the employee experiences his or her job as valuable and worthwhile. It is measured by four items, such as "The work I do on this job is very meaningful to me," and "Most of the things I have to do on this job seem useless or trivial." Employees are left to define "meaningful," "useless," and "trivial" for themselves.

The Job Characteristics Model postulates that meaningfulness is created by skill variety, task identity, and task significance. Whether this is true or not depends on the worker's values. A job with high skill and task identity is not necessarily meaningful. This is sometimes the case with activities that produce no visible product. Many former schoolteachers report that teaching became meaningless for them even though they used a variety of skills and performed a "whole" task. Housework and child care also provide numerous opportunities for skill variety and task identity. Some mothers think these activities are meaningful and fulfilling while other mothers feel trapped in a frustrating routine of trivia and endless demands.

In summary, even though the content of the job is an important element in determining its meaningfulness, meaning depends primarily on personal values. No job, highly enriched or specialized, has independent meaning. It acquires meaning through its association with a personal value system that says certain actions or conditions are desirable and good.

Responsibility. In the Job Characteristics Model, job responsibility is defined rather narrowly. It refers to the degree to which the employee feels personally accountable for the results of the work he or she does. This variable is measured by such items as "I feel a very high degree of *personal* responsibility for the work I do on this job," and "Whether or not this job gets done right is clearly *my* responsibility." The model claims that greater autonomy will create greater responsibility. In many instances, this is true. When employees are free to decide what to do and are allowed to do it alone, they usually feel personally responsible for the outcome—*if* it gets done. Autonomy is no guarantee of action. Workers not only need to feel accountable for the result; they also need to feel that the task is meaningful and they must be motivated to do it well.

A major problem with defining responsibility as accountability for a specific activity is that the definition does not encompass the broader values of organizational commitment, company loyalty, personal initiative, and personal control. When supervisors talk about responsibility, they are usually referring to these broader values. To most supervisors, "responsible" employees do more than feel like their efforts determine the success or failure of the task. "Responsible" employees accept personal responsibility for the success or failure of the company. "Responsible" employees also have the initiative and self-discipline to do all they can to accomplish an assigned task.

This form of responsibility is not developed by greater autonomy. The issue is similar to the development of social responsibility in children (reported in Chapter 7). For many years it was assumed that independent, creative, freethinking children were the product of permissive parents. Not until overwhelming evidence indicated otherwise did we come to understand the need for discipline, self-control, and firm parental expectations.

A similar caution ought to be stated with respect to job enrichment. More autonomy may not produce "responsible" employees. Removing controls, eliminating time schedules, taking away procedures manuals, and reducing the amount of supervisory observation will not necessarily increase satisfaction, performance, attendance, or motivation. Giving employees greater autonomy is appropriate as the employees develop better work values—that is, as they recognize the importance of their work to themselves, the company, and society, and as they develop a commitment to doing their jobs well. As noted in Chapter 8, greater autonomy plays a significant role in the development of work values, but by itself it is more likely to lead to greater disinterest in work than commitment to it.

WORKER PARTICIPATION IN JOB REDESIGN

The research evidence indicates that it is generally unwise to use a crude measure such as urban-rural background to estimate how employees will respond to job enrichment. Both urban and rural workers respond about the same. Work values are also poor indicators of how a worker will respond to a job enrichment program. Instead, a direct assessment of the worker's desires is preferable. Employees ought to be involved in any attempt to redesign their jobs.

This approach is obviously simplistic and lacks the elegance of other moderator variable explanations. But what is the value of a sophisticated theory if it does not explain any better? The desire for an enriched job is influenced not by a single set of causal variables, but by a complex combination of situational and/or personality variables.

Who wants an enriched job? The evidence suggests that almost all workers want more variety, autonomy, feedback, and task identity. After conducting 19 major job enrichment studies at AT&T, researchers reported that they did not find a single job that was already too enriched.[13] All workers identified at least some change, large or small, desired in their jobs. My own interviews with workers indicated that most people want more job enrichment. But this condition is not universally true. Some workers claim their jobs are too enriched, especially top-level managers, research scientists and engineers, and some project directors who work independently.

The complexity of trying to discover who wants and will respond favorably to job enrichment is illustrated by the comments of different workers.

> "I've got too many things to worry about at home. I just don't need any more responsibility here."

This comment was made by a 35-year-old homemaker and mother of three children. She was quite content to perform a very routine job, since it seemed to add stability to her life.

> "My job will probably be phased out in five years from now. If I don't learn how to do other things I probably won't have a job before too long."

This comment was made by a 40-year-old man whose desire for an enriched job was motivated by economic security. He was interested in any form of job enrichment or job rotation that would help him secure a new job.

> "I've been doing the same thing for twenty years. Now that I've put my kids through college I'm thinking of going back myself. I'm looking for a new challenge."

"When I read this stuff on job enrichment it makes me shake my head. My job is already too enriched for me or anyone else. Every day I'm being called on to make decisions I'm not prepared to make. I don't have enough time and I've got too many things to do. It's frustrating to be spread so thin."

These comments were made by two middle-aged male professionals working in the same work group. The differences in their attitudes cannot be attributed to differences in their jobs, since the jobs were essentially identical.

"They tried to get us to do different jobs, but no one liked it except _____. We couldn't get near as much done that way. This way is lots better. My job is coating and I can do it just about twice as fast as anyone else. I don't think I could ever learn to do other people's jobs as fast as them. We like it the way it is now."

This comment was made by a 65-year-old woman who worked with eight other women in a small electronics manufacturing plant. The extremely repetitious nature of the tasks, the rural location of the company, and the generally strong work-oriented attitudes of these women would lead some to conclude that here was an ideal opportunity to reap the benefits of job enrichment. But a combination of vertical and horizontal enrichment had been tried earlier at the company and had not succeeded. The women were happier with efficient, specialized jobs than with inefficient, enriched jobs.

The New Ethic.   Several authors have suggested that a new ethic has developed in America, particularly among young adults, which stresses autonomy, participation, the pursuit of money, greater mobility within and between organizations, and less personal involvement or commitment.[14] This new ethic seems to call for greater job enrichment and exhorts everyone to aspire to an enriched job simply for the sake of having an enriched job. Autonomy and participation seem to be the most

241

important elements of enrichment. The new ethic suggests that employees should be supervised more indirectly and should participate more democratically in organizational decision making, especially in their own work group. In earlier decades job enrichment was primarily a means to an end—highly work-oriented employees desired enriched jobs because added responsibility, autonomy, and participation were necessary to achieve vocational success and greater control over their lives. With the new ethic, however, job enrichment is an end in itself.

One implication of this new ethic is that satisfaction should increase with greater job enrichment, but not performance. The productivity of employees with enriched jobs should not necessarily be any greater than that of employees with unenriched jobs. This is because the purpose of holding an enriched job is simply to "have" it, not to "use" it. There is some question, however, about how generally accepted the new ethic is. Most employees who want an enriched job still desire it to achieve success and greater self-determination.

ASSESSING JOB REDESIGN

There are five important criteria to be considered in deciding whether to redesign a job and in evaluating the results of a change.

1. *Job satisfaction.* Which job design contributes most to job satisfaction? Some job arrangements are superior to others because they help the work flow more smoothly, eliminate points of conflict between workers or departments, require less effort, improve working conditions, and make life more comfortable. The argument that most job enrichment programs increase satisfaction is the major justification used by behavioral scientists to advocate greater job redesign. Managers do not always think job satisfaction is the most important consideration in job enrichment, although most agree that positive attitudes are important from a humanitarian point of view.

2. *Productivity.* Which job design produces the greatest quantity and quality of performance? The important point to

remember here is that many jobs have intentionally been highly specialized to increase productivity. If job enrichment reduces the degree of specialization it might make such jobs less productive. Therefore, job redesign projects should take into account the probable effects on productivity. Occasionally, productivity is not materially reduced by greater enrichment; but managers ought to think carefully about the amount of productivity they are willing to sacrifice to gain other rewards.

Specialization usually increases productivity. But productivity can also be increased by enrichment. The most frequently stated argument for job enrichment is that it increases employee motivation. Carefully designed jobs which are so highly specialized that workers refuse to do them are not very productive. Overspecialization of jobs was blamed for the labor problems at the General Motors assembly plant in Lordstown, Ohio in 1972. This new plant was an engineering showplace, but many new workers refused to perform the same task 101.6 times each hour. It is obvious that some jobs can be too specialized and need to be enriched. Productivity can also be increased through enrichment when the need for close coordination and control is reduced and fewer supervisors are required.

3. *Attendance.* Which job design reduces absenteeism, tardiness, and turnover? Most job redesign programs that increase job satisfaction also improve attendance, since these variables are related. One particular change, flextime, virtually eliminates tardiness, since it allows workers to set their own hours, within certain constraints. Companies which have measured the financial costs of absenteeism, tardiness, and turnover have shown how important good attendance is—the costs of absenteeism and turnover are staggering.

4. *Quality of life.* Which job design contributes most to the long-term development of workers? This criterion encompasses numerous aspects of a person's life, including developing new skills and talents, improving the quality of family and social relationships, becoming involved in civic affairs, and maintaining good physical and emotional health.

5. *Internal work motivation.* Which job design will stimu-

late the development of work values? Some job enrichment projects promote organizational commitment, pride in craftsmanship, and personal initiative. Other projects focus on nonwork activities or ways to avoid work. The following discussion examines the effects of various job enrichment projects on the development of work values.

Job Enrichment Projects. The principles involved in teaching work values were presented in Chapter 8. These principles included:

Creating a favorable organizational climate.
Developing explicit behavioral expectations.
Providing a good role model.
Teaching by induction.
Carefully selecting and delegating task assignments.
Providing continuous feedback.
Rewarding appropriate behavior.
Encouraging personal growth and development.

Job enrichment projects that foster these eight principles contribute to the development of work values. Projects that focus on leisure activities and work-avoidance strategies tend to weaken the development of the work ethic.[15]

1. *Autonomous work teams.* Several companies have eliminated the traditional assembly line and changed to a production system based on autonomous work teams. The two most widely known experiments in autonomous work teams are the Swedish car companies Volvo and SAAB. Autonomous work teams consist of small groups of workers who are responsible for performing a set of jobs. The groups are usually directed by their own informal leadership rather than through a layer of supervisors. Members of each team are free to rotate jobs as they choose. Someone might perform the same repetitive job day after day, while someone else might shift from one job to another or even build a complete unit alone. Some groups handle their own personnel functions, hiring new people, evaluating each other's performance, and deciding about each member's pay increase.

Autonomous work teams are a radical departure from the traditional assembly line. Some workers do not like to work in such teams, and serious problems, such as invidious forms of racial discrimination, have occasionally been observed. But most of the evidence suggests that autonomous work teams contribute to the satisfaction, productivity, and attendance of members and promote the development of work values.

2. *Job enlargement.* Jobs can be redesigned in many ways to provide more variety, responsibility, and autonomy. A job can be enlarged by adding tasks from other jobs at the same organizational level (called horizontal enrichment) or by adding elements from jobs at higher or lower organizational levels (called vertical enrichment). Most of the studies in job enrichment have examined these two forms of job enlargement. By itself, job enlargement probably has a small influence on the development of work values. But most job enlargement changes carry with them implicit expectations about good performance, commitment to one's job, loyalty to the group or company, and personal responsibility to produce a high-quality product. Thus job enrichment projects can, and frequently do, contribute to the development of work values.

3. *Membership on the board of directors.* Many companies have placed production workers on the board of directors. These people are elected by the workforce to represent the workers' interests. In many European companies, this practice has been mandated by federal law. In Sweden, for example, a law passed in 1973 requires all corporations with more than 100 people on the payroll to have worker representatives on their board. West German companies adopted this practice many years ago to minimize labor disputes. It seems to be effective, since the number of lost days due to strikes has been reduced. Placing production workers on the board of directors is a useful way to obtain greater information about worker interests. But it probably does little to strengthen the work values of either the representatives or the people they represent.

The following job redesign programs, which alter the amount of time a worker spends on the job, tend to inhibit the development of strong work values. Their deleterious effects on the work ethic are probably quite small, and other benefits usually override this concern. Even so, it is useful to consider their effects on the meaning and importance of work.

4. *Flextime*. Flextime is a modification in the normal hours of work. Some companies have allowed workers to start and quit whenever they want, subject to certain constraints. For example, one company set the following conditions: each employee had to work 40 hours a week, but not more than 10 hours in any one day; everyone had to be at work during the core hours, between 10:00 A.M. and 2:00 P.M. As long as they followed these rules, employees were free to set their own work hours, which did not have to be the same each day. Tardiness was virtually eliminated and traffic problems were reduced. There is no evidence about the effect of flextime on self-discipline, personal initiative, or workmanship, but there is little reason to expect it to be positive.

5. *Job sharing*. Job sharing and work sharing are old ideas, dating back to the days when two workers shared the same job on different 12-hour shifts. In the modern form of job sharing, two people share one 8-hour job by working part time. This arrangement is convenient for people who do not want to work full time because of family or health considerations. At one university, two women filled a librarian's job. Neither was able to work full time and the library could not find a qualified replacement. The women arranged their own hours, divided the pay, and shared responsibility for the job. The only problem was the benefits. To receive full benefits, each woman had to contribute part of the school's cost. The women liked the arrangement and the work got done. Many companies could attract more women into the workforce with such a plan, but it will not do much to strengthen work values.

6. *Leaves of absence*. Sabbaticals have been popular among college professors for many years. But only recently have companies allowed managers to take time off from work. Executives who go on leave may or may not be paid their full salaries while they are away, depending on the remuneration they receive from other sources. The sabbaticals are used for many purposes. Some managers and engineers return to

school, either as students or as visiting faculty members. Other managers become involved in social improvement projects, such as urban renewal, Indian tribal council projects, and business roundtables. Finally, some managers are given time off (one proposal is six months' leave for every 14 years of service) to combine travel, study, vacation, and visits to other companies for the purpose of intellectual stimulation and emotional rejuvenation. The value of these leaves depends on the individual manager. But regardless of the cost-benefit considerations, sabbaticals will probably not strengthen work values.

7. *Crafts programs.* Participating in hobbies and crafts at work is a bit unusual. But when the employees of one company were asked how they wanted to change their working conditions, they requested a place to learn new hobbies after they completed their assigned jobs. Many employees, when given the incentive of time to pursue a hobby, were able to complete their regular jobs in five or six hours. The employees and management agreed that workers had to remain at the plant during the full eight-hour shift, even if the work was finished. The company provided a separate room for working on hobbies and crafts. The employees paid for their own instruction or taught each other. Two of the most popular hobbies were leatherworking and woodworking. The program was strictly voluntary, and employees had the options of hurrying through their work and going to the hobby shop, hurrying through their work and sitting idle, or not hurrying through their work. Although such a project may be popular with employees, it does little to strengthen work values. The situational pressures are not to do outstanding work but to hurry through a job in order to have more leisure time. In the long run, projects of this kind will most likely reduce the commitment to high-quality work.

GENERAL VALUES VERSUS SPECIFIC ATTITUDES

Some job enrichment programs have been shown to create favorable job attitudes—employees like the changes and are more satisfied with their specific jobs. There is also evidence suggesting that some job enrichment programs have created general work values—employees are more reliable and feel a stronger motivation to perform their jobs. However, all job enrichment programs do necessarily foster general work values, even though they create positive attitudes about a specific job.

To illustrate, a company manufacturing air conditioners attempted to enrich the jobs of workers by increasing the number of tasks each person performed and telling workers more about the product. The assembly line was eliminated and each worker performed various tasks at his or her work station before the unit moved to the next work station. The company also attempted to stimulate responsibility and strengthen the meaning of work by having groups of workers visit places where the air conditioners had been installed and then serve as representatives for potential buyers.

The program seemed to significantly change many of the employees' attitudes about the value of the work they performed. One employee reported that the program helped him realize that the tubes he bent were necessary to make air conditioners to cool people's homes and make them more comfortable. He also learned that if the coils were not made correctly, the air conditioners would not function properly. But the important question here is whether these specific attitudes will develop into more general values about the importance of work and pride in craftsmanship. Will the association of "good coils create comfort" generalize to "good work contributes to quality of life for myself and others"? Likewise, will the idea that good coils avoid defects generalize to the belief that high-quality craftsmanship is a benefit to society and something that ought to be done?

Research on the development of moral behavior suggests several answers to the above questions. One early study attempted to determine whether honesty was a generalizable personality trait, like IQ, or whether it was determined by the situation.[16] In the study, 7,000 children between the ages of 8 and 16 were observed as they worked on several games and

248

puzzles designed to test their honesty. For example, one test involved a "planted dime." Each child was given a box containing a dime and other items. The dime was supposed to be used in one of the puzzles. After the boxes were returned, a check was made to determine which children had "stolen" the dime.

The most significant conclusion of this study, a conclusion which had a major impact on later research, was that honesty was not a generalizable personality trait. The authors stated that any correlation between honesty in one test and honesty in another test was due to similarities in the situations and not to a consistent personality trait.

More recently, however, the original data have been reanalyzed by Roger Burton, who concluded that for some people honesty is a general and consistent personality trait but for other people honesty depends on the situation.[17] Burton attributed the difference to two characteristics in the child's moral training. The first characteristic was the degree of consistency in reinforcing honesty and punishing dishonesty. Honesty develops best as a general moral trait when parents and teachers are consistent in rewarding honest behaviors and punishing dishonesty. The second characteristic was the degree of consistency in defining honest behavior and situations that call for honest responses. Thus, if parents consistently reward and encourage honesty and if they define honest and dishonest behaviors, children will develop a general trait of honesty. If parents simply punish or reward moral behavior without giving it a label or explaining a principle, and if their standards of honesty are inconsistent, then children's behavior will also be inconsistent. This research on honesty helps to explain how job redesign programs can be implemented to facilitate the development of general work values. Work values need to be defined as general values and consistently rewarded. This process requires a patient and persistent dose of induction, as explained in Chapter 8. Workers need to see that their efforts have significance beyond the specific item being produced. Bending air conditioner coils contributes to the comfort of people and the good of society, and so do a lot of other activities required in making air conditioners. Furthermore, making cars, baking bread, selling shoes, delivering mail, and many other forms of work also contribute to the comfort of people, the betterment of society, personal self-esteem, eternal salvation, or whatever. Carelessly made coils do not just mean defective air conditioners; they are also indicative of sloppy work habits that result in massive waste and inefficiency.

In short, the benefits of job enrichment programs may not extend beyond the specific situation unless efforts are made to help workers generalize from their individual jobs to the meaning of work as a whole. That is, not only does a specific job have value in contributing to people's comfort, but work itself also has value for various reasons. Diligence and effort are morally good and contribute to the betterment of society.

REFERENCES

1. Paul Dickson, *The Future of the Work Place* (New York: Weybright and Talley, 1975).
2. Taylor's major publications are *The Principles of Scientific Management* (New York: Harper & Brothers, 1911) and *Shop Management* (New York: Harper & Brothers, 1911). For an excellent description of the development of the factory system, see Daniel Nelson, *Managers and Workers* (Madison: University of Wisconsin Press, 1975).
3. Studs Terkel, *Working* (New York: Avon Books, 1972). See also reference 14 below.
4. Arthur Turner and Paul Lawrence. *Industrial Jobs and the Worker: An Investigation of Response to Task Attributes* (Boston: Graduate School of Business Administration, Harvard University, 1965).
5. Charles L. Hulin and Milton R. Blood, "Job Enlargement, Individual Differences, and Worker Responses," *Psychological Bulletin,* Vol. 69 No. 1 (1968), pp. 41–55.
6. Milton R. Blood and Charles L. Hulin, "Alienation, Environmental Characteristics, and Worker Responses," *Journal of Applied Psychology,* Vol. 51 (1967), pp. 284–290.
7. These studies are reviewed in J. Kenneth White, "Individual Differences and the Job Quality–Worker Response Relationship: Review, Comments, and Integration," *Academy of Management Review,* Vol. 3 (1978), pp. 267–279.

8. David C. Cherrington and J. Lynn England, "The Desire for an Enriched Job as a Moderator of the Enrichment–Satisfaction Relationship," *Organizational Behavior and Human Performance*, Vol. 25 (February 1980) pp. 139–159.

9. This section is a summary and adaptation of the Job Characteristics Model which is presented in the following publications: J. Richard Hackman and Greg R. Oldham, "The Job Diagnostic Survey: An Instrument for the Diagnosis of Jobs and the Evaluation of Job Redesign Projects" (Technical Report No. 4, Yale University, School of Organization and Management, 1974) J. Richard Hackman and Greg R. Oldham, "Motivation Through the Design of Work: Test of a Theory," *Organizational Behavior and Human Performance*, Vol. 16 (1976), pp. 250–279; J. Richard Hackman, Greg R. Oldham, Robert Janson, and Kenneth Purdy, "A New Strategy for Job Enrichment," *California Management Review*, Vol. 17 (Summer 1975), pp. 57–71; and Greg R. Oldham, "Job Characteristics and Internal Motivation: The Moderating Effect of Interpersonal and Individual Variables," *Human Relations*, Vol. 29, No. 6 (1976), pp. 559–569.

10. According to the Job Characteristics Model, the fourth outcome is "internal work motivation." Since this is really a personal value, I have replaced it with a more general work outcome that has been carefully described in the literature. See Daniel Katz and Robert Kahn, *The Social Psychology of Organizations* (New York: John Wiley and Sons, 1965), chap. 12.

11. Hackman *et al.*, "A New Strategy for Job Enrichment," *op. cit.*, p. 60.

12. Hackman and Oldham, "Motivation Through the Design of Work: Test of a Theory," *op. cit.*

13. Robert N. Ford, "Job Enrichment Lessons from AT&T," *Harvard Business Review* (January-February 1973), pp. 96–106.

14. See, for example, Alan Gartner and Frank Riessman, "Is There a Work Ethic?" *American Journal of Orthopsychiatry*, Vol. 44 (1974), pp. 653–657; James F. Murphy, "The Future of Time, Work, and Leisure," *Parks and Recreation*, Vol. 8 (November 1973), pp. 25–26; Erwin R. Smarr and Philip J. Escoll, "Humanism and the American Work Ethic," *Today's Education*, Vol. 63 (January–February, 1975), pp. 83–85.

15. Most of the job redesign experiments mentioned in this section are discussed more fully in Paul Dickson, *op. cit.*; Edward M. Glaser, *Productivity Gains Through Worklife Improvements* (New York: Harcourt Brace Jovanovich, 1976); Waino W. Suojanen, Gary L. Swallow, Mackey J. McDonald, and W. William Suojanen, *Perspectives on Job Enrichment and Productivity* (Atlanta: School of Business Administration, Georgia State University, 1975).

251

16. Hugh Hartshorne and Mark A. May, *Studies in Deceit,* Vol. 1 (New York: Macmillan, 1928).

17. Roger V. Burton, ''Generality of Honesty Reconsidered,'' *Psychological Review,* Vol. 70, No. 6 (1963), pp. 481–499.

THE WORKAHOLIC
AND LEISURE

The preceding chapters have examined the meaning of work and have proposed ways to increase its importance. The survey described in Chapter 4 indicated that most workers believe it is important to do a good job and to have pride in their work. To some extent, they also believe in the moral importance of work—in having a job, being productive, and making a social contribution. But the evidence indicates that the vitality of the traditional work ethic is declining. The moral importance of work is not endorsed as strongly as the importance of pride in craftsmanship. Especially troublesome are the data indicating significant differences in the values of different age groups: young workers are not as work-oriented as older workers. As a group, they do not accept the traditional work ethic as wholeheartedly as older workers. This difference is partly due to a failure to teach work values to young people. The work ethic has not been advocated as frequently or as enthusiastically in recent years as it has in earlier times.

The failure to inculcate the work ethic was regarded in earlier chapters as a serious social failure. Dignity in labor, pride in craftsmanship, and personal responsibility are desirable values for all workers, and principles for developing them were discussed in Chapters 7 and 8. The justification for this stand was defended in part in Chapter 6—people who espouse the work ethic tend to be happier and more productive.

Previous chapters have argued that the best interests of the individual, the organization, and society are furthered by strengthening the meaning and importance of work. The work ethic was advocated as a general social norm where social pressures and personal self-esteem are, in part, related to an individual's work role. The purpose of this chapter is to qualify the earlier advice by suggesting certain limitations and placing the issue in a broader context of the quality of life.

How busy is a diligent person? He or she is probably quite busy. But this is not a useful question to ask, because it assumes that a certain degree of busyness is optimal. The work ethic in early America did not entail a particular pace of activity so much as an attitude about the importance of work. If the work ethic is to be relevant today, it cannot focus on a state of busyness, but rather on a value of work derived from a broader meaning of life. Focusing on a state of busyness creates a compulsion to work wherein work is neither satisfying nor meaningful. Work becomes a displaced terminal value and the employee becomes a work addict.

THE WORKAHOLIC

While dedicated work is clearly important, it is also important to identify some of the abuses of work. The advice to work harder is not sound advice for everyone. Some people already work too long and too hard. Their work occupies too much of their time and interest. Their lives are so distorted in the direction of excessive work that the situation is unhealthy and unwise.

In 1971, a word was coined to describe this condition: "workaholic." The term was immediately popular, for good reasons. First, it seemed to accurately describe a growing problem among a sizable number of people whose lives revolve around their work. Second, it carried a negative connotation about work consistent with the growing disaffection for the traditional work ethic. Finally, it provided a convenient contrast for and, in some sense, a legitimation of the person who was not overly enthusiastic about work, did not work long hours, and had numerous off-the-job interests. Social awareness of workaholism as a serious problem was considerably enhanced because, like alcoholism, many who wrote about it were "reformed addicts," such as Wayne Oates, author of the original treatise on the subject: *Confessions of a Workaholic*.[1]

Most descriptions of a workaholic's life are quite similar. The scenario changes to fit the audience of the journal, but the essential features of the story are the same.[2]

The Addict. Jack Almond was a hard-driving, energetic _____ (fill in the blank—engineer, accountant, executive, salesman). At the age of 35, Jack was promoted, and his apparent success was envied by many. Jack always arrived at work early, and his breakfast often consisted of coffee and paperwork. Lunch and dinner were usually connected with business, and Jack was always conscious of the need to plan his mealtimes around work opportunities. During the day, Jack's life was a dizzying round of conferences, meetings, reports, and deadlines. When he finally went home in the evening, he routinely took a briefcase filled with papers from the office. Jack worked late into the evenings and every weekend. He was too busy for more than a one-week vacation every few years. Besides, he did not like vacations; they were unpleasant experiences. When he was not at work, he felt irritable and cross. He spent his time longing for the vacation to end. Golf and other recreations were always tied to business affairs, and he attacked the golf course with the same aggressiveness that he attacked business problems.

Jack's wife and family seldom saw him. When they did, he showed little interest in their problems. If they wanted to see him, they had to fit themselves into his work schedule. If they wanted to talk with him, they had to discuss topics related to his work. When Jack went to a social event or met old friends, he could converse informally only about his work.

At the age of 50, Jack died of a heart attack—a surprise to most people, since Jack did not drink, smoke, or overeat. At his funeral, he was eulogized as a hard worker, a loyal employee, and a person committed to his profession. But in spite of his untimely death, he was not missed six months later. The company replaced him with someone else—a man who worked only half as long, but did the important matters. Jack's wife had always been alone and considered his absence an extended business trip. His children, who had grown up without a father, still wondered what he was really like.

Workaholics are usually considered very valuable employees. Indeed, most of them accomplish a lot of work. But their self-sacrifice is not always in the best interest of the company. Workaholics can be both inefficient and ineffective if they fail to distinguish between being busy and being productive. Sometimes workaholics engage in "empire building," taking on too many responsibilities without delegating adequately. Occasionally they are self-serving and unwilling to subordinate their personal goals to the good of the organization. They have also been criticized for their lack of creativity and imagination.[3]

Workaholics and Hard Workers. A workaholic has been loosely defined as anyone who works long hours and has an intense interest in work. However, such a definition is like calling anyone who drinks alcohol an alcoholic. The concepts of addiction and an inability to function normally are missing. A lot of confusion has resulted from this loose definition. Many outstanding workers have been mistakenly called workaholics. Some people consider work their real hobby; it satisfies their ambitions and is an exciting and exhilarating activity. Many hard workers think their work is not really work; it is play to them. When Mark Twain was nearly 73, he wrote: "I have always been able to gain my living without doing any work. I enjoyed the writing of books and magazine matter; it was merely billiards to me."[4] To analyze the abuses of work, it is necessary to distinguish between a workaholic and a hard worker.

Workaholism refers to a compulsion to work. By definition, it is an unhealthy condition in which the individual is addicted to work and feels an uncontrollable need to work incessantly. The need to work can arise from many different sources. People may feel anxious and guilt-ridden and turn to work as a means to salve their conscience. Or they may suffer from feelings of insecurity and turn to work to obtain a sense of permanence, usefulness, and competence. Some people rely on their work activity to support their feelings of self-righteousness and self-worth.

The central element defining a workaholic is an irrational commitment to excessive work. Workaholics are unable to take time off from work or to comfortably divert their interests. Several other characteristics of workaholics are also characteristics of hard workers. But not every hard worker is a workaholic. The hard worker may put in long hours or take an extra job in order to meet a mortgage payment or support a child in college. The workaholic puts in long hours all the time, not to earn extra money or to oblige a supervisor, but to satisfy an inner compulsion. Both may arrive early, leave late, take work home, and prefer short vacations. But a hard worker retains a sense of meaning and purpose in work and can place it within the larger context of the meaning of life. The workaholic either is unable to find meaning in life apart from work or cannot maintain a perspective on work and life. For the workaholic, work is a displaced terminal value; the meaning of life revolves around the meaning of work. Hard workers can stop working when they want to and turn to some other activity without suffering acute withdrawal pains. When workaholics go on vacation, it is not the natives but the tourists who are restless.

Although few workers are pure workaholics, most hard workers tend to behave like work addicts at various times. Several journals have published short quizzes to help people assess their tendencies toward workaholism. The following 25 statements supposedly measure workaholism, although the last 8 statements are also indicative of a hard worker.[5] A 5-point scale is used to measure each statement (always = 5, frequently = 4, occasionally = 3, seldom = 2, and never = 1).

1. I get restless and irritable on a long weekend.
2. I find myself drinking too much, smoking too much, or feeling restless or irritable when I am not working.
3. I have a habit of looking at my watch.
4. I am impatient when things don't go exactly as I planned.
5. I compete to win at everything, including playing games with my family.
6. I take an annual vacation, and look forward to it. *(opposite)*
7. My spouse and family would agree that I leave my worries at the office. *(opposite)*
8. I feel "lost" when I am away from my work.
9. I talk about my work more easily than I talk about other subjects.
10. I think hobbies and recreation are a waste of time.
11. I dread the idea of retiring.
12. My family has accused me of being more interested in my work than in them.
13. Family problems can be blamed on my work.
14. I bring work into the bathroom.
15. I telephone friends in the evening just to chat. *(opposite)*
16. I interrupt people who are talking to me.
17. When someone is talking to me, I let my mind stray to some other lines of thought.
18. I work more than 50 hours a week at my job.
19. I feel that no one can do my job as well as I can.
20. I prefer to work alone rather than as part of a team.
21. I spend a lot of time thinking about my work.
22. My work prevents me from taking part in community or social activities.
23. I see more of my co-workers or employees than family or friends.
24. When I leave the office at the end of the day, I take my work with me.
25. I feel time passes too quickly for what I want to do.

A casual examination of these statements reveals that most concern the relationship between work and leisure. Work-aholics are unable to use leisure hours in a meaningful or personally enriching way. They cannot find contentment or satisfaction in life away from work. The quality of life is greatly influenced by leisure activities, and people need to carefully consider how they spend their leisure time.

LEISURE

American moralists have always been suspicious of leisure time: the idle mind was said to be the devil's workshop. Corruption, crime, and immorality were thought to accompany increased leisure hours. Two centuries ago, Alexander Hamilton argued in his famous "Report on Manufactures" that factory work made women and children more useful to society and prevented crime and immorality.[6] More recently, leisure time was said to be related to urban riots.[7] Free time seems to present special problems to many people, who have difficulty spending it in socially acceptable ways. Earlier in the century, particularly during the 1920s, there was a lot of concern about how Americans would spend their leisure time. A shorter workday was condemned by many who doubted that the working man would know how to use his leisure properly.[8]

Worthy Use of Leisure. In spite of the concern about idleness, there has been a growing recognition of the value of recreational programs. For example, a study of black neighborhoods in 1925 indicated that the crime rates were high in areas lacking playgrounds and recreational programs. The study concluded that society had the choice of spending money on police, court, and prison expenses or spending it on playgrounds and community recreation programs. Recreation was advocated especially for youth. But the need for leisure education showing adults how to pursue worthwhile hobbies and recreations was also recognized.[9]

Astute observers from abroad have often remarked on the intense pace of work and activity of Americans. In 1882, the British sociologist Herbert Spencer traveled extensively in America to observe American life. At a farewell banquet in

259

New York City, he summarized his impressions of the country and its people. He said he found an intense absorption in the mere making of a living and the accumulation of wealth such as no organism could stand: "We have had somewhat too much of the 'gospel of work.' It is time to preach the 'gospel of relaxation.' " Other foreign visitors have made simliar observations, but their advice did little to slow the pace of life. Americans took pride in their lifestyle and seemed to think their frantic pace of work and leisure was cause for national congratulation. Americans worked hard and played hard.[10]

To avoid the excesses of work, numerous authors have called for more leisure. The "gospel of relaxation" has been preached over the past century by an assortment of politicians, philosophers, ministers, psychiatrists, and foreign visitors. Most of these people were not preaching against the work ethic. They were calling for a better balance between the gospel of work and the pursuit of a meaningful life. For example, one of the nineteenth century's most colorful ministers, Henry Ward Beecher, surprised his New York City newspaper readers in 1854 with a fanciful article in praise of rest: "The chief use of a farm, if it be well selected, and of a proper soil, is to lie down upon. Mine is an excellent farm for such uses, and I thus cultivate it every day. . . . Though but a week here, I have lain down more hours and in more places than that hardworking brother of mine in the whole year that he has dwelt here."[11] Ten years earlier, the same Henry Ward Beecher had published a collection of sermons on work called *Seven Lectures to Young Men*. Anxious parents placed this volume in the hands of their children to teach them the moral preeminence of work and the sins of idleness. Like a pendulum swinging in both directions, Beecher's writings advocated work as well as leisure.[12]

After the turn of the century, when the workweek became noticeably shorter, there was a growing concern about how Americans would spend their leisure hours. Nothing attests to the vitality of the work ethic in America more than the anxiety that was shown over the proper use of leisure time. Again and again, Americans were reminded that idleness contributed to crime, wasted moments could not be regained, and significant social accomplishments usually came from using one's spare time. On every hand editorials reminded readers about the wise use of leisure. Abraham Lincoln acquired much of his education studying in his spare time. Thomas Edison and Alexander Graham Bell made significant discoveries in their spare time. "Most of the world's great men have achieved their true life work, not in the course of their needful daily occupations, but—in their spare time." Americans were reminded that the worthy use of leisure was no less important than diligence at work.[13]

Occasionally, however, lone voices would cry out against the move toward scheduled leisure time. Leisure, by definition, was time not spent in labor or in pursuits that engrossed one's thoughts or attention. Therefore, the "worthy use of leisure" was considered to be a contradiction in terms. "Leisure is not leisure if you *use* it; leisure is to be spent." Instead of taking piano lessons, starting a stamp collection, reading the book of the month, or attending a lecture, people were urged to pursue unalloyed leisure in the form of good, old-fashioned, praiseworthy daydreaming.[14]

Leisure Constrained by Work. Moralists generally agreed that people ought to be free to do anything they wanted during their leisure hours. But many argued further that people needed instruction on the proper uses of leisure so they could make informed choices. The research evidence suggests that most people do not use their leisure time to improve the quality of their lives.[15] Without the encouragement of external forces, such as organized recreational programs, church activities, and social clubs, the life of the worker away from the job seems to follow the same rut as life at work. It is obvious that leisure hours can be profitably used to benefit society or to enhance personal wealth. But the value of leisure activities for increasing the quality of life is not so obvious.

The meaning of life and the fulfillment derived from it

depend partly on your work and how you respond to it. However, they are also influenced by how you spend your leisure time. The quality of life is determined by the combination of work and nonwork activities, a fact that has been recognized for many years. Numerous studies have shown how repressive working conditions and impoverished social environments create a meager existence for many workers.

An early study of how work influences nonwork activities was Margaret Byington's classic description of life in Homestead, Pennsylvania.[16] Through a series of interviews, a trained field staff investigated the family life, culture, and social interactions of people living in a mill town. Wages provided only a bare subsistence, and the work varied from 12 hours a day, seven days a week, to no work at all. Byington's report showed how work dominated the personal lives and family interactions of the workers. Life in the community was also dictated by the steel mill. The long hours of heavy work and the dangerous, inhospitable conditions surrounding it served as social constraints on all aspects of life in the community. The long arm of the job reached out to direct both work and nonwork activities. The workers had only limited opportunities for leisure, but many tried to use what little time they had to good advantage. Through creative uses of leisure, some families were able to provide a happy home environment, with music, games, and group activities.

Three hypotheses have been proposed to describe the relationship between work and leisure activities: the compensatory hypothesis, the carryover hypothesis, and the no-relationship hypothesis.[17] The compensatory hypothesis claims that people have stable needs for certain activities. Some needs are satisfied through work activities in the normal course of the day. Needs that are not filled at work are supposedly filled in leisure hours. Since people control their own leisure time, it is assumed that they will choose activities that compensate for any deficiencies in their work environment.

The carryover hypothesis is the opposite of the compensatory hypothesis. It claims that people spend their leisure time performing the same sort of activities they perform at work and practice day after day. Thus the style of life a worker learns at work tends to spill over into his or her leisure hours.

The no-relationship hypothesis claims that work and leisure activities are largely determined by local business organizations and civic programs rather than by the individual. Therefore, people spend their leisure hours in activities not necessarily of their own choosing, but as provided by the community.

Research on these three hypotheses supports the carryover thesis. Employees seem to choose leisure activities with characteristics similar to their jobs. Three aspects of work and leisure activities have been examined: the amount of discretion the person has to direct his or her actions; the extent to which the person's actions are instrumental in producing a fixed product as opposed to a unique creative product; and the degree of social interaction the person has at work. The research findings indicate that people who have a lot of social interaction at work tend to choose leisure activities that also entail a lot of social interaction. People who work alone on creative tasks do not seem to exhaust their creative urges at work, since they generally pursue similar activities in their leisure time. And rather than asserting their independence, people who have little discretion over their work tend to choose leisure activities in which their actions are again controlled externally—by the rules of the game, a coach, a time schedule, and so on. Thus the strengths or weaknesses that are built into a worker's job seem to carry over into the person's leisure activities. Unfortunately, a poor quality of life at work tends to indicate a poor quality of life in general.

Goals of Leisure. How much time should be devoted to leisure and recreation? All leisure activities are not the same. Some activities are qualitatively superior to others. Thus the question is not how much time a person should spend in leisure activities, but what form of enrichment the person needs in his or her life that leisure activities will provide. There is a dramatic difference between watching a professional baseball game on television and watching a Little League game at the neighborhood park. There is a big difference in the athletic talent of the ballplayers. But the important difference for the spectators comes from their own involvement rather than from the quality of athletic talent they observe. There is also a qualitative difference between playing music yourself and listening to the music of someone else. Many people do not have the talent to make their own music. The important question is whether their lives would be more enriched if they developed this talent

There appears to be sound support for the "worthy use of leisure" idea. To achieve a healthy balance in life, people need to pursue leisure activities that supplement their work activities. Each person needs to analyze his or her situation and select a combination of leisure and work activities that maximizes the quality of life. Below are some of the most important considerations involved in achieving a healthy balance between work and leisure.

1. *Physical activity.* Everyone needs some physical activity to maintain good health. Many doctors advocate at least 30 minutes of exercise three times a week—exercise that uses large muscle groups, increases the heartbeat and rate of breathing, and develops the cardiovascular and respiratory systems. Some occupations satisfy needs for physical exercise. But the trend is toward jobs requiring less physical effort. Several years ago a number of studies examined the effects of fatigue and the maximum limits of exertion before work became damaging to the worker's health. Today studies are examining the effects of inactivity and the minimum exercise required to maintain reasonable health. The need for physical exercise either on the job or through leisure activities is becoming increasingly obvious.

2. *Social interaction.* It is important for people to develop a circle of friends who can provide meaningful companionship and social support. People need to learn how to make new friends, cultivate the friendships, and handle themselves in social situations. It takes experience to develop the social grace

to feel comfortable among strangers. Occupations that restrict a person's social interaction tend to inhibit social development. Membership in outside organizations, however, can help a person meet new people and encourage greater social interaction.

3. *Emotional stability.* Social norms inhibit the public expression of emotion. When stress, frustrations, and disappointments come, people are not able to "get in touch" with their feelings. These social constraints are not all bad. Every time people get angry, they should not hit somebody; nor should they cry every time they do not get their own way. But people do need time to analyze their feelings and develop a proper perspective on what is important and what should be overlooked. The time to control and direct your anger or sadness is not in the "heat of battle" but when you can calmly reflect on your feelings and the situation. You need time to decide how you want to respond. Some occupations, such as assembly-line work and truckdriving, provide ample time for contemplation and reflection. Other jobs, such as executive management and air traffic control, are often so fast-paced and highly pressured that people do not have much reflection time. Many vacationers praise the therapeutic value of hiking in the mountains, walking along the beach, camping alone in the desert, or fishing in a secluded stream.

4. *Intellectual development.* Life is a constant process of learning and growing. Periodically, people need to be intellectually challenged, either at work or in their leisure activities. Intellectual stimulation helps people adjust to a changing environment, improves their conversational abilities, and contributes to their personal growth.

Daily living presents numerous intellectual challenges— such as buying a home, filing your income tax, visiting a large city via public transportation, and investing money in stocks or bonds. Even making home repairs can be a challenge. The difference between "doing it yourself" and hiring an expert is usually a willingness to tolerate a little ambiguity and frustration. Learning can be an uncomfortable and frustrating experience at first, but it is rewarding in the end. Some occupations provide very little intellectual stimulation. Others provide a lot of stimulation but in a very narrow technical area. People should consider how much intellectual stimulation their occupations provide and choose leisure activities that supplement deficiencies in the mental demands of their work.

5. *Cultural refinement.* The arts can make an enormous contribution to the quality of a person's life. An appreciation of music, drama, dance, painting, and sculpture can be acquired only through exposure. Some people question the value of the arts in their lives, and find attending a concert or ballet a boring waste of time. People who have developed an appreciation for the arts, however, find such activities meaningful and enriching. It is interesting to watch a music lover describe how a piece of classical music enriches his or her life to a person who does not care much for music. People who have not developed an appreciation for the arts cannot understand why someone would stand silently staring at a painting several centuries old; or why one piece of music can cause a person to cry and another piece can motivate, inspire, and redirect the person's behavior. Art can make a significant contribution to the quality of life. Since most occupations do not provide good cultural experiences, people must use leisure hours for cultural pursuits.

In summary, leisure activities ought to contribute to the quality of a person's life. For some people, the ideal form of leisure is supervising a Little League baseball program in the community. For others, the ideal activity is practicing a musical instrument and playing in a local symphony. On occasion, all of us need time for ourselves—time to be alone, to think, to contemplate, and to daydream. But too much time for daydreaming is not much different from solitary confinement. The important criterion is to achieve a balance of work and leisure that creates a meaningful and fulfilling life.

MEANINGFUL WORK, MEANINGFUL LIFE

There is a growing awareness of the relationship between a meaningful life and meaningful work. A question being asked with increasing concern is: "How can work have meaning if life has no meaning?" Several surveys have attempted to assess the quality of life for American workers to see if it is related to job satisfaction and other work-related attitudes. The results indicate that general life satisfaction is declining, even though working conditions and employee benefits are improving. Employees are generally satisfied with specific job factors (working conditions, pay, benefits, the job), but the decline in their general life satisfaction suggests that the quality of life is deteriorating. Cleaner bathrooms and better dental coverage do not compensate for the sense of worthlessness a person feels in following an endless daily routine or the futility a worker feels in knowing that the money from his or her paycheck is already spent. The research findings suggest that the meaning of life in its broad context has a significant influence on a person's work attitudes (and vice versa).[18]

A Matrix of Meaning. The relationship between the meaning of work and the meaning of life is shown in Figure 12.1. The way a person responds to work is largely determined by how work fits into the person's larger value system. Work can have meaning to a person as a terminal or instrumental value. Or work can be a meaningless activity that the person dislikes and would prefer to avoid. For simplicity, the work portion of Figure 12.1 is divided into two categories: work is either meaningful or meaningless. Also for simplicity, the meaning of life is divided into two categories: life is either meaningful or meaningless. Such a crude dichotomy violates many elegant ideas from both philosophy and religion. But it provides a sufficiently simple conceptualization to examine the work ethic, meaningless work, and workaholism.

Life can be meaningful for many reasons. Many people find meaning in life through religion. A poll by *People* magazine revealed that 95 percent of its readers thought religion was important in American life. Half the respondents were described as being "positively evangelistic on the subject."[19] For those who have intense religious faith, life can possess considerable meaning and purpose. The belief in a life after death, formerly relegated to the tenets of religious faith, has become a popular topic in literature, as evidenced by a book describing

267

Figure 12.1. Matrix of meanings.

	Work Is Meaningful	Work Is Meaningless
Life Is Meaningful	**I** Strong work ethic. Happy and productive workers. Work is a terminal and/or instrumental value. 50% of workforce	**II** Work is an obligation that is not consistent with the meaning of life. Solution: inculcate work values, redesign the job, or change jobs. 20% of workforce
Life Is Meaningless	**III** Work is a displaced terminal value. Work is the reason for existence. Solution: enforced rest, reassessment of priorities, diversification of interest. 10% of workforce	**IV** Work is soulless, mind-numbing drudgery. Welfare is preferred to work. Solution: "right actions" and "contributing to life" 20% of workforce

the experiences of people who recovered after being pronounced medically dead.[20]

Personal goals and ambitions can also add meaning to life. Family relationships, especially raising children, provide many parents with a unique sense of purpose. People in the helping professions—psychiatrists, clergy, counselors, doctors—often feel that their service to others adds meaning and fulfillment to their lives. Unique accomplishments, such as developing a new theory, making a scientific discovery, writing a book, or producing a work of art, often give the creator a sense of mission in life.

Many people find meaning in both life and the work they do. These people are in the first quadrant of Figure 12.1. Approximately 50 percent of the American workforce might fit in this category. This figure is only a rough approximation, based on the responses of workers to national opinion polls and other surveys, such as the one described in Chapter 4. These workers generally have strong work values and would be expected to be happy and productive employees. They accept work (1) as a terminal value, where work is an attribute of good character; (2) as a generalized instrumental value, where work contributes to the good of society; (3) as a specific instrumental value, where work contributes to the worker's immediate benefit; or (4) as an indication of personal competence and self-esteem. Since they also think life is meaningful, these people often enjoy a healthy quality of life.

In quadrant IV, at the opposite extreme, are people who think that life is meaningless and that the work they do (if they work at all) is equally meaningless. These individuals, who probably represent up to 20 percent of the workforce, find work a form of mind-numbing drudgery. They would like to avoid work and would prefer to live off welfare, gambling, or any other means of obtaining money without working.

In quadrant II are people who think life in general is meaningful, but work (their work, at least) is meaningless. These individuals, perhaps 20 percent of the workforce, respond to work as an obligation. Work is not an activity that is consistent with the meaning of life as they define it. The problem might be due to their present job or past work history. The cure for the problem depends on its cause. Some workers have been stuck in dead-end jobs so long that they have learned from experience that work is useless. Other workers have simply never been taught to find meaning or purpose in work. Many young workers have never held permanent full-time jobs or had sufficient work experiences to acquire work values. Diligence, perseverance, and industry are foreign concepts to them. Thus the cure may be to redesign the job, find a new job, or inculcate the work ethic in the worker's system of values.

In quadrant III are people who think work is meaningful, but its meaning is shallow or tenuous because it is not based on a broader meaning of life. These people, approximately 10 percent of the workforce, are often workaholics who attack their work with an ill-founded enthusiasm. Work is immensely important to them, but it is a displaced terminal value: they work for the sake of working. Work is a positive activity, but they do not always understand why, since it has become an inner compulsion. Most workaholics can provide some justification for working so long and hard, even if it is irrational. "I'm only doing it for my family" is perhaps the poorest justification, since families usually suffer the most. This and other glorifications of work distort the quality of life. In elevating work so high, workaholics ignore other positive values that contribute to the quality of life, such as family relationships, cultural experiences, community involvement, religion, friendships, and personal development.

The cure prescribed most frequently for workaholics is enforced rest, a reassessment of priorities, and a diversification of personal interests. When they first begin a hobby, most workaholics experience a similar addiction to activity. They pursue it with the same aggressiveness that they pursued work. A simple watch collection becomes an enormous compilation of timepieces. A leisurely walk through the park becomes a daily forced march in record time. Because people who suddenly change from work to leisure tend to develop a variety of physical and psychological illnesses, it is usually recommended that they ease into it gradually by a series of shorter vacations. Returning to hobbies formerly pursued in adolescence has also been recommended.[21]

Contributing to Life.   A useful therapy for finding meaning in life is described by Viktor Frankl, an Austrian psychologist, in his highly acclaimed book *Man's Search for Meaning*. Frankl spent three grim years in Auschwitz and other Nazi prisons during World War II. His book describes the painful experiences he and other prisoners endured and their physical and psychological struggle for survival. As a psychiatrist, Dr. Frankl was able to use the intense suffering he observed and experienced to develop some valuable ideas about the meaning of life.

Under such trying circumstances, the meaning of life and its effects on behavior become very apparent. Death came quickly to those who lost the will to live. Starvation and illness were constant threats, and only those who had an intense resolve to live were able to survive. Frankl suggested that the secret of endurance was contained in the words of Nietzsche: "He who has a *why* to live for can bear with almost any *how*."[22]

According to Frankl, the "*why* to live for" is unique to each person. Life cannot be defined in a general way; nor is it something vague. The meaning of life is "very real and concrete, just as life's tasks are real and concrete." It is to be found by each individual in responding to the unique problems and opportunities before him. Frankl stated that despair could not be countered by attempting to explain what life had to offer. Instead what was needed was a fundamental change in one's attitude toward life. "*It did not really matter what we expected from life, but rather what life expected from us.* We needed to stop asking about the meaning of life, and instead think of ourselves as those who were being questioned by life—daily and hourly. Our answer must consist, not in talk and meditation, but in right action and in right conduct. Life ultimately means taking the responsibility to find the right answer to its problems and to fulfill the tasks which it constantly sets for each individual."[23]

Frankl's philosophy, sometimes called "logotherapy," provides many useful insights for people who think work is demeaning drudgery. The three elements in Frankl's logotherapy are (1) learning to love—to develop meaningful and close associations with family members and friends; (2) learning to work—to produce, to master, to create, and to direct one's own destiny; and (3) learning to endure pain gracefully.

Two profound insights come from Frankl's philosophy. First, the meaning of life comes from within. Second, people can choose how they wish to respond to their environment. The walls of Auschwitz did not chain Frankl's mind. The guards who limited his physical movement could not destroy his spirit, his creative ideas, or the joy he found in such little things as a beautiful sunset and a wild flower.

DIAGNOSING DISLIKED JOBS

Meaning and fulfillment in life need not depend on having ideal work conditions or a glamorous occupation. Many workers are able to find purpose in life even though they are required to perform menial tasks. Boredom is a psychological response to the environment, and repetitive work does not have to be boring. There are times when every job is frustrating and unpleasant, and it is only natural for workers to occasionally feel dissatisfied with work. But if a worker says "I hate my job" day after day, something ought to be changed—the job, the person's reaction to it, or both.

If you do not like your job, what should you do? The first step in improving your situation is to examine what you dislike and why. The changes that need to be made should be determined by a careful diagnosis of the problem. In some cases, you may need to change your job. But in other cases, you may need to reassess the value of work and how it fits into the meaning of life for you. There are times when it is appropriate to consider the advice of the early moralists who so extensively influenced the work values of Americans: "An hour's industry will do more to produce cheerfulness, suppress evil humors, and retrieve your affairs than a month's moaning."[24]

Many workers say they dislike their jobs because the pay is low. Low pay can create intense dissatisfaction, because workers feel they are not being treated fairly and their work is not appreciated. You may be unhappy with low pay—it may contribute to your poverty, and you may be forced to change jobs out of economic necessity. But low pay should not make the work itself unattractive. Nor will higher pay necessarily make the work itself more interesting.

Antagonistic supervisors and obnoxious co-workers can also make life at work unpleasant. Changing the job itself and developing a stronger commitment to the work ethic will not solve this problem. The most challenging and rewarding solution is to change supervisors and co-workers by being supportive, patient, considerate, informative, persistent, and whatever else it takes to help them develop better interpersonal skills. The easiest solution is to find a more compatible social environment and change jobs. But if you find one unpleasant situation after another, perhaps you are the one who needs better interpersonal skills.

Many workers say they dislike their jobs because of the work itself. This can be a difficult problem to analyze, since most workers feel that a better job would be more satisfying and fulfilling and every job has something that could be changed. But is the problem really with the job? In this situation you should try to determine why you dislike your job. Does the job require you to do something you dislike? Is there something you want to do that you do not have an opportunity to do on your present job?

Some workers feel that their jobs do not offer adequate opportunities for growth, enough challenge to their knowledge and skills, or a meaningful career. Many jobs are criticized for being stultifying, boring, and dead-ended. Some jobs obviously need to be restructured. But the question is whether the problem is caused by a dead-end job or a dead-end worker.[25] In this situation, the following questions need to be considered: Are your expectations realistic? Could any job measure up to your expectations? If you continually find that one job after another is meaningless and frustrating, you ought to ask yourself whether it is really the job that is meaningless or if it is life itself that is meaningless. Many people go from job to job, disliking each one, and thinking the next one will be the charm. Young workers, especially college graduates, have lofty aspirations about the ideal occupation. They have not had enough experience to realize that "good" jobs are ultimately made by good workers. Organizations create job opportunities, and some opportunities are better than others. But personal growth and career advancement are primarily determined by the individual.

Many jobs are criticized not for what they lack but for what they require. The critical question is whether the requirements are necessary and legitimate. Most jobs have some aspects that people find objectionable, such as punctuality, the discipline to avoid making mistakes, and the need to perform the same task over and over. Whether workers like them or not, these requirements are part of the job. Reliability and dependability are important in every job, especially for self-employed people.

If you dislike your job, you need to decide if the things you dislike are really necessary. If they are, you should accept them as part of life and seek fulfillment within those constraints. But if the things you dislike do not have to be accepted, such as meeting the public, writing reports that are dishonest, working night shifts or on Sundays, or working in an office, these things can be changed by either redesigning your job or finding another job. The prayer that was first offered by Reinhold Niebuhr many years ago may sound too glib for comfort, but if we take the trouble to hear the message behind the familiar ring, we'll find some very sound advice: "Lord, give us the serenity to accept what cannot be changed, courage to change what should be changed, and wisdom to distinguish the one from the other."

REFERENCES

1. Wayne Oates, *Confessions of a Workaholic* (New York: World Publishing Company, 1971).
2. See, for example, Paul Martin, "Hooked on Work: America's Secret Habit," *Science Digest,* Vol. 80 (December 1976), pp. 72–77.
3. Warren Boroson, "The Workaholic," *Money,* Vol. 5 (June 1976), pp. 32–35.
4. Quoted in Boroson, *op. cit.,* p. 32.
5. This questionnaire comes primarily from Boroson, *op. cit.;* Marilyn Machlowitz, "Workaholics," *Across the Board,* Vol. 14 (October 1977), pp. 30–37; and Jean Rosenbaum, "Are You a Workaholic?" *Family Weekly* (March 4, 1979), p. 11.
6. Alexander Hamilton, "Report on Manufactures," speech presented to the House of Representatives on December 5, 1791. In Walter Lowrie and Matthew Clarke, eds., *American State Papers, Documents, Legislative and Executive, of the Congress of the United States,* Vol. 5 (Washington, 1832), pp. 123–144.

7. I. J. Hutchison, "Leisure Time and the Riots: Are We Contributing?" *Parks and Recreation*, Vol. 4 (July 1969), pp. 11, 23.

8. See Helen McAfee, "The Menace of Leisure," *Century*, Vol. 114 (May 1927), pp. 67–76.

9. Emmett Scott, "Leisure Time and the Colored Citizen," *Playground*, Vol. 18 (January 1925), pp. 593–596.

10. Herbert Spencer's farewell banquet address, New York, November 9, 1882. Quoted in Daniel T. Rodgers, *The Work Ethic in Industrial America, 1850–1920* (Chicago: University of Chicago Press, p. 94). See also Lee Russell, "Live While You Live," *Scribner's Magazine*, Vol. 78 (September 1925), pp. 273–280; and William Attwood, "The American Male: Why Does He Work So Hard?" *Look*, Vol. 22 (March 4, 1958), pp. 70–75.

11. Henry W. Beecher, *Star Papers, or Experiences of Art and Nature* (New York: J. C. Derby, 1855), p. 268.

12. See Clifford E. Clark, Jr., "The Changing Nature of Protestantism in Mid-Nineteenth Century America: Henry Ward Beecher's *Seven Lectures to Young Men*," *Journal of American History*, Vol. 57 (1971), pp. 832–846; and William G. McLoughlin, *The Meaning of Henry Ward Beecher: An Essay on the Shifting Values of Mid-Victorian America, 1840–1870* (New York: Alfred A. Knopf, 1970).

13. The quotation comes from Albert P. Terhune, "If You Ask Me, You Can't Afford to Spare Your Spare Time," *American Magazine*, Vol. 107 (January 1929), p. 21. The number of articles advising Americans about the proper use of leisure was staggering. In the 1932–1935 index of the *Reader's Guide to Periodical Literature*, there were 121 entries on leisure.

14. Lawrence H. Conrad, "The Worthy Use of Leisure," *The Forum*, Vol. 86 (November 1931), pp. 312–314.

15. Martin Meissner, "The Long Arm of the Job: A Study of Work and Leisure," *Industrial Relations*, Vol. 10 (October 1971), pp. 239–260.

16. Margaret F. Byington, *Homestead: The Households of a Mill Town* (New York: Charities Publication Committee, 1910).

17. Meissner, *op. cit.*

18. Graham L. Staines, "Is Worker Dissatisfaction Rising?" *Challenge*, Vol. 22, No. 2 (May–June 1979) pp. 38–45; Graham L. Staines and Robert P. Quinn, "American Workers Evaluate the Quality of Their Jobs," *Monthly Labor Review*, Vol. 102, No. 1 (January 1979), pp. 3–12.

19. "A Surprising Readers' Poll," *People* (March 5, 1979), pp. 25–36.

20. Raymond A. Moody, *Life After Life* (Harrisburg, Pa.: Stackpole Books, 1976).

21. Martin, *op cit.*; Boroson, *op cit.*

22. Viktor Frankl, *Man's Search For Meaning* (Boston: Beacon Press, 1959), p. 121.
23. Frankl, *op. cit.*, pp. 122–123.
24. *Benjamin Franklin: The Autobiography and Other Writings* (New York: Signet, 1961).
25. See William Raspberry, "Dead-end Workers Make Dead-end Jobs," *Worklife*, Vol. 3 (May 1978), p. 23.

INDEX

279

DATE DUE

6. 15. '82	
5. 2 7. '82	
3. 10. '83	
7. 5. '85	
6 22 '88 APR 2 5 '90	
MAY 30 '90	
JUN 2 0 '90	
MAY 0 6 1996	
2 2 2001	

BRODART, INC.   Cat. No. 23-221